THE UNDERMINING OF THE SANDINISTA REVOLUTION

Also by Gary Prevost

CUBA: A Different America (*co-editor with Wilber Chaffee*)

DEMOCRACY AND SOCIALISM IN SANDINISTA NICARAGUA (*with Harry E. Vanden*)

THE 1990 NICARAGUAN ELECTIONS AND THEIR AFTERMATH (*co-editor with Vanessa Castro*)

Also by Harry E. Vanden

A BIBLIOGRAPHY OF LATIN AMERICAN MARXISM

DEMOCRACY AND SOCIALISM IN SANDINISTA NICARAGUA (*with Gary Prevost*)

MARIÁTEGUI: Influencias en su Formación Ideológica

NATIONAL MARXISM IN LATIN AMERICA: José Carlos Mariátegui's Thought and Politics

The Undermining of the Sandinista Revolution

Edited by

Gary Prevost
Professor, Department of Political Science
St John's University, Minnesota

and

Harry E. Vanden
Professor, Department of Government and International Affairs
Director, Caribbean and Latin American Studies Center
University of South Florida, Tampa, Florida

Published in Great Britain by
MACMILLAN PRESS LTD
Houndmills, Basingstoke, Hampshire RG21 6XS and London
Companies and representatives throughout the world

A catalogue record for this book is available from the British Library.

ISBN 0–333–64837–4 hardcover
ISBN 0–333–75199–X paperback

Published in the United States of America by
ST. MARTIN'S PRESS, INC.,
Scholarly and Reference Division,
175 Fifth Avenue, New York, N.Y. 10010

ISBN 0–312–16112–3 clothbound
ISBN 0–312–21705–6 paperback

The Library of Congress has cataloged the hardcover edition as follows:
The undermining of the Sandinista Revolution / edited by Gary Prevost
and Harry E. Vanden.
p. cm.
Includes bibliographical references (p.   ) and index.
ISBN 0–312–16112–3
1. Nicaragua—Politics and government—1990–   I. Prevost, Gary.
II. Vanden, Harry E.
F1528.U6   1996
972.8505'3—dc20   96–16523
                                                                       CIP

© Gary Prevost and Harry E. Vanden 1997, 1999

First edition 1997
Reprinted (with new preface and minor alterations) 1999

This book is printed on paper suitable for recycling and made from fully managed and
sustained forest sources.

10   9   8   7   6   5   4   3   2   1
08   07   06   05   04   03   02   01   00   99

Printed and bound in Great Britain by
Antony Rowe Ltd, Chippenham, Wiltshire

Contents

List of Plates

Acknowledgements

The editors acknowledge the assistance of many people in the preparation of this book. Professor Prevost conducted his field research in 1994 and 1995 with the support of two Dillon Research Grants from St John's University. In Nicaragua the assistance of various individuals and organizations was invaluable to the editors. Organizations to be credited include the Institute for the Development of Democracy and its director, Luis Carrión, the Institute for International Studies and its director, Alejandro Bendaña, and the Secretariat of the Sandinista National Liberation Front. Individuals who provided valuable help included Vanessa Castro, Ramón Meneses, Daysi Moncada, Colleen Littlejohn, Rhina Mayorga, Edgar Paralles, Francisco Campbell, Victor Hugo Tinoco, Miriam Hooker, Dr Emilio Alvarez Montalván, Trevor Evans, Henry Ruíz, Patricia Elvir, Leonidas Pulidas, Dora Zeledón, Judy Butler, and Sr Rita Owczarek. At St John's University, Shirley Zipoy provided valuable office assistance including the typing of parts of the manuscript and handling correspondence with our publisher in London. Both editors wish to thank Anne Ladia for completing the index. John Howell prepared the bibliography. Additional office assistance, including detailed translation of several key Sandinista documents, was provided by Carlos Velez. Professor Prevost is particularly indebted to the support of his companion Catherine Kocy, who has backed this project in many ways. Harry Vanden thanks his sons for their critical support and Susan Cashman for inspiration. Professor Vanden also thanks Delores Bryant for her invaluable secretarial assistance in this and many projects. Likewise, he wishes to thank the political and economic officers in the US Embassy in Managua for sharing data and insights.

Pierre LaRamée and Erica Polakoff wish to acknowledge the assistance of the following people: Hilda Bolt, General Secretariat, FSLN; Enrique Picado, Coordinator of the Movimiento Comunal (MC); Máxima Bermudez, Vice-Coordinator of the MC; Dora Zeladón, Coordinator, AMNLAE; Daniel Nuñez Rodríguez, President, UNAG;

Manuel Cano, MC Department Coordinator, Masaya; Jeanette Castillo, MC Municipal Coordinator, Matagalpa; María Auxiliadora Chiong, Associate Director of the Institute for Women and Community, Esteli; Aurelila Cruz, MC Department Vice-Coordinator, Carazo; Miguel Espinosa, MC Community Coordinator, 'Tierra Prometida', Managua; Sérgio Obando, MC Department Coordinator, Granada; Noel Palácio, MC Adult Education Coordinator, Esteli; Maria Auxiliadora Romero Cruz, MC Community Daycare Center Coordinator, Matagalpa; Blanca Sevilla, Director, Unemployed Women's Center, Esteli; Francisco Silva, MC Department Coordinator, León; Juanita Silva, MC Preschool Coordinator, León; T. M. Scruggs, Music Department, University of Iowa, for logistical help; Nicolás Burgos and family, Managua, for generous hospitality; and Bloomfield College, Bloomfield, NJ for travel grant.

Richard Stahler-Sholk wishes to thank Gary Prevost, Harry Vanden, Kent Norsworthy, Oscar Neira, Trevor Evans, Rose Spalding and all of the participants in the LASA 1995 research seminar in Nicaragua. Cynthia Chavez Metoyer acknowledges Sheryl Lutjens, Richard Stahler-Sholk, Gary Prevost and Harry Vanden for their useful comments on earlier versions of her chapter.

Notes on the Contributors

Gary Prevost is the author of *Democracy and Socialism in Sandinista Nicaragua* (co-authored with Harry E. Vanden), *The 1990 Nicaraguan Elections and Their Aftermath* (co-edited with Vanessa Castro) and *Cuba: A Different America* (co-edited with Wilber Chaffee). His numerous articles on Nicaragua have appeared in such journals as *Latin American Perspectives, Conflict Quarterly, Scandinavian Journal of Development Alternatives, Annals of the Southeastern Council of Latin American Studies*, and *NACLA – Report on the Americas*. He has received numerous research grants including a Fulbright Central American Republics award. He holds a PhD from the University of Minnesota and is in the Department of Political Science at St. John's University in Collegeville, Minnesota.

Harry E. Vanden is Professor of Political Science and Director of the Caribbean and Latin American Studies Center at the University of South Florida, Tampa. In the 1970s, he was a Fulbright Scholar in Peru where he worked in the National Institute of Public Administration. His articles have appeared in the *Latin American Research Review*, the *Journal of Inter-American Studies and World Affairs, Latin American Perspectives, New Political Science*, and *The Annals of the American Academy of Political and Social Science*. Topics include Latin American politics, ideology and foreign policy. His books include *National Marxism in Latin America: José Carlos Mariátegui's Thought and Politics, A Bibliography of Latin American Marxism*, and with Gary Prevost, *Democracy and Socialism in Sandinista Nicaragua*. Recent research was focused on Nicaragua and Central America, and different forms of democracy. He is a former president of the South Eastern Council of Latin American Studies and the Society for Iberian and Latin American Thought, and currently a member of the Latin American Studies Association's Central American task force. He completed his undergraduate work at Albright College and the University of Madrid. He holds the MA and Certificate in Latin American Studies from the Maxwell School of Syracuse University and the PhD from the New School for Social Research.

Pierre M. LaRamée is director of the North American Congress on Latin America (NACLA) in New York. He was previously an Assistant Professor of Sociology and has written on grassroots democracy and economic development policy in the Nicaraguan revolution and the mass organizations and squatter settlements in Managua. He has also published articles on economic policy and agricultural development and land distribution in North America and Latin America. He holds a BA and an MA from McGill University (Montreal) and received his PhD from Cornell University (Ithaca, NY).

Erica G. Polakoff is Assistant Professor of Sociology and Sociology Coordinator at Bloomfield College (New Jersey). She has published several articles on poverty and underdevelopment in Bolivia and on squatter settlements and grassroots democracy in Nicaragua. She holds a BS, an MS, and a PhD from Cornell University.

Richard Stahler-Sholk is Assistant Professor of Political Science at Eastern Michigan University. During 1985–89 he was Research Associate at the *Coordinadora Regional de Investigaciones Económicas y Sociales* (CRIES) in Managua. He has written a number of articles and book chapters on Nicaraguan political economy. He has a BA from Brandeis University and an MA and a PhD from the University of California, Berkeley.

Cynthia Chavez Metoyer is Assistant Professor at California State University San Marcos in the Department of Political Science. Her ongoing research in Nicaragua explores the political transition of state power and the gendered impacts of state policies. Her current research examines the policy outcomes of structural adjustment policies for Nicaragua in general, and for rural women in particular. She is the author of 'Can Democracy Be Exported?', in David E. Camacho (ed.), *U.S. Policy and Democracy* (1994). She completed her undergraduate work at New Mexico State University and holds an MA and a PhD from Northern Arizona University.

Preface to the 1999 Reprint

In 1998 Nicaragua was still the second poorest country in the hemisphere. Estimates of unemployment ranged as high as 60 per cent. Politically, Nicaraguans were suffering from the general *malaise* that was settling over the Latin American electorate in the 1990s – a population alienated from politics. The effects of the economic crises and structural reforms had been severe. The populations had lost confidence in their governments and most traditional parties because they had not been able to deliver programmes that improved the deteriorating conditions of the masses. Governmental performance and effectiveness were generally perceived as low. Nicaragua was very much part of this trend.

The first edition of this book went to press as the Nicaraguan people were going to the polls in the October 1996 national elections. In an election marked by considerable irregularities in the voting, Constitutional Liberal candidate Arnaldo Alemán, won the presidential election with 50 per cent of the vote, defeating FSLN leader Daniel Ortega who gained 38 per cent. Promising better times, the Liberals also emerged as the largest party in the National Assembly with 42 deputies, compared to 36 for the FSLN. Of the 145 municipal governments, 92 are in Liberal hands and 51 in Sandinista hands. As the election neared and the FSLN displayed a genuine interest in the real conditions of the people, Daniel Ortega's standing in the polls had begun to increase and it seemed for a while that he would have a chance to try to restore the economic well-being that the masses had enjoyed in the early eighties. This possibility mobilized many supporters, but also was exploited by the Liberals to mobilize votes against a return of Sandinista rule. This accounted for the fact that there was a turnout of almost 80 per cent of the electorate. Yet, there were considerable delays and irregularities in the vote count leading to an initial call by the FSLN for voiding the election. In Managua alone there were anomalies in more than 50 per cent of the polling stations. However, the FSLN ultimately accepted the results and its solidified position as the primary opposition in what may become a two-party dominant system. The FSLN has continued to press for reform of the Supreme Electoral Council but any change has been blocked by the Liberals.

In the run up to the 1996 elections the FSLN warned that the election of Alemán would lay the groundwork for the return of Somocismo. As Alemán neared the end of his second year in office this dire prediction had not proven true, but those gains of the Sandinista revolution that had survived the Chamorro years have in most cases been further eroded. The hard-line neo-liberal policies pursued by the Alemán administration further undermined the social gains of the Sandinista period in areas such as health care and education. One million children were not attending school. In 1998, university students joined physicians who had gone on strike to protest against deteriorating wages and conditions in the public hospitals. Significant street demonstrations ensued. The process of further reducing Sandinista influence in both the police and army continued, though there did not appear to be any significant danger of military interference in civilian affairs. Workers in the privatized companies generally did not fare well. By 1993, 137 companies were partially or wholly privatized in favour of the workers. By 1998, only 50 of the 'workers' companies' have managed to survive under the neo-liberal model. President Alemán favoured the opening of more enterprises in the free trade zone around the Managua airport even though wages were low and many of the companies threatened to leave when faced with unionization or other labour generated demands for better working conditions.

At this writing, the single most important event of the Alemán administration was the achievement of an accord on property rights between the Liberals and the FSLN in September 1997. The surprise agreement came on the heels of massive anti-government demonstrations in April 1997 organized by the popular sectors and the demonstrated un-willingness of the FSLN to join the national dialogue with the Alemán government. The character of the property issue in many ways captured political reality. The FSLN and the popular classes were in sharp retreat, largely unable to defend the gains that were won in the eighties, but were able to maintain just enough political power to prevent the Liberals from implementing their full programme and eliminating the Sandinistas from the Nicaraguan political scene.

On the positive side, the property agreement did result in the titling of a significant number of properties to poor Nicaraguans who had lived on them since the Sandinista revolution. In Managua, for example, eleven neighbourhoods were fully deeded and nation-wide tens of thousands of poor families materially benefited. Moreover, by signing the agreement the Alemán government acknowledged the legitimacy of Sandinista laws, something it claimed that it would never do. However, on the downside the FSLN signed off on an agreement that left unprotected a vast number of the poor that the party has always claimed to represent. In the rural area the accord presumed a review of the entire agrarian reform process and in the city at least twenty thousand families in some seventy poor settlements of Managua faced eviction in the name of new urban planning criteria. The agreement also opened the way for further return of property to the Somoza family. As the agreement was reached, the last of Somoza's sons returned to Nicaragua to claim family lands that had been taken by the Sandinistas.

As could be expected, both the Liberals and the Sandinistas were manoeuvering with an eye to the 2001 presidential elections. There were slight improvements in macroeconomic indicators in 1997 and 1998 and in March 1998 the PLC widened its advantage over the FSLN with a convincing victory in the Atlantic Coast regional elections. Yet the message was mixed indeed, since 50 per cent of the voters stayed away from the polls. By later in the year armed resistance groups were appearing throughout the country. Alemán and the Liberals' popularity continued to be buffeted by general economic conditions and the painful effects of new structural adjustment agreements (Nicaragua's $7 billion external debt gave it the highest per capita debt in the world in 1998 and necessitated difficult repayment terms). In the beginning of 1998 the suitability of the FSLN's leader was brought into question when Daniel Ortega was accused by his stepdaughter of sexually molesting her for some years. Several Sandinista leaders eventually resigned from the Party's National Directorate and Ortega's public popularity fell, but be was reaffirmed as the General Secretary of the party in a May 1998 Party Congress.

The Party Congress also failed to carry out any significant reforms that might have signalled that it was ready to reverse its sagging fortunes and make a serious bid to win the 2001 elections. At the same time, presidential and cabinet use of a drug-tainted Lear jet also involved the government in a major scandal. Dissatisfaction with both parties, if not the political system itself, made it difficult to predict the exact direction of Nicaraguan politics, but the Liberals' Atlantic Coast election victory, combined with the continuing disarray within the ranks of the FSLN, gave Alemán and the Liberals the opportunity to be the likely holders of political power in Nicaragua for the foreseeable future.

Introduction

Like a distant region in Gabriel García Márquez's *One Hundred Years of Solitude*, Central America is often seen as an area bypassed by history – a backwater dominated by the production of bananas and coffee. And until recently, Nicaragua was seen as one of the most traditional of the Central American states. It was a land where macho dictators and their mercenary guard ruled over an unsophisticated populace who were little able to initiate change.

But as history plays out in different epochs and locales, nations, like people, are presented with critical junctures in their evolution. Paths taken at these times are decisive in determining the speed and direction of national evolution. Forces that have been brewing for decades burst forth and shatter the traditional *status quo*, offering opportunities for rapid change and restructuring. New vistas appear and avenues for advancement that seemed impossible a few years before are now within the realm of possibility. In Central America, several nations have experienced these historic junctures. Guatemala experienced a decade of radical change from 1944 to 1954, but this process was truncated by the US-engineered coup of 1954. The reforms were abolished and the organizers persecuted. The United Fruit Company and the CIA condemned the most Indian of the Central American states to four more decades of military-dominated rule. In 1948 José Figueres initiated a reformist revolution in Costa Rica that restructured that nation into one of the most enlightened social democracies among the southern nations. For a time after 1978, Panama experienced a period of enlightened social policy under the rule of Omar Torrejos. This experiment also came to an end when Torrejos was killed in a very suspicious plane crash as Reagan was coming into office.

Nicaragua also experienced an historic turning-point in these years. Previously, this nation had been so traditional that the beginnings of a modern nation-state did not appear until President José Santos Zelaya took office in 1893. Frequent US interventions and several conservative leaders retarded the growth of a liberal movement until guerrilla leader Augusto

1

César Sandino led an uprising against the conservative elite and the US Marines from 1926 to early 1933. But the first Sandinistas' heroic struggle was not ultimately successful. From soon after Sandino's assassination in 1933, until 1979 the Somoza dynasty ruled Nicaragua more like a traditional family business than a modern nation-state. Their close ties to the United States helped make their dictatorship one of the longest and most hated in Latin American history. Their excesses and gluttony were as legendary as the brutality of the National Guard. And so it was that the people of Nicaragua were ready for a radical break with the past by the 1970s. Led by a vanguard of Sandinista militants, they overthrew a hated dictatorship and tried to transform their small tradition-bound nation. As this process developed, Nicaragua became a symbol of national struggle and a focal point of social transformation. For a time in the early eighties, people had hope and the future looked bright. During these years, Nicaragua was one of the centres of attention in the Third World. It was a leader of progressive forces in Central and Latin America and an active member of the Non-Aligned Movement. Under Sandinista leadership the nation rid itself of the avarice and corruption of the Somoza years. The people were freed and mobilized for what all hoped would be a bright future. Literacy and health care were radically improved. Daycare was made available and a modern, progressive educational system was instituted. Resources began to flow to the masses for the first time since the conquest. Women began to be treated as equals and became ever more assertive. For the first time in its national history, Nicaraguans could dream of living in a modern nation that provided the equality, support and services many other nations took for granted. They could regain their dignity and take pride in their many accomplishments.

But outside forces began to darken Nicaragua's bright vistas. With the election of Ronald Reagan, conservative forces in the United States began to plot the demise of the Sandinista experiment. CIA head Bill Casey came to Central America soon after Reagan's inauguration to begin a concerted experiment in low-intensity conflict designed to topple the new Nicaraguan leadership. What followed was the Contra war. It eventually took 30 000 Nicaraguan lives, cost more than $12 billion in damages and bankrupted the Nicaraguan treasury.

Combined with a powerful US economic embargo imposed in 1985, it exacerbated authoritarian, anti-participatory tendencies among Sandinista leaders and caused an ever stronger outcry from the Nicaraguan masses as their sons and daughters and economic well-being were sacrificed to the war effort and unsuccessful attempts at external appeasement. Top-down verticalist tendencies within the FSLN stopped governmental and party leaders from continuing the radical participatory experiment begun in the early eighties. This same orientation and the urban bias of the Sandinista leadership caused the new leaders to turn a deaf ear to rural demands and ignore peasant needs. Pressured by the Reagan and Bush administrations, Western European nations, and Latin American supporters like Venezuela and Mexico, the new Nicaraguan leadership moved towards a Western-style system of representative democracy that ultimately made it increasingly hard for the ever more entrenched political elites to heed the pleas and lamentations of their own people. The popular mobilization through mass organizations that had been an essential part of the original revolutionary vision was in large part abandoned. By doubting the wisdom and strength of their own mobilized people, the Sandinista leadership lost its greatest strength and primary political support.

With the coming of the late eighties, these external and internal factors were combining to work against the initial successes of the Sandinista government. Ever darker clouds loomed on what had been a bright Nicaraguan horizon. The masses were becoming disillusioned but the leadership did not have sufficient organizational lines of communication to know it. Even their polls were faulty. The Sandinista defeat in 1990 was inevitable, given the context in which the vote occurred. The election of the US-backed opposition candidate Violeta Chamorro represented a triumph for US policy, the local quislings who backed it, and a few reformers outside the Sandinista National Liberation Front (FSLN). It also pointed to the arrogance of many Sandinista leaders and the pervasive authoritarian tendencies in Nicaraguan political culture.

Violeta Chamorro proved to be a benign leader who nonetheless presided over the massive rollback of most of the gains the Nicaraguan masses had achieved during the Sandinista years. Sovereignty and national dignity became ever more subordinated to US pressure and to the requirements imposed by international lending agencies like the International Monetary Fund. Chamorro's term in office (1990–96) has witnessed the reincorporation of Nicaragua into the US sphere of influence and its reinsertion into an international economic system increasingly dominated by aggressive capitalist powers. Nicaragua has been returned to the status of a small Central American state whose role it is to produce coffee, bananas and other export commodities for the new metropolitan powers and to provide a product market and investment opportunities for international corporations in the globalized neoliberal economy. No longer the focus of international attention, it has begun to slip away from its period of change and renovation. By 1996, its historical horizons have been very much reduced.

Gary Prevost begins the work by providing a balance sheet of the gains and losses that the revolutionary process suffered through the Sandinista years and during Chamorro's term in office. He continues by assessing the current status of the primary positive results that have emerged from the revolution in the areas of agrarian reform, political democracy and popular participation, women's rights, workers' rights, education, health care, Atlantic Coast autonomy, national identity, and the creation of a more democratic economy. The purpose of the chapter is not to provide an overall balance sheet on the Sandinista revolution by focusing on its achievements and failures but rather to begin from the point of its legitimate successes and then to analyse how well those gains have been protected during the years of the Chamorro government. Those seeking a more comprehensive analysis sheet on the Sandinista years can look to the co-editors' *Democracy and Socialism in Sandinista Nicaragua* and Vanessa Castro and Gary Prevost (eds), *The 1990 Elections in Nicaragua and their Aftermath.*

Prevost's basic conclusion is that the Sandinista achievements have been rapidly undermined by the Chamorro government and its supporters in Washington. The rollback of gains is especially significant in the social sector and in the re-establishment of a conservative political economy in Nicaragua. In the areas of women's rights and Atlantic Coast autonomy the formal legal gains of the Sandinista period have remained in place, but the Chamorro government has exploited weaknesses in the Sandinista approach in this area to undermine practical gains. Prevost concludes that the elimination of the historic repressive apparatus of the Somoza regime and the continued distribution of Nicaraguan farmland to small- and medium-sized producers are the gains which have been best protected during the last six years. However, even in the latter two arenas, the status of these achievements is fragile in Nicaragua's volatile political climate.

Harry Vanden's chapter builds directly on his previously stated argument from *Democracy and Socialism in Sandinista Nicaragua* that a significant factor in the Sandinista revolution's failure to achieve its stated goal of a fundamental transformation of Nicaragua was its abandonment of grassroots, participatory democracy in favour of standard representative democracy. Vanden argues that a clear strength of the Sandinistas was the power and dynamism of a myriad of grassroots movements that participated in the overthrow of the Somoza regime and then pushed forward early gains of the revolution in a variety of areas. However, beginning with the 1984 elections, the FSLN began to marginalize the direct political role of the movements and concentrated on constructing a representative democratic system along Western lines. Such an orientation was carried out in the context of the US war on Nicaragua and the FSLN's attempts to gain legitimacy in the international community, especially Western Europe. The Sandinistas succeeded in the short run by winning the 1984 elections and fending off the Contras but ultimately opened themselves up to defeat in the 1990 elections. Vanden argues that the Sandinistas were defeated in the 1990 elections because the United States and its sympathizers within Nicaragua were able to manipulate the election to their advantage. The Sandinistas' ability to resist that manipulation was undercut by their abandonment of revolutionary principles and their willingness to compete in an arena favourable to their political enemies.

Vanden argues that the 1990 elections marked the beginning of a return to political decision-making by political and economic elites that was conducted far from institutions in which the masses could exercise any real power. He demonstrates how the Chamorro period witnessed the development of a political system that was increasingly characterized by intense competition among political elites about issues that were often irrelevant to the daily lives of the Nicaraguan people. As the Chamorro period comes to an end, he sees a widespread sense of alienation among the populace from the primary political actors, including the Sandinistas.

Richard Stahler-Sholk's chapter focuses on the struggle in Nicaragua between the 'structural adjustment' programmes of the IMF and World Bank and the resistance by popular organizations within Nicaragua. He argues that the incoming Chamorro government moved quickly to implement an orthodox stabilization and adjustment programme which brought financial support from a variety of international lending agencies and USAID. However, the Sandinista era had left a legacy of high levels of mobilization. Initially this provided a base from which organized labour and other sectors could resist, forcing some backing off from the harshest plans in 1990–91. However, the strength and coherence of this resistance was gradually eroded by the dynamic of economic adjustment itself and by a combination of legitimacy problems and divisions within the Sandinista party. Meanwhile, by the end of its six-year term the Chamorro government was politically weak and economically dependent on external financing that was drying up. Inflation had been brought under control, but unemployment had soared and there was serious doubt about the sustainability of a project that could not deliver economic growth or alleviate the poverty of a majority of the population.

The chapter by Cynthia Metoyer Chavez begins from the theoretical premise that men and women experience governmental policies differently. From that perspective the transition from Sandinista power to the Chamorro government is analysed. The basic conclusion of the chapter is that Chamorro's neoliberal policies have hit women harder than similarly situated men. Chavez arrives at this judgement using a mixture of qualitative and quantitative data. The qualitative data takes the form of extensive interviews carried out with peasant women who provide a litany of the challenges they face – lack of credit, delays in receiving land titles, high prices for food, and so on. The personal observations are backed up by statistical data demonstrating the unequal impact of Chamorro's policies. For example, historical structures of dis-

crimination in Nicaragua dictate that women typically receive less education than men. Consequently UNO's redistribution of state property has mainly benefited well-educated men: of the total of 5000 who received some allotment of land by 1992, only 1221 were women (24 per cent). Women have also been harder hit by economic policies that have raised unemployment. Some 56 per cent of the unemployed and underemployed are women.

The final chapter by Pierre LaRamée and Erica Polakoff focuses on the current status of grassroots organizations by placing their development in an historical context and within the framework of Sandinista efforts to expand popular participation within the revolutionary process. Two of Nicaragua's many grassroots organizations are the primary focus of the study – the Nicaraguan Women's Association (AMNLAE) and the Sandinista neighbourhood organization (now called the Community Movement, originally Sandinista Defence Committees (CDS)). LaRamée and Polakoff argue that while the Sandinistas were committed in a broad sense to popular participation they had no viable large-scale or national-level model of democracy – with a genuine participatory element – to draw on. Capitalist democracies more or less limit participation to periodic voting exercises between largely ideologically similar parties. Capitalist systems tend to reduce competition for power to contests between factions of the political and economic elite. On the other hand, socialist countries are primarily authoritarian, highly centralized and bureaucratic party states. Communist parties operate on the Marxist-Leninist principle of democratic centralism which concentrates power in the hands of party cadre and state managers.

In the absence of a clear framework for placing the mass organizations that developed during the revolutionary overturn of Somoza into a revolutionary political framework, these organizations created a dilemma for the FSLN. Although intent on empowering the masses and leading the country down the road to democratic socialism, the FSLN wanted to do so on the basis of the same broad alliance that brought down Somoza. As a result, the mass organizations were seen as instruments to achieve the aims of the FSLN in the context of this struggle with its class opponents who constantly wanted to moderate the revolutionary change. However, as the

Sandinista mass organizations were subordinated to the goals of FSLN state power they became less and less vibrant organizations drawing in the creative power of their members. As a result, even before the 1990 electoral defeat, sharp debates occurred over the proper relationship between the FSLN and organizations such as the CDS and AMNLAE. However, the electoral defeat forced more immediate and drastic changes. During the Chamorro period, Nicaragua's grassroots organizations have become far more dynamic with the renamed Community Movement (MC) leading the way. The MC has been in the forefront of struggles by urban dwellers to retain ownership of their homes in the face of efforts by the Chamorro government to return properties to their former owners. The Community Movement's largest and most widespread project focuses on children in very poor neighbourhoods through over 200 'Children's Community Centres'. The LaRamée/Polakoff chapter concludes by placing the experiences of Nicaragua's grassroots movements within the larger context of current literature on 'new social movements' and the emergence of 'civil society' in Latin America.

1 The Status of the Sandinista Revolutionary Project

Gary Prevost

On 25 April 1990, Violeta Chamorro assumed the presidency of Nicaragua, two months after her National Opposition Union (UNO) coalition scored a decisive electoral victory ending 11 years of rule by the revolutionary Sandinista National Liberation Front (FSLN). The backers of President Chamorro, both inside and outside Nicaragua, expected her administration to move quickly to dismantle the revolutionary projects of the Sandinistas. This chapter will give an assessment of Nicaraguan society based on the questions: what gains of the Sandinista revolution have been overturned by the Chamorro administration and what gains have been protected by the Sandinistas and their supporters. Additionally, it will analyse the current relationship of political forces within Nicaragua with an eye towards the prospects for social change in the coming years.[1]

SANDINISTA ACHIEVEMENTS

To answer the two questions that have been posed, it is first necessary to draw a balance sheet on the 11 years of Sandinista rule with an eye to cataloguing the transformations of Nicaraguan society that did emerge during this period. Transformations in ten areas will be discussed briefly: agrarian reform, workers' rights, creation of a more democratic economy, women's rights, elimination of the historic repressive apparatus, democratic political processes, education, health care, Atlantic Coast autonomy process, and the re-establishment of a Nicaraguan national identity. In analysing the successes of the Sandinista revolution and ultimately assessing the success and failure of the current government to overturn these gains, it is important to acknowledge that many of the gains of the Sandinista period had already been eroded by the effects of the Contra war and the Sandinistas' own policies even before Chamorro assumed office. This chapter does not seek to draw a balance sheet on the years of Sandinista power. That has been accomplished elsewhere;[2] rather this work begins with the accomplishments of the Sandinista revolution and analyses those changes that have occurred since 1990.

Agrarian reform is at the top of the list of Sandinista achievements because it is often cited as the single most important development of the 1980s in Nicaragua. Nicaragua is primarily an agrarian country. By 1990 the agrarian reform had affected more than half of the country's arable land, benefiting some 60 per cent of all rural families. Also, by 1990 the majority of farms were in the hands of small- and medium-sized producers, in contrast to the historic maldistribution of land going back to colonial times. Initially the Sandinista land reform had concentrated on creating a significant state sector for agroexport but beginning in 1985 much greater emphasis was placed on land distribution to individual *campesinos*, and by 1989 the small private producers and the cooperatives were responsible for 47 per cent of all agricultural production (Baumeister 1989: 34). The *campesino* sector benefited from the government's policy of easy credit terms and technical assistance along with state-run processing and storage facilities. This step forward was partially offset by commercial policies that kept producer prices low. In one of its final acts, the outgoing Sandinista-led National Assembly passed laws designed to protect the agrarian reform from its possible dismantling by the Chamorro government. While the laws could not make up for ten years of failure to grant the necessary titles, they have provided a legal basis to struggle for the maintenance of this gain.

A significant expansion of workers' rights, especially the right to form unions and engage in collective bargaining, was a definitive achievement of Sandinista power. Prior to 1979, only about 30 000 Nicaraguans (less than 10 per cent of the workers) were trade union members and strikes or even collective bargaining were made virtually impossible by the Somoza regime. By the end of the 1980s there were more than

2000 workplace unions with some 55 per cent of the working population unionized (*Barricada Internacional* 1989: 2). New laws enacted by the National Assembly guaranteed the right to strike and collective bargaining. Some trade union rights, including the right to strike, were suspended during the Contra war, but strikes occurred throughout the 1980s. Most labour confrontations were settled through dialogue with the FSLN.

During the Sandinista years, a considerable transformation of the Nicaraguan economy occurred in the direction of the interests of Nicaragua's poor majority. Through government intervention, unemployment was sharply reduced, basic necessities such as food and clothing became accessible to a much greater proportion of the population, and the gap in the standard of living between rural and urban areas was narrowed. These gains were achieved through a combination of government credit policies and a subsidization of basic necessities with export revenues. This achievement, probably more than any other, was always fragile, and by 1990 the combination of the Contra war and Sandinista economic policies undermined this transformation.

In the area of women's rights, the gains of the 1980s were numerous including paid maternity leave; equal access to education; legal equality in relation to divorce, adoption, and parental responsibility; a measure of economic independence; and the inclusion of sex education in the school curriculum. Of course, these gains occurred in the context of a very traditional male-orientated society and with a Sandinista government that often resisted women's demands out of a lack of commitment to women's rights and a deference to the Roman Catholic hierarchy. However, even with those limitations, women had emerged by 1990 as much greater players in Nicaraguan society than ever before.

Sometimes overlooked in recitations of revolutionary achievements, especially by outside observers, was the elimination of the repressive apparatus of the Somoza regime and its replacement by an army and police force under civilian political control. The brutality of Somoza's National Guard is well chronicled and one of the Sandinista government's first acts was the establishment of the Sandinista Army and the Sandinista Police without any involvement of persons connected to the National Guard. In many bureaucratic areas the

Sandinistas were forced to depend on some Somoza holdovers, but not in the police and army. As a result, when the Sandinistas handed over state power in 1990, they left behind army and police institutions imbued with a revolutionary consciousness and insulated from penetration by North American institutions. The Sandinista Army and Police were not immune from human-rights abuses. Rather they were under strict political supervision and their human-rights record compared quite favourably with their Central American neighbours. Disappearances and killings by government forces were commonplace in the 1980s in El Salvador, Guatemala, and Honduras. This simply did not happen on any comparable scale in Nicaragua.

Another Sandinista achievement hailed by virtually all analysts was the establishment of a democratic constitutional and electoral process that resulted in Nicaragua's first truly peaceful and legal transfer of political power from one party to another. During the Somoza era and before, Nicaragua had the façade of a democratic constitution and elections, but the political reality was a dictatorship that rigged elections and operated outside the law. The 1987 constitution, which combined Western liberal democratic norms with a revolutionary social conscience, was the centrepiece of the new political progress. In addition, Nicaragua conducted two honest elections, in 1984 and 1990, the second of which saw the Sandinistas defeated but committed to the democratic will.

In the area of education the 1980s saw significant gains, particularly in the early years. The 1980 Literacy Crusade, cited as a model campaign by the United Nations, dramatically reduced illiteracy, particularly in the rural areas. The Nicaraguan government also committed a greater share of resources to education than any previous administration. By 1989, the school population had grown from 300 000 to 1 million and the government launched a follow-up to the Literacy Crusade in the form of 17 000 education collectives providing adult education to 200 000 Nicaraguans (Norsworthy 1991: 109). Education was, however, undermined by the Contra war as resources were diverted away to the military and schools were forced to close in areas of heavy fighting.

Provision of health care to the whole of the Nicaraguan population was greatly expanded, especially during the early years of the revolution. For the first time, Nicaragua gained a true national health system under the Sandinistas. During the Somoza era only about 15 per cent of the population received care. Substantial expansion was achieved in both curative and preventative medicine. More than 400 new health clinics and several major hospitals were built around the country. Government expenditure on health care more than tripled (Norsworthy 1991: 116).

After initial serious mistakes, the Sandinista government enacted an autonomy statute for Nicaragua's Atlantic Coast that is a significant achievement for the rights of the indigenous peoples of the Americas. Nicaragua's eastern coast, rich in minerals and other natural resources, had long been exploited with no care for the environment nor the non-Hispanic population that lived there. Initially the Pacific Coast-based Sandinistas continued the same pattern of dominant relations with the coast. After serious confrontation with CIA-sponsored Indian rebel groups in the early 1980s, however, the government entered into dialogue with the Atlantic Coast residents. This dialogue resulted in a 1987 Autonomy Statute that guarantees the rights of the indigenous groups to their own language, culture, and communal forms of land ownership. In addition, the statute recognizes the rights of the different groups in regard to the development of natural resources. Also established were regional governmental assemblies with direct representation from each ethnic group. The statute intended for the transference of considerable authority to these governments, especially in the areas of taxation and resource development.

Finally, the Sandinista revolution provided for the reestablishment of a Nicaraguan national identity. The revolution allowed Nicaragua to significantly break free of the United States economically, politically and culturally. Through culture and education, the country was able to reclaim some of its own history, including the story of the struggle of Sandino against the US invaders. Nicaragua was also able to gain a much greater identity in the world community. Somoza's government had had only limited diplomatic contacts, but the Sandinistas expanded Nicaragua's relations to encompass important African and Asian nations, including the People's Republic of China. Nicaragua assumed a leadership role in the Non-Aligned Movement and hosted several international conferences. For the first time Nicaragua established significant aid and trade relationships with a variety of Western European governments. These contacts, combined with the other achievements of the revolution, began to generate a national pride in Nicaragua that had largely been lacking in the earlier years.

CHAMORRO'S VICTORY

The Chamorro election victory, while not fully anticipated either by Chamorro or her Washington backers, laid the groundwork for a fundamental assault on the projects of the Sandinista revolution. The Chamorro candidacy was a transparent political initiative fostered in Washington when it became clear in 1988 that the Contra war had fallen short of Reagan's intent. The 14-party UNO coalition was brought together under the auspices of the US embassy and was united only in its hatred for the Sandinistas.[3] The coalition contained political parties from the far right to the far left. It became clear soon after the election that Chamorro and her closest advisers would dominate the political decision-making. Even Chamorro's running mate, Independent Liberal leader Virgilio Godoy, was quickly marginalized. The isolation of Godoy and his alliance with the most pro-Contra right wing elements led many observers to give Chamorro and her advisers, primarily Antonio Lacayo, a moderate label. In reality they are deeply conservative and have worked closely with the United States to reverse the policies of the Sandinistas. Chamorro and many of her advisers were members of a right-wing fundamentalist Catholic cult called 'The City of God'. Chamorro's conservatism manifested itself very well in the appointment of fundamentalist Humberto Belli to the Ministry of Education. Belli, working closely with the US Agency for International Development (USAID), moved quickly to marginalize Sandinista influence in the schools on the grounds that the previous government had promoted an 'atheist humanist view of life'. With AID funding, the Ministry quickly replaced Sandinista-era texts with books imported from the United States. The fundamentally conservative and anti-Sandinista strategy was also evidenced by the government's headlong drive to reprivatize the economy. Within weeks of taking power, Chamorro and her advisers moved to privatize virtually all state-run property, from farms to factories, against the strong resistance of the labour movement. In many instances the properties were returned to their former owners, including persons who had been closely associated with the Somoza dictatorship. The privatization occurred within the framework of a neoliberal policy of 'structural adjustment'. Such a policy was not unique to Nicaragua but rather was part of a worldwide initiative of the United States and international lending agencies like the International Monetary Fund (IMF). It should be noted that a form of 'structural adjustment' was begun by the Sandinistas in 1988 and 1989 under the pressure of the Contra war and pressure from the West European donor countries. However, the policies pursued by the new administration were qualitatively harsher and contained no safety net for Nicaragua's majority poor.

Since assuming office, the Chamorro administration has introduced two stabilization programmes – economic policies designed to reduce inflation and eliminate the balance of payments deficit. (Nicaragua earns around $300 million a year and spends about $700 million a year on imports.) The programme involved large cuts in public spending, tight controls on credit to producers, and big devaluations. The initial programme was vigorously opposed by a renewed labour movement in 1990 with a resulting retreat by the government. However, in 1991 similar measures were successfully implemented. Virtually all government controls of the economy have been lifted. Prices and the currency have been significantly stabilized, but largely as the result of massive foreign aid received in 1991–2 rather than any serious effort to reactivate production. Between 1990 and 1994 Nicaragua received the highest per capita foreign aid of any developing country: $182 annually, though this has now dropped to $130. But the huge foreign-debt service the country was paying meant that even that capital flow could not cover the current payments gap, so the debt kept on growing. By 1994, 96 per cent of all cash aid went to service the foreign debt (*Envío*, May 1995: 5).

The Chamorro administration has had a very important ally in its anti-Sandinista campaign – the government of the United States. A prime vehicle for US involvement has been USAID. AID officials saw Nicaragua as an excellent venue for its strategy of counter-reform. AID's profile in Nicaragua was thus very political and ideological as it sought to place the Sandinistas in irreversible retreat. As part of its Central American strategy for the 1990s, US officials sought to eliminate governmental obstacles to trade, to promote reform of political and military institutions to meet US needs, and to encourage Central American economic and political integration under North American dominance.

AID used its promises of assistance to influence Nicaraguan government policy on all levels. US assistance has been provided only after Nicaragua has complied with all IMF rules in regard to domestic economic policy. In addition, the United States has used aid as a weapon to pressure the government on issues where Washington and Managua have been at odds. For example, in acknowledging the reality of the strength of the FSLN in national politics, Chamorro decided to retain Sandinista Humberto Ortega as chief of the army. The US government never agreed with this decision and for more than three years sought to have it overturned. In so doing, US officials made a tactical alliance with the far right forces of Godoy. On the Humberto Ortega issue, the Chamorro government, with aid from the USA temporarily suspended, announced in late 1993 that Ortega would be removed. US funding was renewed.

Not surprisingly, AID money has been used to favour institutions in Nicaraguan society that are anti-Sandinista and pro-US government. Some of the recipients include conservative trade unions, the Supreme Council of Private Enterprise (COSEP), and conservative nongovernmental organizations such as Save the Children and Project Hope (Webbels 1993: 10). In the last two years US pressure has taken a new direction. With Senate Foreign Relations chair Jesse Helms taking the lead, the US government began to champion demands for the return of confiscated land to former supporters of the Somoza dictatorship. Many of these people became US citizens after fleeing Nicaragua in 1979 and now support for their claims is being based on that citizenship. US Ambassador John Maisto has stated on several occasions that future US aid will be conditional on the settlement of these land claims. AID officials have stated that no US assistance can be given to any land that may have been illegally confiscated (*Barricada Internacional,* July 1995).

BALANCE SHEET ON THE GAINS

Agrarian Reforms

A balance sheet on the defence of the gains of the revolution begins with agrarian reform. Key Sandinista leaders believe that this is the most important achievement that remains in place five years after the loss of Sandinista state power. Their view may be overly optimistic, but it is based on the fact that, according to recent statistics, 78 per cent of Nicaraguan farmland remains in the hands of small- and medium-sized producers. Property is still more equitably distributed in Nicaragua than before the revolution (52 per cent of the land in 1978 was controlled by large landholders), and the number of large estates remains small, especially in comparison to other Central American states.[4]

However, the agrarian reform programme is under attack from the government and this achievement remains in jeopardy. Formally, the new administration was committed to respecting the land tenure arrangements of the previous government. In practice the counter-reform began almost immediately. Decrees 10–90 and 11–90 of May 1990 created a commission charged with reviewing the land confiscations of the previous government. Former landlords were given six months to petition for the return of their lands, though lands confiscated from Somoza were to be excluded. By the end of June 1990, the government approved requests by 57 former owners to rent some 86 000 acres of land on state farms (Norsworthy 1991: 82).

The large-scale return of former owners, mainly self-exiles who had developed business interests in Miami, led to many confrontations and mobilizations. These mobilizations led to the July 1990 general strike which demanded the repeal of Decrees 10–90 and 11–90. The National Workers' Federation (FNT) received assurances that no further land would be returned, but in reality the government continued its privatization and land-return policies behind the scenes. The ability of the union movement to carry out a resolute struggle against the return of lands was undermined by crosscutting interests. In some instances farm workers welcomed former landlords, hoping that their return would bring new capital into their farms. In other instances, the government's firmness in moving forward with privatization persuaded some farmers to accept what they thought was the best deal they could get.

At the end of the Sandinista period, nearly 12 per cent of the country's farmland was state-owned under the rubric of the Area of People's Property (APP). This area was declining slowly after 1985 as Sandinista agrarian policy shifted towards the distribution of individual plots, but it remained largely intact and became a key target of the Chamorro counter-reform. Many of the 70 000 workers on state farms were affiliated to the Sandinista-led Rural Workers' Association (ATC) and were seen as a significant Sandinista power base to be attacked.

Initially, the ATC sought to prevent the privatization process entirely, but retreated from this position as the result of the previously discussed division within its ranks. Eventually, the union accepted the government's policy with several stipulations. No property was to be returned to people who had close links with Somoza, and smallholders and cooperatives who had benefited from agrarian reform would be protected. In the latter case, former owners were compensated with shares in public utility companies (water, electricity, and telecommunications). After considerable negotiation, the union agreed to a formula for the privatization of the APP lands – workers (32 per cent), demobilized army personnel (17 per cent), ex-Contra (21 per cent), and former owners (30 per cent). However, the workers on many farms that were to be returned to their former owners refused to accept the agreement. They argued that they were the legitimate owners and feared the loss of their jobs, homes, and personal plots. This led to serious conflicts in which former owners tried to take possession of the disputed properties with the aid of the police and army. According to 1993 union figures, this has resulted in over 130 arrests and seven fatalities (Evans 1993: 10). Many of the farms are in dispute and cases are still being fought out in the court system. The speed with which this privatization was carried out is demonstrated by the fact that by the end of 1993 the ATC reported that the agricultural APP had been 100 per cent privatized.[5]

While it is clear that large numbers of medium- and small-sized producers retain control of their land, the long-term future of this pattern of land tenure remains in doubt. In what seems to be a blatant government tactic, many peasants still do not hold the actual title to their land. Without the title, the current banking system will not grant credit to such farmers in most instances. This situation has left many farmers unable to plant their crops and facing bankruptcy and foreclosure. During 1995, many protests were staged to highlight the gravity of the situation regarding land titles. In June, more than 6000 small farmers from throughout Nicaragua marched on President Chamorro's office, and the ATC staged long-term occupations at two sites in Managua to underscore their plight.

The problem of credit is not limited to the untitled farms. Credit cutbacks have fallen particularly hard on the rural poor. The number of *campesino* families served by the National Development Bank, BANADES, had expanded from 16 000 in 1978 to a peak of 102 000 in 1988 under the Sandinista government. By 1991 this was cut to 31 000 families (Baumeister 1995: 259). The combination of less money allotted by the government to small producers and the tighter lending policies of the banking system have conspired to place many small producers in a precarious financial situation where they are highly vulnerable to being bought out by larger landholders. Privatization reached its zenith in November 1995 when the National Assembly voted to sell the government's most profitable business, the Nicaraguan Telecommunications and Postal Service (TELCOR). In December 1995, The National Development Bank announced the creation of a trustee office to recover outstanding debt. The agency will have the power to seize the debtor's property and auction it off to repay the debt. Farming organizations estimated that some 3.4 million acres of land, belonging to small and medium-scale producers are in danger of being seized. Many of the producers are behind on payments because the Government has established high interest rates (44 per cent a year) (*Barricada Internacional*, December 1995).[14]

Under the laws enacted during the transition in 1990, no lands were to be returned to persons connected to the Somoza family. In practice, however, this law has been violated, and now the Somocistas have gained an important ally in the US government which is lobbying on their behalf. Members of Somoza's own family have become active in attempts to reclaim property, including farms.[6] In the face of these policies and pressures, it is not clear how long Nicaragua's relatively democratic distribution of land can be maintained.

The privatization process has not been limited to the agricultural sector; state-owned manufacturing, utility and service industries were also targeted. As in the rural areas, the initial instinct of the union movement was total opposition to privatization, and large demonstrations, including factory occupations, occurred during the summer of 1990. However, divisions within the working class and the absolute commitment of the government led to the privatization process going forward. The union movement concentrated on winning agreements allowing all workers to purchase all or part of the privatized enterprises. This process of full and partial workers' ownership has turned out to be highly controversial and contradictory. An agreement between the government and the FSLN in 1991 established the principle that when an enterprise is privatized a minimum of 25 per cent of the value of the enterprise must be available for purchase by the employees. No provision of the agreement blocked full purchase of the enterprise if the workers could raise the capital. A good example of the complexity and difficulty of this process is the food industry where the Sandinista Workers' Federation (CST) represents 1200 workers in 11 enterprises that were previously state-owned.

By mid-1995, five of the enterprises were 100 per cent worker-owned, and three were mixed with worker-owned shares from 25 to 50 per cent. The remaining three were completely privatized. The Secretary-General of the Food Workers' section detailed how government policies and the overall economic crisis have combined to create a very mixed picture for the workers.[7] On the positive side, the food processor Delmor has been a success. The fully worker-owned company is profitable. Having paid its debt to the government, it is now expanding to export to other Central American countries. However, even its relatively good position is threatened by low-priced foreign competition and antiquated machinery. Other worker-owned industries in the food sector are not as fortunate as Delmor. In one case, the El Mejor coffee processing plant is fully worker-owned but carried out no production for almost two years as the government directed coffee production to those processing plants that were wholly private. Production was resumed in 1994 after an agreement with a worker-owned coffee plantation, but production remains modest. In another worker-owned coffee processing plant, El Caracol, the government and the banks made operation of the enterprise almost impossible during a lengthy dispute over ownership. Basic services were cut off, and vehicles were confiscated. Worker-owned enterprises have usually found it very difficult to obtain credit, even with formal ownership. In many cases, particularly with farmland, the government has been slow in granting formal title to the workers, thus undermining their ability to obtain credit. The unions have sought to secure financing directly from abroad, but so far this approach has had little success, in part because of the overall chaotic economic situation in the country.[8]

Union leaders that were interviewed remain convinced that full and partial worker ownership represents an important achievement and a primary battleground for the union movement, but it seems to be a questionable position. By compromising their initial demand against privatization, the union movement forfeited the momentum and bargaining power that it had in 1990. When the union movement enters the arena of ownership and management, it is not playing its strongest card. In the arena of financial capital, the government and the private sector have both the money and the expertise. The unions are working hard to adjust to their new role, but it seems that the amount of time and resources devoted to privatization has come at the expense of their representation of workers in traditional owner-management situations. Even if the union movement can make some of the enterprises successful, it is estimated that these efforts can only benefit five to ten per cent of the workers.[9] Any process that benefits such a small percentage only further divides the working class and ultimately weakens the union movement.

Neoliberal Economic Reforms

The overall democratization of the Nicaraguan economy that occurred in the Sandinista era has been significantly undermined by the new government's neoliberal economic model. As noted earlier, the Sandinistas themselves had retreated from a more democratic economy by 1988, but the counter-reforms of the Chamorro government have deepened the process of reconcentration of wealth in the hands of fewer people. The strategy has been 'structural adjustment', a redistribution of resources to the capitalist sector as the favoured way of reactivating the post-war economy (see Chapter 3). Virtually all government controls of the economy have been lifted. Food prices are now almost entirely market-driven with all remaining government food subsidies eliminated. Supermarkets have sprung up all over Managua with well-stocked shelves of primarily imported foodstuffs. However, the price of goods is comparable to North American standards and is, therefore, out of the reach of ordinary Nicaraguans. Because the stores are stocked with imported goods, local producers are not the ones to benefit from this revival of commerce. The beneficiaries are primarily the private commercial intermediaries who have re-emerged.

What is obvious to any visitor to Managua these days, is that the conspicuous consumption of the middle class has returned with a vengeance. New businesses – auto parts shops, restaurants, computer stores – have popped up throughout the city. The symbols of American capitalism are featured in newly painted billboards on the road in from the airport – Firestone, Goodyear, Motorola. During the 1980s vehicle traffic in Managua was generally light, but today traffic jams have begun to occur as wealthy Nicaraguans return with luxury automobiles from Miami. In the last two years several cable television operations have opened throughout the country and Nicaragua's middle class now enjoys multiple channels from the United States and Latin America. During the Sandinista era Nicaragua had begun to move in the direction of a more democratic economy by controlling the import of luxury goods and redistributing wealth through government policy, but today the country has clearly returned to an orientation that benefits the wealthiest sector of Nicaraguan society.

The reconcentration of wealth has also occurred in other ways, particularly in changes to the banking system. Existing state-owned banks could not be privatized because of constitutional provisions. As a result, the government encouraged the establishment of a parallel private system and by 1995 ten private banks were in existence. To prop up the new banks the government assigned most of the foreign financing to these institutions. Also, to undermine the viability of the state banks, a sharp reduction in personnel was carried out. The progressive lending policies of the state banks that supported agrarian reform through generous loans to poor peasants have been eliminated. The National Development Bank now operates on strictly commercial criteria. The new economic policies also seek to reverse Sandinista efforts for Nicaragua to become more self-sufficient as part of a Central American common market. In 1990 Chamorro cut import duties from an average of 80 per cent to 30 per cent. As a result, there was a flood of imported textiles, shoes, and metal goods with which domestic producers could not compete. The subsequent closing of plants has only worsened the country's staggering unemployment. 50 per cent of the economically active population was underemployed in 1992 and 1993, and figures rose to nearly 52 per cent in 1994. Open unemployment also grew considerably in 1994, reaching almost 24 per cent of the labour force (*Envío*, May 1995: 5). The job cuts in the formal sector have been dramatic. The number of people paying social security dropped 23 per cent between 1990 and 1994 in absolute terms, without even factoring in the growth of the employable population. According to a UN study, 70 per cent of the population is living in poverty, with 40 per cent in acute poverty (Evans 1993: 12).[10]

Social Reforms

The Sandinista revolution received considerable international attention and praise for its efforts in the field of education, particularly the successful 1980 National Literacy Crusade and the expansion of adult education. How is education faring under the new government? Education policy has been highly controversial under Minister of Education Humberto Belli. Within the wider context of reduced spending on education, the main feature of Chamorro's programme has been curriculum revision and an offensive against the Sandinista-led teachers' union, ANDEN.

The curriculum changes being implemented in Nicaraguan schools seek to marginalize Sandinista influence and to promote a world-view closer to the ideological outlook of Chamorro and her advisers. Belli has spoken of the need to create an education system 'permeated with Christian-inspired values'. Within weeks of the government's arrival in power, thousands of new school books appeared in Nicaragua funded by USAID. By the 1991 school year, these books and the new school curriculum were well entrenched. Typical of the new curriculum is the 'Civic Morals' text that teaches conservative values of subservience and obedience to church and state authorities.

The Ministry of Education recognized that there would be resistance to the changes because of strong Sandinista influence among the nation's 30 000 teachers primarily through ANDEN, the teachers' union. The Ministry of Education used harsh tactics to break down ANDEN's resistance to the curriculum changes. Within the first four months of the new government, ANDEN reported that 420 teachers had either been arbitrarily dismissed or transferred to schools far from their homes (Norsworthy 1991: 108). ANDEN has fought the government's actions and some teachers have won reinstatement through the courts, but the strong-arm tactics have largely succeeded in taming the resistance of the teachers. A six-week teachers' strike was conducted in early 1995, but the union was only able to win a very modest pay increase. Most teachers, including Sandinistas and their sympathizers, have been forced to implement the new curriculum in order to retain their employment in very desperate economic circumstances.[11] The combined impact of the years of war and the further cutbacks in education spending during the last five years have almost totally reversed any gains that may have been accomplished in the early 1980s. In 1979, approximately

22 per cent of those students who began primary school completed sixth grade; in 1992 the same figure was being cited by the Ministry of Education. For both years, less than 10 per cent of rural populations completed primary school. In another telling statistic, the 1993 illiteracy rate was already equivalent to or greater than the 54 per cent rate in 1980, when the national literacy campaign took place. In absolute numbers there were approximately half a million more illiterate Nicaraguans in 1993 than in 1980.[12]

Efforts have also been undertaken to undermine Sandinista influence in higher education. In one of its final acts, the outgoing Sandinista-dominated National Assembly passed the University Autonomy Law guaranteeing 'academic, financial, organic, and administrative autonomy' for the country's institutions of higher education. The passage of this law was the culmination of years of efforts by university students and faculty to have greater control over their own affairs. Chamorro attempted to reverse these gains but was largely unsuccessful when she faced massive resistance from virtually everyone connected to the universities. Failing to be fully successful in this manner, the government has moved to reduce funding for higher education and to raise fees so that students from poorer families are less able to attend school. In the summer of 1993, *Barricada Internacional* reported that more than 8000 students were denied entry to institutions of higher education due to a lack of government funding (Duarte 1993: 15–17). In late 1995 and early 1996 the struggle over the funding of higher education dominated Nicaraguan politics. Militant demonstrations and building takeovers resulted in violent confrontations between university students and the government. These demonstrations occurred as the students sought to force the government to implement a constitutionally mandated expenditure of 6 per cent of the national budget on higher education.

The Nicaraguan people had made significant health gains in the first years of the revolution, but the Contra war began a process of eroding those gains that continues now under the Chamorro administration. The current regime's dismantling of the Sandinista system is again based on a privatization process. In part because of constitutional provisions requiring a public health system and in part because of resistance from well-organized health care workers, the government has not fully succeeded in implementing their privatization plans. Notwithstanding, they are definitely moving forward. The system is clearly favouring those who have the resources to pay for health care over those that do not. This is being done in a variety of ways. At public hospitals and clinics only the visit to a doctor remains free; all other services, including diagnostic tests and medicines, involve significant charges, usually beyond the means of the majority of the population. Visits to a doctor are by no means guaranteed because the number of appointments available has been severely reduced as a result of the sharp cutback in government funding for public hospitals and clinics. The overall budget of the Ministry of Health has been cut from $130 million in 1989 to $70 million in 1994 (Nicaraguan Ministry of Health 1994). As a result many medical personnel have been laid off from the public health system and forced to seek work in the growing private system. The government actually subsidized the transfer of medical talent from the public to the private sector by giving doctors cash incentives to leave the public system and move into private practice. Many doctors remain committed to the public system but find it necessary to split their time between a presence at the public hospital and a private practice. This obviously limits the number of appointments available in the public system.

Other privatization tactics are also being employed. Private doctors are permitted to rent space and equipment from the public hospitals at favourable rates. In some hospitals, a certain percentage (up to 50 per cent) of the beds are now reserved for private patients. Many of the pharmacies in the public facilities are now operated by private concerns who own the drugs that they sell, and therefore gain a majority of the profits. The government is also funnelling money from workers' health payments into the private sector. In the past, the social security tax paid by workers went entirely to support the public system. Now the Social Security Institute is developing its own institutions in the private sector. Medical workers will no longer be state employees but rather organized into cooperatives selling services. This effort is a union-busting strategy and dovetails with the ideological drive towards privatization. Ending the status of medical personnel as public employees is allowing the government to fire those workers who are union activists. The Sandinista-led health workers' union, FETSALUD, has fought against the privatization and the union-busting but its membership has been reduced from 23 600 in 1990 to 18 000 in 1995.[13] Finally, in mid-1995 the Ministry of Health announced that it would begin charging for basic health services on a sliding scale.

All these cutbacks have had an impact on the health of the Nicaraguan population. According to statistics released by the Office of Nutrition of the Ministry of Health, more than 60 per cent of Nicaragua's children under the age of one year are anaemic and 4 per cent of all children under five years old suffer from irreversible mental retardation because of malnutrition. In 1988 more than 40 000 children received nutritional attention in government daycare centres. Many of those centres are now closed and only 7000 children are receiving the same attention. Infant mortality rates have increased from 62 deaths per 1000 live births in 1987 to 107 in 1994.[14]

Women's Rights

How have the gains in women's rights achieved in the Sandinista years fared during the last five years? On the positive side, the legal framework has largely been maintained. The UNO parties and the Catholic Church have sought to restrict the right to unilateral divorce by either party but so far the Sandinista-era law has been sustained. However, the legal framework put in place by the Sandinistas had many serious limitations for women's rights and now Nicaraguan women's organizations are seeking to strengthen their rights but are doing so in a generally unfavourable political climate. Examples of loopholes in the legal code of the revolutionary period included abortion, violence against women, democratization of the family, lack of an equal pay provision, and protection for gays and lesbians. In spite of pressure from some women, abortion was never decriminalized. The Sandinista leadership made it clear that it was unwilling to go against the Catholic Church on this issue. However, during the 1980s abortion became widely tolerated and few prosecutions occurred. In the last five years the Managua women's hospital stopped performing therapeutic abortions, and the procedure has been driven entirely underground. The pro-government media have presented powerful anti-abortion measures, and this has dovetailed with the Catholic Church's wider campaign of promoting a more traditional role for women. Nicaragua has also taken a backward step with the recent passage of anti-sodomy laws. Prior to this new measure, Nicaraguan law had been silent on such questions. After a heated internal debate, the Sandinista bench opposed the sodomy law in the National Assembly, but the conservative forces prevailed. The Women's Commission of the National Assembly, dominated by Sandinista legislators, has proposed a democratic family code and a law forbidding violence against women, but the passage of these proposals seems unlikely. The conservative framework of laws on women and the family allowed the Nicaraguan delegation at the UN Population Conference in Cairo in 1994 to line up with the Vatican against the mildly progressive majority document.

Nonetheless, the greater involvement of women in the public life of Nicaragua, an important advancement of the 1980s, remains strong. The women's movement is probably stronger today than ten years ago, with the Nicaraguan Women's Association (AMNLAE) strengthened and many new organizations on the scene, including several which have clearly labelled themselves as feminist. AMNLAE operates 57 centres throughout Nicaragua that promote programmes in health, economic development, gender consciousness, political involvement, the environment, and legal rights. In 1994 the programmes reached 108 000 women.[15] That these centres continue to function and provide services to women that were not available prior to 1979, is a significant achievement.

However, on many fronts the position of women is under strong attack in today's Nicaragua. The country's economic crisis bears heavily on women because so many are heads of households and because they bear a disproportionate burden of household production and reproduction. Desperate economic circumstances have resulted in the greater occurrence of prostitution. AMNLAE's service orientation has benefited some women but there seems to be little defence of women's rights in the political arena. The Catholic Church and its allies in government seem to have the upper hand in implementing their anti-feminist agenda. Countering this trend are a variety of new groups organized around concrete issues such as violence against women and women's health, including abortion.

Atlantic Coast Autonomy

The autonomy process is under direct challenge from the Chamorro government. Basically, Managua has used flanking tactics to undermine the rights of the residents of Nicaragua's Atlantic Coast. Rather than seeking any formal reversal of the Autonomy Statute, the central government has simply ignored the law and created its own approach to the region. In April 1990, Chamorro created the Institute for the Development of the Atlantic Coast (INDERA) and appointed former Miskito Contra leader Brooklyn Rivera as its head. For four years the meagre resources allotted for the coast were channelled through INDERA rather than the regional Autonomous Councils. The Managua government used INDERA to divide the different coast groups by pitting them against each other. With shifting political alliances, both regional governments passed motions rejecting INDERA in 1994, and the central government eliminated the agency and proceeded to carry out all programmes for the coast through national-level ministries. This strategy is aided by the control of the south region government by the anti-autonomy Liberal Constitutional Party (PLC). The February 1994 regional elections brought the PLC to power in the south, while an FSLN/Yatama alliance governs in the north. Yatama's commitment to autonomy, in spite of its Contra roots, has allowed tactical alliances with the FSLN against the anti-autonomy parties.

The greatest challenges to the coast today are growing environmental destruction and the lack of control over its natural resources – fishing, forestry, and mining. According to the spirit of the autonomy law, control over the coast's resources was to be vested with the regional governmental bodies. In the last four years, the central government has either ignored this aspect of the law or used local leaders sympathetic to the central government to conclude deals on the exploitation of resources that are detrimental to the region's interests. Virtually all the fishing rights for the coast have been placed in the hands of Oceanic, a company run by Diego Lacayo, brother of the presidential adviser. Oceanic does not actually carry out significant fishing operations. Rather, it subleases its rights for an exorbitant profit to primarily US-based fishing companies who do the actual work. Because the US operators have their own processing plants in Honduras and Costa Rica, the Bluefields processing facility is operating well below capacity with more than 250 people out of work. Another previously government-owned facility, the COMABLUSA sawmill has been privatized to a US owner. Its level of operation, however, is still in doubt. Its future may hinge, in part, on an effort of the central government to sell 150 000 acres of forested communal lands that indigenous people claim should be protected by the Autonomy Statute.[16]

Supporters of the autonomy process, headed by former diplomat Francisco Campbell, have launched an ambitious project to create the Autonomous University of the Caribbean Coast (URACCAN). In March 1995, after several years of planning, URACCAN opened its first year with over 400 students on three campuses in Bluefields, Puerto Cabezas, and Rosita. When fully operational, the university plans to train local people in a variety of fields needed in the coast including mining, forestry, and fishing. URACCAN has significant support from NGOs in North America and Europe and modest funding from the National Assembly, but the Chamorro government has given its support to another new institution, the Bluefields Indian Caribbean University (BICU). BICU is not a direct competitor to URACCAN because it is a two-year college with a primarily business curriculum, but it does compete for the scarce resources for higher education on the coast.

Efforts in the National Assembly to achieve constitutional reform come from a variety of political directions and may yet prove to be an important battleground for the legal and political future of the autonomy project. The Sandinista years ended without the passage of laws to implement fully the process outlined in general principles in the 1987 statute. This failure gave the anti-autonomy forces in the Chamorro government and the National Assembly the handle with which to stall the process. Atlantic Coast National Assembly members, Mirna Cunningham and Ray Hooker of the Sandinista Renovation Movement (MRS), have embarked on an effort to raise the 1987 statute to the level of constitutional status. If the effort eventually succeeds, it will be a step forward for autonomy, but constitutional reforms are a two-edged sword. In a political context dominated by conservative forces, constitutional principles could be established that would explicitly block further autonomy for the coast. Strong sentiment clearly continues to exist among the indigenous residents of the coast, but it is far from clear that their hopes for autonomy and sustainable resource development will be achieved.

Changes in the Police and Army

The elimination of Somoza's National Guard and the repressive police force of his rule was clearly an important achievement of the Sandinista revolution. How has this gain fared during the last six years? Maintenance of Sandinista influence in the army and the police was at the centre of the transition negotiations after the February 1990 elections. Sandinista leaders were fearful that the Chamorro administration would bring former Contras directly into the government apparatus and exact revenge on their people for the military defeat that the Contras suffered at the hands of the Sandinista army. Aware of the importance of the issue to the FSLN and mindful of their considerable power even in defeat, Chamorro allowed Sandinista Humberto Ortega to remain as the head of the army. The President herself assumed the position of Minister of Defence. Chamorro argued that retaining Ortega as head of the army would maintain social peace and allow for an orderly reduction in the size of the military. The reductions have been dramatic. At the time of the elections there were about 96 000 soldiers and by mid-1994 the number stood at 17 000 (Evans 1993: 16–17). The retirement of Humberto Ortega in early 1995 and his replacement by a less controversial Sandinista officer, General Joaquín Cuadra, has been hailed by many as a further depoliticizing of the armed forces. Cuadra is from a Nicaraguan oligarchic family, and is a cousin of Antonio Lacayo. By the end of 1995 the label of Sandinista had been removed from the organization.

The maintenance of the army as a progressive force has met with mixed results. On the positive side, up until late 1995 the army has not been absorbed into the framework of US domination that is true for every other Latin American army except that of Cuba. Nicaraguan officers are not trained at the infamous School of the Americas in Georgia. US leaders clearly hope for the long-term integration of the Nicaraguan army into their sphere of influence but remain sceptical about the character of an army still dominated by Sandinistas. Nicaraguan military officials have sought full participation in Central American military manoeuvres but so far they have been rebuffed.

Also on the positive side, the army has not engaged in systematic human-rights abuses so common to Nicaragua's northern neighbours in Central America. Nicaraguan citizens do not have to fear arbitrary death or detention as they did during the Somoza era. The army also remained strictly neutral during the protracted political stalemate between the executive and legislative branches in 1994 and 1995. The professionalism of the army helped to defuse the potentially volatile confrontation. However, there were also some disturbing trends that led many Sandinistas to question the leadership of Ortega and the trajectory of the army. In numerous incidents the army has been deployed in labour disputes, especially in the countryside where it has acted in support of former landowners attempting to recover their land from occupying workers. There is also a developing bitterness within the Sandinista ranks towards senior army officers who have apparently acquired considerable amounts of land. Senior army officials have also established a number of private companies including a bank located in the former EPS press headquarters in front of the Intercontinental Hotel in Managua.

The deterioration of the police as a progressive force has occurred with even greater speed. The Ministry of Interior was renamed Ministry of Government and the Sandinista Police became the National Police. Chamorro appointee Carlos Hurtado, became the new high official replacing Tomás Borge. New uniforms were issued, and police units in riot gear were commonly deployed in the capital, a departure from the Sandinista era. In 1992 Managua mayor Arnoldo Alemán created a new municipal police force (highly visible in the capital with their red berets). After initial hesitation, the police have increasingly come to be used as strikebreakers. In the most dramatic confrontation to date, three people were killed when a force of over 600 anti-riot policemen opened fire on protesters in the Managua neighbourhood of Villa

Progresa during a transportation strike in May 1995 (*La Prensa*, 19 May 1995; *Barricada*, 20 May 1995). Earlier in 1995, police used force against a peaceful demonstration of the La Fosforera match workers and also against the national teachers' strike (*El Nuevo Diario*, 15 February 1995). In early 1996, the Annual Reports of the three major Nicaraguan human rights groups declared that in 1995 the major violator of human rights in the country was the National Police. (*Barricada*, 14 January 1996). During the 1980s the Sandinista Police gained a reputation for honesty and discipline. Much of that reputation is now gone. Bribery and corruption have developed on a widespread basis in the context of the desperate economic situation and low police salaries.

Nicaragua and the World

Any objective analysis of Nicaragua's standing in the world must come to the conclusion that the gains for Nicaraguan sovereignty that were achieved during the Sandinista period have been significantly eroded in the last four years. The most dramatic example is Nicaragua's case against the United States in the International Court of Justice at The Hague. In 1984 Nicaragua initiated a suit against the United States at the ICJ charging that US support for the Contra rebels violated international law and US treaty commitments to Nicaragua. In June 1986 the Court ruled in Nicaragua's favour, and Nicaragua formally petitioned the Court to demand $17 billion in reparations. The United States never responded to Nicaragua's petition, and soon after the February 1990 elections the Bush administration began pressing Chamorro to withdraw the suit. Chamorro initially resisted but in 1991 she bowed to US pressure and abandoned the case without receiving any compensation. The Nicaraguan government was widely criticized within the country for its action, but the concession fully demonstrated how Nicaragua was again becoming quickly reintegrated into the US sphere of influence.

Further evidence of renewed US involvement in Nicaraguan internal affairs has been demonstrated in the process by which US foreign aid has been provided. Interference in internal Nicaraguan affairs was graphically shown by the FY 94 Foreign Aid Appropriations Act passed by the US Congress on 25

September 1993. Section 567 of the law places a series of strict limitations under which Nicaragua can receive its appropriated dollars. The provisions include proof of civilian control over the Nicaraguan army and police. This condition was a thinly veiled demand for a further reduction in Sandinista influence in these institutions and specifically the removal of Humberto Ortega as head of the army. Soon after this legislation was passed, Chamorro announced that Ortega would be leaving his post sometime in 1994. (He actually left the post in early 1995.) Aid was also tied to further investigation of a 23 May 1993 explosion in Managua of a weapons cache. The US government, without any plausible proof, has attempted to link the explosion with alleged Sandinista involvement in international terrorism, including the World Trade Center bombing. Additionally, North Carolina Senator Jesse Helms slipped into the foreign aid bill an amendment, which was adopted by 92 votes to four, that would have required cutoff of US aid to countries that have expropriated property or nullified contracts with any US citizen or corporation. This provision was a direct attack on the Nicaraguan law that prohibits return of property to supporters of Somoza. Many of these people emigrated to Florida, became US citizens and are now attempting to use this citizenship as leverage to have their property returned. The Helms amendment was later removed in conference committee, but Helms vowed that the issue is not dead. In 1995 Helms introduced legislation that would tie future US aid to the successful resolution of land claims of all US citizens in Nicaragua. The citizens include many who fled the Sandinista revolution and were naturalized in the 1980s. The United States government has also continued to press the Chamorro government to uphold its discredited policy of isolating Cuba. In January 1995, Minister of the Presidency, Antonio Lacayo, announced that Cuban-Nicaraguan relations were on hold (*Barricada*, 3 January 1995). This hold comes in spite of the strong relations that developed between the two countries in the 1980s and demonstrates Managua's subservience to Washington.

The Ruling Coalition

Five years into the presidency of Violeta Chamorro, what is the state of her ruling coalition and how is her primary opposition, the FSLN, faring? Chamorro's UNO coalition has been fractured almost from the beginning. The electoral alliance that included Vice President Virgilio Godoy of the PLI did not even last until the government assumed power in April 1990. Godoy never actually assumed any real duties as Vice President. Along with his party and several others, Godoy has moved into the opposition on the grounds that Chamorro and Lacayo were making too many concessions to the Sandinistas during the transition process. Godoy was joined in his withdrawal of political support from the government by two other prominent political figures on the right – Alfredo César and Arnoldo Alemán. César, leader of the conservative Social Democratic Party, was a Contra political leader and was elected President of the National Assembly in 1991. However, his presidency was controversial and in January 1993 the Sandinista members of the Assembly allied themselves with a small group of centrist, pro-Chamorro delegates to oust César from his position. After his ouster César declared himself officially in opposition to the government, a further deepening of the division in the UNO.

In the last four years, Godoy's prominence has declined and Managua mayor Arnoldo Alemán emerged as the leader of Nicaragua's conservative forces. Formerly a supporter of Somoza, Alemán achieved notoriety for his attempts to eliminate symbols of the Sandinista revolution such as street names, public murals, and the eternal flame at the grave of Carlos Fonseca. He used AID money and new local taxes to finance showy public works projects, aimed at gaining popular backing for himself. In the tradition of Cook County, Illinois politics, the mayor's office appears prominently on billboards near all of his new projects in Managua. Even Sandinista officials admit that his efforts in Managua made grassroots organizing there more difficult.[17] In mid-1995 Alemán, encouraged by the performance of his Liberal Constitutional Party (PLC) in the 1994 Atlantic Coast elections, resigned his mayor's position and formally announced his presidential candidacy. Running independently of UNO, the PLC emerged as the largest single party in both regional councils, with 19 seats in the north and 18 seats in the south. Public opinion polls have shown Alemán to be the leading candidate in the period leading up to the October 1996 election.[18]

The State of the FSLN

Key questions on the minds of most Nicaragua-watchers are: Are the Sandinistas maintaining their base of support and do they have any prospect of returning to power? These are difficult questions to answer but some patterns are beginning to emerge. The FSLN remains the largest and best-organized political party in Nicaragua, but the election defeat and its aftermath have taken a heavy toll on the organization, making its long-term prospects unclear at this time.

Sandinista success in the war against Somoza and in the years of state power was nurtured by a broad unity built around certain basic principles. This unity emerged from years of factional warfare in the 1970s and held up fairly well until the election defeat. However, since 1990 the divisions have re-emerged, though not along the same lines as in the 1970s. After a bitterly divisive party congress in May 1994, the FSLN broke into two separate political organizations in January 1995 with the departure from the party of several key figures, including former Vice President Sergio Ramírez and National Directorate members Dora Maria Téllez, Luis Carrión, and Mirna Cunningham. Also many prominent intellectuals, including Ernesto and Fernando Cardenal, left the party. Many of those who left formed the Sandinista Renovation Movement (MRS) which was formally launched as a political party at a congress in May 1995. The gulf between those who stayed in the FSLN and the newly formed MRS is quite wide. Reconciliation seems unlikely and both parties are likely to field candidates in the 1996 elections. The MRS claims a membership of 24 000 (*El Nuevo Diario*, 22 May 1995), compared to the current membership claim of 350 000 for the FSLN (*Barricada Internacional*, February 1995: 3). At any rate, the MRS now dominates the Sandinista bench in the National Assembly. Of the 38 Sandinistas in the Assembly, only seven are clearly affiliated with the FSLN. While not all the rest have formally joined the MRS, they tend to vote with them on key legislative matters including the 1995 reform of the constitution.

It is too early to draw definitive conclusions about the split in the FSLN, but a review of some developments in the party since 1990 may shed some light on the division. During 1992 and 1993, divisions developed within the party over the political course that the party's National Directorate was pursuing as an opposition party. Arguing that the main threat to the gains of the revolution was the activity of the far-right Godoy-Alemán forces, the FSLN leadership pursued a tactical alliance with Chamorro and Lacayo against the far right. The policy was implemented through an ongoing National Dialogue and through an alliance in the National Assembly that removed César as parliamentary leader in January 1993.

It is the view of many Nicaraguan political observers that this alliance resulted in considerable political cost to the Sandinistas. The alliance gave the FSLN no real control over Chamorro-government policies (it was not co-governance), but it meant that the FSLN was seen as bearing some of the responsibility for the dire economic circumstances of the country. In practice, the FSLN's support for social and economic stability has meant that the economic interests of the popular sectors have taken a back seat in the political priorities of the FSLN. Important elements in the resurgent popular movements, especially the trade unions, have shown marked displeasure with the FSLN leadership. This opposition came out into the open in July 1993 with the publication of an open letter signed by 29 prominent Sandinistas that called for the party leadership to distance itself definitively from the Chamorro government and resume close affiliation with the social base of the FSLN, the workers and peasants. The document was signed by many prominent Sandinistas including Victor Hugo Tinoco, Political Secretary of Managua; Doris Tijerino, former chief of police; Gustavo Porras, head of FETSALUD; Fanor Herrera, party head in León; Felipe Pérez, Mayor of León; Henry Petrie, former head of the Sandinista Youth; and Lumberto Campbell, former presidential delegate to South Zelaya. The document spurred considerable discussion throughout the party and received especially strong support from Sandinista unionists and within the Sandinista Youth.[19]

Following the publication of the letter of the Group of 29, Daniel Ortega made an important tactical shift. Fearing a challenge from the left, Ortega began to reposition himself within the party debates. Beginning with his 19 July 1993 revolution commemoration speech that responded to the Group of 29,

Ortega began to identify more closely with popular sectors and to distance himself somewhat, at least in rhetoric, from Chamorro and Lacayo. Ortega's shift to the left made FSLN leaders with more clearly social democratic tendencies (that is, Ramírez, Carrión, and Téllez) vulnerable. Two events in the autumn of 1993 heightened the division. At a meeting of the National Directorate, Ramírez declared an interest in running for the presidency in light of his positive standing in the polls in comparison to Ortega.[20] In hindsight, Ortega may have seen this declaration by Ramírez as the signalling of a power struggle for control of the party. In addition, sharp divisions of opinion within the National Directorate raged publicly over a national strike that turned violent. Ramírez and others criticized the tactics of the strikers, while Ortega clearly sided with those in the streets. These differences were formalized with the emergence of two tendencies prior to the special May 1994 party congress. Ramírez formed the group 'For the Return to a Sandinista Majority' and Ortega led the 'Democratic Left' tendency. The Ramírez group made it clear that it felt the FSLN needed to move towards the political centre if it was to regain political power in the 1996 elections, a task which was considered to be of the highest priority. The Democratic Left group also stressed the importance of winning the 1996 elections but questioned the more definitively centrist leaning tactics of the Ramírez group. It stressed the importance of maintaining the historic principles of the FSLN and identifying with the popular sectors. The Democratic Left was clearly responding to the challenge from the Group of 29. In reality, the Ortega group had re-established its revolutionary credentials without really questioning or changing its conservative alliance strategy.

The May 1994 congress represented a solid victory for the Democratic Left tendency, which dominated the elections to the new Sandinista Assembly and National Directorate. The congress, however, also laid the groundwork for the split that occurred several months later. The spirit of the congress was deeply divisive and marked by harsh personal attacks. In a seemingly vindictive act, Ramírez was excluded from an expanded National Directorate in spite of his prominent position in the party and his leadership of an obviously important minority grouping. Many rank-and-file Sandinistas were shocked by the harshness of the divisions at the congress and hoped that the differences would not lead to a split, but such a break-up may have been inevitable. Since the Sandinista movement incorporated the relatively conservative 'Group of Twelve' in 1978, it had been a broadly heterogeneous political party. That heterogeneity had been suppressed during the years of state power, but the disorientation caused by the electoral defeat and the challenges of being a revolutionary party in the post-Cold War era were too great to overcome without a split.

The party's alliance strategy is not the only target of discontent with the FSLN. The party is still suffering from the widespread belief, both inside and outside the party, that individual members of the party unfairly benefited from the distribution of goods that occurred during the transition to the Chamorro government. Known as the *piñata*, this process apparently resulted in the transfer of considerable property and goods to the leadership ranks of the FSLN throughout the country. Many of the transactions may well have been justified by years of low-paid services, but it was ultimately viewed as unjust by many rank-and-file Sandinistas who did not materially benefit during the transition and by the wider population.[21] The long-term impact of the *piñata* is difficult to assess, but it appears to have significantly undercut the moral authority of the Sandinista movement and has also helped to magnify class divisions within the FSLN that make it almost impossible for the party to mount a sustained alternative to the neoliberal economic policies of the government.

The split, combined with the FSLN's loss of moral authority and failure to articulate a credible alternative to the neoliberal economic policies of the government, makes a return to power through the 1996 elections unlikely. The FSLN leadership seems determined to prevent an Alemán victory at all costs and seems ready to make whatever electoral alliance is necessary to deny Alemán the presidency. Remarkably, the alliance which seems least likely would be one with Ramírez and the MRS. Forming an electoral alliance with Antonio Lacayo has a much greater probability in spite of its obvious political opportunism and Lacayo's very low standing in the polls. The 1996 election remains difficult to predict because of the high level of political alienation on the part of the Nicaraguan populace. At one time the strength of the FSLN was its image as a challenger to the old political elites that had ruled Nicaragua for decades. Today, most Nicaraguans see the FSLN as part of that political elite that has failed to solve their problems. Divided as it now is, it will be hard for the FSLN to change that image, at least in the short term. Widespread alienation plays into the hands of an Alemán candidacy and points to a potential marginalizing of the Sandinista movement.

Popular Organizations

It should be noted that the organized defence of the revolutionary gains is not limited to the formal activity of the FSLN party. Since the 1990 electoral defeat the activities of the popular sectors have actually been strengthened. This activity is a direct legacy of the Sandinista era and is one of the most enduring realities of the revolution. Most of the popular organizations were set up by the FSLN, but since 1990 they have become increasingly independent of the party. This independence has reflected not only the growing maturity of some of the organizations but also discontent with the alliance strategy of the FSLN's national leadership.[22] The strongest of the popular organizations are the unions. The Sandinista unions, organized under the National Workers' Front (FNT), have emerged as the principal opponents of the government's economic policies. However, the power of the unions has been weakened by widespread unemployment and concentration on the establishment of 'areas of workers' property' within privatization. In spite of these limitations, the unions are still a potent force and a factor for positive social change. The strongest of the peasant organizations is the National Union of Farmers and Ranchers (UNAG). Although it has ties with the FSLN, this organization has had an independent power base among small landholders from its origins in the early 1980s. UNAG has always had a private-sector orientation and is now establishing its own bank. There have always been class divisions within the UNAG and this tended to favour the large farmers over the marginalized ones. As a result, it would not necessarily be a strong voice as government policies drive marginalized farmers off their land. It has specifically opposed takeovers by the landless peasants (Evans 1993: 16).

In many ways the organized women's movement has been strengthened since 1990. Many new initiatives were launched in the late 1980s as a response to AMNLAE's close identification with the FSLN's vacillation on women's rights. The growth of a women's movement independent of AMNLAE was highlighted by a women's conference in 1992 that drew over 800 activists. The new organizations are working on a variety of women's issues ranging from reproductive rights to legal services (Quandt 1993). Many grassroots organizing campaigns have been launched in the last four years. Some of the more successful have come from the Community Movement (MC), a reincarnation of the Sandinista Defence Committees (see Chapter 5). While still an FSLN-dominated operation, the organization has a new vitality based around struggles to defend property rights and neighbourhood development. The MC has apparently achieved its greatest successes in smaller towns and cities where the FSLN is well-organized.[23]

Conclusion

To summarize the balance sheet on the Nicaraguan revolution six years after the electoral defeat, it can be said that the future course of Nicaragua has yet to be definitively determined but the prognosis is not good. At this time the counter-revolutionary forces have clearly gained the upper hand in the context of a world situation favourable to the neoliberal programme and the continuing failure of the FSLN leadership to provide a coherent alternative. However, the final chapter of the Nicaraguan revolution has yet to be written. Some crucial gains of the revolution, especially in land tenure and democracy, remain alive. Nicaragua's population, while beaten down, has shown considerable willingness to struggle. The biggest question mark may be the FSLN itself. The split in the party makes its return to power highly unlikely in the short term. It is not clear that the party can recover to again become an inspiration for the majority of Nicaraguans seeking fundamental social change. At the base of the party there remain many dedicated people through whom the organization may be able to recover its lost credibility, but it is not clear that a national leadership exists to

42   *The Undermining of the Sandinista Revolution*

formulate a strategy for the return to power. The FSLN is now seen as part of the political problem by most Nicaraguans and therefore not looked to as a solution. Those who left to form the MRS believe that they can rebuild the people's trust but their limited base among the country's intellectuals makes this unlikely. The grassroots movements alone, however well-organized, are not capable of defending the gains of the Sandinista revolution. Organizations like unions, cooperatives, and women's movements are all capable of militant struggle within their own sectors, but they face an enemy that has control of the state apparatus and the backing of powerful foreign governments and international organizations. As a result of this relationship of forces, the grassroots organizations can be isolated and in some instances played off against each other. Because of Nicaragua's unsolved social and economic problems, radical change can return to the agenda in Nicaragua and build on the gains of the Sandinista period. However, it will require a new political force that does not now exist. It could be a revitalized FSLN or it could be a new political movement that comes from the militancy of the current grassroots organizing.

REFERENCES

Arnove, Robert. 1993. *Education as Contested Terrain: Nicaragua 1979–1993.* Boulder, CO: Westview Press.
Barricada, 3 January 1995.
Barricada, 20 May 1995.
Barricada, 14 January 1996.
Barricada Internacional, May 1989.
Barricada Internacional, February 1995.
Barricada Internacional, July 1995.
Barricada Internacional, December 1995.
Baumeister, Eduardo. 1989. 'y las Tierras Cambiaron de Dueños', *Pensamiento Propio,* July.
Baumeister, Eduardo. 1995. 'Farmers' Organizations and Agrarian Transformation in Nicaragua', in Minor Sinclair (ed.), *Politics of Survival: Grass Roots Movements in Central America.* NY: Monthly Review/EPICA.
Castro, Vanessa and Gary Prevost (eds), 1992. *The 1990 Elections in Nicaragua and Their Aftermath* Savage, MD: Rowman and Littlefield.
Duarte, Vilma. 1993. 'University Crisis', *Barricada Internacional,* August.
Dye, David, *et al.* 1995. *Contesting Everything, Winning Nothing.* Cambridge, MA: Hemispheric Initiatives.

Envio, May 1995.

Evans, Trevor. 1993. 'Nicaragua: An Introduction to the Economic and Social Situation', *CRIES Working Paper*, Managua, October.

Nicaraguan Ministry of Health. 1994. 'Spending on Health 1980–1994', Managua.

Norsworthy, Kent. 1990. *Nicaragua – A Country Guide.* Albuquerque: Inter-Hemispheric Education Resource Center.

El Nuevo Diario, 15 February 1995.

El Nuero Diario, 22 May 1995.

La Prensa, 15 March 1995.

La Prensa, 19 May 1995.

Quandt, Midge. 1993. *Unbinding the Ties: The Popular Organizations and the FSLN in Nicaragua.* Washington, DC: Nicaragua Network.

Robinson, William I. 1992. *A Faustian Bargain: U.S. Intervention in the Nicaraguan Elections and American Foreign Policy in the Post-Cold-War Era.* Boulder, CO: Westview Press.

Vanden, Harry and Gary Prevost. 1993. *Democracy and Socialism in Sandinista Nicaragua.* Boulder, CO: Lynne Reinner Publishers.

Webbels, Erik. 1993. 'Misguided Aid Policy toward Nicaragua' *Nicaragua Monitor*, November.

NOTES

1. The conclusions drawn here are primarily based on field work conducted in Nicaragua in 1991, 1994, and 1995. The research focused primarily on studies done by Nicaraguan social scientists and interviews with the leaders and the rank-and-file of the political parties and grassroots organizations.

2. See Vanden and Prevost (1993) and Castro and Prevost (1992).

3. For a complete review of the 1990 election campaign see Vanden and Prevost (1993: 129–51) and Robinson (1992).

4. These statistics on agrarian reform come from the Nicaraguan Institute of Agrarian Reform (INRA), 'Consideraciónes generales sobre la evolución reciente de la tenencia de la tierra en Nicaragua' (mimeo, May 1995), and were cited in David Dye *et. al.*, *Contesting Everything, Winning Nothing* (Cambridge, MA: Hemispheric Initiatives, 1995). Land numbers in Nicaragua are approximate and the 1995 numbers probably do not include several important privatizations that have placed some land back in the hands of large-scale producers.

5. Interview with Lily Soto, official of the Rural Workers' Union (ATC), Managua, 5 January 1994.

6. In an interview in *El Nuevo Diario* (25 March 1995) Luis Ramón Sevilla Somoza, the first of the Somoza family who is publicly reclaiming his family's confiscated property, stated the value of the claim at over $250 million. The claim has been made in part through a formal petition to the Interamerican Commission on Human Rights in Washington.

7. Interviews with Leonidas Pulidas, Secretary General of the Food Workers' Section of the Sandinista Workers' Federation, Managua, 7 January 1994 and 5 July 1995.
8. Ibid.
9. Interview with Trevor Evans, CRIES, 4 January 1994.
10. Evans (1994: 12). A similar study released by the Nicaraguan Center for Human Rights in February 1995 reported figures of 44 per cent and 75 per cent.
11. Interview with William Schwartz, FSLN Regional Secretary and former ANDEN official, Bluefields, 8 January 1994.
12. Figures quoted from Arnove (1994: 207). Arnove's book is a detailed analysis of Nicaraguan education under both the FSLN and Chamorro.
13. Interview with Dr Andrés Zamora Peralta, Financial Director, FETSALUD, Managua, 5 July 1995.
14. Nicaraguan Ministry of Health Statistics quoted in *Barricada*, 5 May 1995.
15. 1994 Report of the National Executive Committee of AMNLAE and interviews with Dora Zeledón, National Coordinator of AMNLAE, 7 January 1994 and 5 July 1995.
16. Interview with Francisco Campbell, Secretary-General of the Autonomous University of the Caribbean Coast (URACCAN), Bluefields, 8 January 1994.
17. Interview with Enrique Picado, Head of the Community Movement, Managua, 5 January 1994.
18. A Borges and Associates poll, reported in *La Prensa*, 15 March 1995, gave Alemán 43.4 per cent of the vote, with no other candidate garnering as much as 20 per cent. In December 1995, *Barricada Internacional* reported that Alemán was leading FSLN candidate 29 per cent to 22 per cent but the reliability of the poll can be questioned.
19. Support for the Group of 29 document was evidenced in many interviews especially Lily Soto of the Rural Workers' Association, Leonidas Pulidas of the CST, and in discussions with Sandinista Youth leaders, but these people did question the motives of some of the signers who were not closely associated with the popular sectors.
20. Interview with Luis Carrión, former member of the National Directorate, Managua, 3 July 1995.
21. This view was confirmed by many interviews especially Ramón Meneses, Sandinista journalist and former DRI official, and Francisco Campbell, Secretary-General of URACCAN.
22. For a good overview of the post-1990 popular sectors see Quandt (1993).
23. Interview with Enrique Picado, Head of the Community Movement, Managua, 5 January 1994.

2 Democracy Derailed: The 1990 Elections and After

Harry E. Vanden

Actions by the Nicaraguan political leadership, both before and after the 1990 election, suggest that the participation and grassroots democracy that had been initially envisioned as part of the Sandinista programme were sidetracked in a rush towards a system of representative democracy that the dominant group in the Sandinista leadership hoped would satisfy the United States and its capitalist allies and thus increase the legitimacy of the Nicaraguan government in their eyes. Nor did the Nicaraguan people recover any greater democratic power in the presidential term of Violeta Chamorro (1990–96). Indeed, by July 1995 some 40 per cent of the electorate were so disillusioned with the existing political parties and their leaders and with the political system in general that they were considering not even voting. As one researcher observed after a July 1995 poll, 'with adults there is despair, deceit, and frustration ... people say "I have been deceived, I feel frustrated, I don't see what good voting is going to do." As one Managua resident put it, 'the way we are going, no government does anything'.[1] These feelings were a far cry from the generalized optimism that characterized the vast majority of Nicaraguans in the first years of Sandinista rule. The pages that follow offer an explanation of what went wrong with Nicaragua's political evolution.

Up to 1979 Nicaragua was one of the most conservative and authoritarian societies in Latin America. It could boast the longest family dictatorship in the hemisphere (1936–79). Indeed, it could be argued that Nicaragua was among the least democratic of the Latin American republics for the longest time and consequently had little experience of democracy or honest elections. Even the ultra-traditional regime in Paraguay could only date its existence to the early fifties. One author even suggested that it not only had an authoritarian political culture, but that the factional nature of party interaction suggested a political system that was characterized by its underdevelopment (Vickers 1990: 19–27). And five years after the successful 1990 election, the subsequent reversion to factionalism and infighting prompted a well-respected observer of national politics to conclude that democracy had still not matured in Nicaragua.[2]

When the FSLN took power on 19 July 1979, the stage was set for a series of changes that included radical experimentation with forms of participatory and direct democracy, two of the most honest elections in Nicaraguan, if not Latin American, history (1984 and 1990), a very open constitution-making process, and the eventual return to representative democratic forms dominated by political elites. But these and subsequent events were in turn conditioned by a political culture that had been extremely traditional and authoritarian, and a political system that had been slow to develop. In his essay on values in Nicaraguan political culture, Emilio Alvarez Montalván lists authoritarianism, elitism and personalism as among the most prominent characteristics (Alvarez Montalván 1995). Even after years of Sandinista rule, many traditional values continued to permeate Nicaraguan political culture.

New values were, however, eventually interjected into the Nicaraguan context. Like many successful revolutions in the Third World, the 1979 Sandinista revolution promised democracy for the Nicaraguan people. Even before the triumph, the 'Historic Programme of the FSLN' (1969) had committed the revolutionaries to political structure(s) 'that will permit the full participation of all of the people at the national as well as the local level' (El Programa Histórico 1981). Further, as an ever wider coalition of forces joined the revolutionary movement in 1978 and 1979, the prospects for Nicaraguan democracy seemed to grow with the inscription of each new political group, many of which had ties with traditional parties, were strongly committed to Western representative democracy, or had already experienced the participatory democracy of the popular Christian movement.[3] Indeed, it could be argued that the particular forms that democracy took in Nicaragua were related to the specific (and very diverse) nature of the class coalition that overthrew the Somoza dictatorship and to the way in which the FSLN's political leadership conceived and interpreted those classes and their role in the continuing revolutionary process. Likewise, external pressures from the United States and other actors would also condition the ways in which democracy would develop during Sandinista rule and also under the Chamorro administration.

In that the triumphant coalition of forces (and classes) became very broad indeed, the invocation of democracy by the new government at the time of the revolutionary triumph was less of a commitment to a specific programme to institutionalize democratic participation than a general commitment to democratic ideals similar to that first invoked by Bolívar at the end of the struggle for Latin American independence. On the practical plane, each group might define democracy very differently and look to very different structures to ensure that the *demos* (the people) would indeed be able to actively engage in the process of governance.

If the new leadership acknowledged a diversity of political groupings ranging from traditional parties to ultra-left movements, it also tacitly acknowledged several different conceptions about exactly what democracy was, or more specifically, which structures maximized its realization. Thus members of the two traditional parties, the Liberals and the Conservatives, wanted Western-style elections and representative government as did most of the bourgeoisie and quite a few in the middle class. Members of the popular classes, who had mobilized for the revolution or who had participated in local community or church organizations, wanted to make sure that their direct participation would continue and would be given effect. Rural and urban workers and peasants wanted more power over where they laboured as well as in national affairs. Sandinistas wanted to ensure the predominant position of the Sandinista movement and make sure that the lower classes would be enfranchised for participation that would guarantee ongoing, effective participation in decision-making and economic justice for the toiling masses. And many Sandinista militants wanted to ensure the hegemonic position of a vanguard party in which democratic centralism would be practised.

Much of the Sandinista leadership was sceptical of a narrow, bourgeois definition of democracy that minimized direct popular participation and did not include a social and economic dimension. They also wanted to make sure that the democracy that was implemented did not block necessary social and economic restructuring and did not facilitate foreign manipulation. 'Democracy neither begins or ends with elections ...'[4] 'Effective democracy, like we intend to practice in Nicaragua, consists of ample popular participation; a permanent dynamic of the people's participation in a variety of political and social tasks ...'[5]

What leading Sandinistas did envision was a popular democracy that would not just allow participation by the few (or domination by the upper classes) but would build democracy from below through the construction of neighbourhood, gender or functional grassroots, mass organizations (Walker 1982: 9–10). The idea of meaningful democratic participation (though sometimes defined somewhat differently) became a strong symbolic value that was readily adopted by wide sectors of the population. As delineated in Chapter 5 of this book, newly formed mass organizations became an important mechanism for popular empowerment. These organizations were also the direct communication link between the masses and the political leadership. They informed the people of new political directions and channelled popular demands through the party to the National Directorate.[6] To hold the victorious coalition together and transform society, some form of political representation that would allow the participation of anti-Somoza elements from the upper and middle classes but would facilitate direct representatives from the lower classes and the Sandinistas was needed. Initially, different organizations were able to send the representatives they chose to an appointed Council of State, which served as the national legislature, albeit with limited powers. After the 1984 election this institution was replaced by an elected National Assembly. Representatives were now chosen by a system of proportional representation and were no longer sent directly by different organizations. Forms of representative democracy began to supplant the attempt at direct democracy represented by the mass organizations and the Council of State. This trend was greatly accelerated by the time of the elections in 1990. By this time, even the Sandinista leadership seems to have assumed that representative structures for national and local government would indeed constitute democracy. Thus, even before the vote in the elections in 1990, it could be argued that traditional, representative forms of democracy had already triumphed at the expense of direct, more participatory democratic forms.

The 1990 election was held after more than a decade of Sandinista rule and after the general outlines of a transformed Nicaraguan society were already in place (see Vanden and Prevost 1993). During these years, in some sectors of the population, many traditional values had been challenged, if not replaced, by modern values.

There were also many external factors that were brought to bear on the electoral process and the ensuing Chamorro administration. The vote occurred as the United States was poised to again extend its power through the region and – as became apparent – further project it in much of the rest of the world. As it turned out, the election occurred in an international and regional context over which the Nicaraguan government had only limited control despite its often brilliant use of diplomacy and the international legal system. From 1982 on, the United States had used military, diplomatic and economic means to impose its will on the Sandinista government and the Nicaraguan people. Although it was often unclear whether the Republican administrations would be able to realize their primary objective of overthrowing the Sandinistas, it was clear that they could make sure that the new government would have very difficult going, would have very limited options, and would be hard put to claim it could be a model for other Central or Latin American countries.[7]

From 1982 to 1990, Nicaragua experienced a Contra war that cost 30 000 lives and in excess of $12 billion in economic losses,[8] a total US economic embargo from 1985 on, and the continual threat of direct US invasion. Responding to such pressures and the Central American Peace Process, the government in Nicaragua not only decided to go ahead with the elections previously scheduled for November 1990, but advanced the timetable to February 1990.

On 25 February 1990, Nicaragua was again tested. Previously, committed Nicaraguans had struggled to change an archaic system and rid the country of a horrid dictator. Next came the struggle to establish a fledgling government and make a whole nation out of a country torn by civil war. Then, after the Reagan administration took office, came confrontation with the United States and a Contra war which lasted in earnest from 1982 to 1990 and eventually forced the Nicaraguan government to devote huge amounts of material and human resources to defend itself (by 1987, 62 per cent of government expenditures were for defence). A further trial began with the economic war whose start coincided with the Contra upsurge, was intensified by the 1985 economic embargo imposed by the United States, and lasted until Violeta Chamorro was inaugurated in April 1990.

Although the FSLN had been able to maintain unity while it was in power, most of the other parties had not been able to overcome the traditional Nicaraguan proclivity for factionalism and internecine struggle. Although only six opposition parties had opposed the FSLN in the 1984 election (encouraged by the United States, the Coordinadora Democrática boycotted the elections), by the beginning of 1988 there were 14 opposition parties plus a few opposition political groupings.[9] The Reagan administration had pushed the military side of low-intensity conflict and discouraged parties from participating in 1984. As Bush took office, US policy began to emphasize an electoral challenge to the Sandinistas.

If traditional factionalism had held sway, there would have been some 20 opposition parties on the ballot. This would have splintered the opposition vote and allowed the FSLN an easy victory. Realizing this, the Bush administration pushed for a unified opposition coalition and strongly encouraged the selection of a fresh opposition candidate who could serve as a symbol around which the opposition could rally. Although lacking political experience, Violeta Chamorro filled this role very well. With US support, she was able to edge out Enrique Bolaños, a traditional political leader and head of COSEP, and become the National Opposition Union (UNO) candidate. By the time of the election, the US-supported unity of the National Opposition Union had held. Included in the new coalition were parties that traced their origins to the old Conservative and Liberal parties as well as social democratic parties, social Christian parties, a party tied to Contra leaders and even two Communist parties – the Nicaraguan Socialist Party (PSN) and the Communist Party of Nicaragua (PC de N).

The campaign proved to be lively and the besieged Sandinista leadership was thrown into a different kind of battle. In order to be able to compete successfully against the

US-supported UNO coalition, the Sandinista leadership had to devote its organizational and human resources to an expensive electoral contest that ate up more than $7 million of very scarce funds. The cost of preparing and administering the election was itself enormous (this will also be the case for the 1996 election). The Supreme Electoral Council, the independent governmental body responsible for overseeing and running the election, spent in excess of $15 million alone.[10] Given the miserable economic conditions in which most workers and peasants found themselves by 1989, they might well have preferred to forgo the election in favour of a direct dispersal of funds that would have guaranteed jobs, increased real wages and thus gained relief from hyperinflation. Many felt they were being crucified on an economic cross wrought from the US-sponsored Contra war, the US trade embargo, lack of economic and administrative expertise on the part of the Nicaraguan government and the international economic conditions that had driven most Latin American states to desperation and governmental change.

The Sandinista leadership knew that conditions were bad, but thought their political base could endure a little longer while they employed the human and material resources at their disposal to win the election. They mobilized their followers well and spent $7 million on a very fancy campaign[11] that featured not only door-to-door organizing and mass rallies, but gave away FSLN baseball caps, straw hats, T-shirts, backpacks and cigarette lighters. The FSLN used outside media and public relations consultants to develop a very slick, rock-star-like presentation of Daniel Ortega. The Sandinistas reasoned that such extravagant spending was necessary to win the election so as to secure their position and legitimize their political system in the eyes of the West. They also realized that they were playing a high-stakes game and that the United States had designated huge sums of money for the UNO Campaign. This was epitomized by the 1989 US Congressional authorization of $9 million in overt funding for the opposition. This was to be dispensed through the National Endowment for Democracy. The result was, however, that the Sandinista campaign presented a stark contrast to the austere, impoverished conditions in which most Nicaraguans found themselves (LASA 1990: 21). This was clearly a contributing factor to the Sandinista defeat.

Up to the time of the February election it seemed that the Nicaraguan revolution might be able to build on the experiment with socialist democracy that developed in Chile in the early 1970s. The Sandinistas would give an expanded electorate the opportunity to decide if they wanted to continue the process of socialist construction or opt for another type of regime. Right up to the eve of the election, most opinion polls suggested that the Nicaraguan people would ratify the socialist, mixed economy experiment and continue with Sandinista democracy. However, the Sandinistas' stunning defeat at the hands of the US-sponsored National Opposition Union (UNO) suggested that the *demos* was not entirely satisfied with Sandinista rule or the type of socialist democracy that was developing in Nicaragua (see Vanden and Prevost 1993, Chapter 7).

The real battle for Nicaragua had become economic and would continue to be economic through 1995. Careful analysis of the facts suggests that the low-intensity conflict that the Bush administration waged against Nicaragua was having disastrous effects on the economy (Vanden and Walker 1991). Nor was the Nicaraguan government well prepared to manage the deteriorating economic conditions. There were three reasons for this. First, as the Sandinistas came to power, few had little, if any, substantial training in economics, administration, planning or management. Second, there were few models of relevant participatory management, planning or administration with which they had any experience or on which they could draw; nor was the acquisition of these skills given a high priority. Third, Cuba and the socialist nations on whom Nicaragua was increasingly forced to rely for material and technical assistance were ill-prepared to supply the necessary training in these areas. Indeed, subsequent events suggest that the training offered to their own government employees might have been sadly lacking in this regard.[12] Nor does the Nicaraguan government appear to have availed itself of much of the expertise that could have been acquired through these states or to have sought it from multilateral aid agencies such as the United Nations. The result was that virtually all levels of government and party were not prepared (or predisposed) to deal with the magnitude of the economic problems that befell Nicaragua (because of the war and the embargo) in ways that were consistent with the form of democracy or the model of humane development that the revolution had set as its goals in July 1979.[13]

As the United States helped to fashion the programme and campaign thrust for the UNO, the economy and the claim that the US-supported candidate was the only one who could improve economic conditions (by enlisting US support and stopping the US-backed Contras) became increasingly prominent. Only with the election of the US-sponsored candidate – it was suggested – could the Nicaraguans hope to begin to recover from the unbearable economic conditions they were experiencing, or end the Contra attacks.

By 1988 inflation had reached some 36 000 per cent, real wages had fallen to 29 per cent of their 1980 value, milk consumption had fallen by 50 per cent, and production had reached levels that were abysmally low (Vilas 1990: 12). In that same year, the deteriorating economy began to have a heavy impact on daily life and increasingly became a subject of intense public concern. The government clearly assigned blame to the US actions. However, like the neoliberal policies the Chamorro administration would later follow, the governmental response was an austerity programme that was modelled on the 'heterodox shock' treatments that Brazil and Argentina employed in 1985 and 1986 and as such fell disproportionately on the poor (Conroy 1990: 21). This marked a shift in Sandinista policy, because it was the first time since the Sandinista insurrection, that 'the Nicaraguan government ha[d] begun a program of economic reforms that d[id] not include steps to protect the poor, the social base of the Sandinistas, from its harshest effects' (IHCA 1988b as cited in Conroy 1990: 21). By the middle of 1988, prices for basic commodities had risen 600 per cent, and the government lifted price controls on the majority of goods and services. The result was devastating for wage earners. 'The Economics minister was forced to admit that average individual worker's wage would cover only 48 per cent of the "minimum market basket" for a family' (IHCA 1988a as cited in Conroy 1990: 22). Other sources that were normally sympathetic to the government estimated that the average worker's wage would cover as little as 7 per cent of the economic basket (Conroy 1990: 22–3). Many criticized these policies because they believed they represented a new policy direction that veered away from previous goals of popular consumption and would transfer resources from internal consumption to the export sector, which would ultimately transfer income from workers, peasants and consumers to those who controlled capital (Conroy 1990: 23–4).

As the economic crisis developed in 1988 and after, the government seemed at a loss to find policies or forms of administration that could stem the crisis and protect the lower classes. For instance, the Sandinistas 'offered broad economic concessions to large private farmers, while attempting to hold back worker and peasant demand' (Vilas 1990: 12). Many members of the bourgeoisie and middle class were unwilling to accept the legitimacy of the societal transformation that the Sandinistas advocated. Yet, as the economic crisis worsened, subsidies to middle-class and wealth entrepreneurs were often financed by 'cutting back the consumption, income, and living conditions of the revolution's natural base of support, the workers and the peasants' (Vilas 1990: 12). The government did not seem to know how to organize service or productive functions in ways that were consistent with a state-directed mixed economy and a participatory democratic model. In a trend that anticipated subsequent events in the Chamorro administration, the market increasingly became the primary means of rationing scarce resources – much to the detriment of the popular classes. And when members of the popular organizations took an independent line against this government policy, they were dissuaded from it. If they persisted, they were often accused of being unpatriotic, or worse still, of being in the service of the United States.

The austerity measures of 1989 did, however, help to stabilize the economy. Inflation slowed and Nicaraguan agricultural exports rose 30 per cent in that year. The economy was beginning to stabilize and there was a more plentiful supply of consumer goods. The problem was that real wages continued to drop, so that few wage earners could afford to acquire the now more abundant goods (Conroy 1990: 23–4). This trend continued and accelerated during the Chamorro years.

By the late 1980s, the harm had been done and there was a growing perception that the Sandinistas were not in control or were selling out their poor supporters to gain the economic cooperation of middle- and upper-class commercial interests.[14]

It seemed that the only response to the economic crisis that the Sandinista leadership could agree to implement was one that sought to activate traditional commercial groups in the hope that they would lead the recovery. But by the end of 1989 it seemed to many that the economic dimension of the Contra war coupled with internal deficiencies in management and allocation had caused the Sandinista government to ignore the economic plight of the masses.

In order to diminish any remaining Sandinista support, the Bush administration orchestrated increased Contra attacks in the summer of 1989. As they rampaged through the countryside they spread political messages for the election: 'Only UNO can end the economic crisis'; 'There will be no peace under a Sandinista government'; 'A Sandinista government means war and a continuation of the military draft. Only UNO can bring peace' (McMichael 1990: 166). The Contras became an active part of the anti-Sandinista campaign that was organized by the United States. In all, the US had invested heavily in supporting opposition forces in Nicaragua – some $26 million in overt and covert aid since the 1984 election (Cook 1989: 2–3). Newsweek suggested that $5 million in covert funds had been used for the 1990 election alone (Newsweek 1989).[15] Overt funding for the election was estimated at $12.5 million (Sklar 1989: 50).

The sophisticated low-intensity conflict campaign was clearly having a dual effect. By January 1990, 52 per cent of those registered voters surveyed believed that the economy was the most important issue for them in deciding how to vote in the coming election. By comparison, 37 per cent thought the Contra war was the most important issue (Conroy 1990: 30).

In order to understand why the vote resulted the way it did, it is necessary to delineate the pressures that were working on the electorate. As it turned out, the economic and human attrition of Washington's economic embargo and the ongoing Contra war against the Nicaraguan people finally did wear down popular Nicaraguan resolve to resist foreign pressure and continue their own brand of democracy. Nor was the example of what happened in Panama lost on the Nicaraguan people.[16] Further, as the economic conditions deteriorated and the political support for the direct, participatory democracy of the mass organizations was diminished by their

exclusion from the legislative body after 1984 and their frequent subordination to FSLN control, there were fewer channels through which the masses could effectively communicate
the gravity of their plight. Thomas Cronin suggests that when
'there is growing suspicion that privileged interests exert far
greater influences on the typical politician than does the
common voter' there is a demand for more democracy
(Cronin 1989: 10). But neither the official party nor the mass
organizations seemed willing or able to provide greater democratic participation. And by lauding the election and the connected Western-style representative democracy, the Sandinistas
themselves seemed to be telling the people that this (and not
participatory democracy) was the only democratic instrument
through which they could express themselves. Meanwhile, the
UNO coalition was arguing that its fundamental objective was
to 'construct democracy' and that it planned to 'profoundly
democratize the nation and the society' (UNO 1989). UNO
was the only party on the ballot that had any chance of challenging Sandinista political hegemony. Since Sandinista dominance appeared to many to be ever less responsive to popular
democracy, there were very limited choices for most voters.

Lower-class Nicaraguans were confronted with a difficult
choice. Vote for the Frente and continue to suffer economically and perhaps risk losing more lives to Contras, or vote for
the National Opposition Union and hope that things would
change. Even the week before the election it was not clear how
many voters were genuinely enthusiastic about Doña Violeta's
administrative or political capacity or the hotchpotch political
coalition that UNO represented.[17] But vote for UNO they did,
hoping the new government would (finally) make peace with
the United States and stop the economic and human attrition
that had been so devastating for the Nicaraguan people. In a
January 1990 poll, 61 per cent thought Violeta Chamorro
could reconcile Nicaragua and the United States and 58 per
cent thought she could end inflation (as compared to 50 and
25 per cent respectively for the FSLN).[18]

Many felt that the Sandinista leaders were isolated from the
hardships of the masses and that their political position facili-
tated access to goods that the poor could no longer afford.
Many were also angered by what they perceived as increasing
bureaucratization in government offices. They saw the forma-

tion of a bureaucratic class that was not particularly sympathetic to popular needs and was the beneficiary of a disproportionate share of scarce resources. This created a considerable amount of resentment. Thus it seemed to many that the Vanguard Party had lost contact with the very people it was supposed to represent and consequently was not responding to their needs and feelings. Rather – they felt – it had become an institution that was ruled from the top down ('the National Directorate commands') and had established a set of interests that was not always the same as those of the people.

As the election results trickled in on the Sunday night, it soon became apparent that – believing they had been abandoned by the Sandinistas – the residents of many working-class neighbourhoods in the capital (Julio Bultrago, Las Brisas and San Judas among them) had given UNO a majority. And so it went in other urban areas and in much of the countryside as well. UNO received 54.7 per cent of the vote while the Sandinistas received only 40.8 per cent (most polls had predicted a substantial Sandinista victory, the ABC/Washington Post poll predicted 48 to 32 per cent).[19] To the FSLN's credit, Daniel Ortega announced early on the day after the election that the government would abide by the election results and would cooperate in transferring power to the new government. Later statements specified conditions for so doing. Nor could the Sandinistas expect to control the National Assembly (they would control only 39 of the 92 seats while the UNO coalition would have 51) or very many municipalities across the country (UNO won 102 of the 131 municipal councils).

It was hard not to feel for the hundreds of thousands of Nicaraguans who stayed with the FSLN through these most bitter of times only to see their dreams shattered by a popular backlash against the economic austerity and the military draft that had been necessary to stem the tide of continuing United States economic and military aggression. But, equally, one must sympathize with the thousands of workers and peasants who were trying to improve their lot so they would not have to continue the impossible task of trying to feed and clothe their families on salaries of $20 to $40 a month, who were out of work altogether (the unemployment rate jumped from 24.4 per cent in 1987 to 32.7 per cent in 1989), or who feared that they or their sons would have to fight in a continuing Contra war. Despite the vote, one of the great ironies of the election was that economic conditions for the masses only continued to worsen after Chamorro was in office.

Careful analysis suggests that it was the US-induced economic crisis and the ineffective way it was handled that most hurt the Sandinistas in their traditional bastions of working-class support. Ironically, the Frente leadership seems to have ignored a fundamental aspect of Sandinista doctrine. As repeatedly emphasized by their founding leader and theoretician, Carlos Fonseca Amador, the vanguard must always stay in touch with the masses and must always represent their interests (in Rousseau's terms, represent the general will). If one is constructing socialism, it is imperative that the interests of the toiling masses are represented and protected. It would appear, however, that the Sandinista leadership felt that the masses would have to suffer a little longer while they stabilized the economy, increased production, persuaded the commercial bourgeoisie to participate more fully, won the election and played out the Central American peace process. Although thousands of party militants and Frente supporters accepted those terms, the vast majority of middle- and upper-class Nicaraguans were far from doing so (despite the fact that many often received preferential treatment in the late eighties). And a growing number of lower-class Nicaraguans did not accept these terms at all. Many began to accuse the Sandinistas of operating with a great deal of arrogance. They thought the revolution was supposed to be for them and seemed to feel that continued support for the Sandinistas would only lead to a further reduction of their already miserable standard of living. By ignoring those aspects of direct, participatory democracy that were part of the initial Sandinista programme and by failing to give economic support to its mass base (and natural constituency), the FSLN only left open more formal Western-style institutional democracy as an avenue of popular expression.

Although complaints about the economy and the war were increasingly vociferous, the masses (in and outside the party) do not seem to have found other avenues to effectively communicate the intensity of their suffering to the governmental and party leadership. The mass organizations had lost the direct representation they held in the Council of State when it was abolished in favour of the National Assembly after the 1984 election. And if any leaders of the mass organizations were elected as deputies in the new National Assembly, it was through the Sandinista Party. Thus, as increasingly was the case in the mass organizations themselves, these deputies were susceptible to Sandinista pressure and the Sandinista programme and were not as closely attuned to the immediate needs of the mass base in the organization. Further, it should be noted that the democracy practised in the formal, Western-style structures of institutionalized representative democracy was a far cry from that which was practised in the heady early days of the revolution when voice and vote counted in mass meetings in the neighbourhood, factory or field, or in the mass organizations themselves.

The newly refined electoral framework was imperfect, but still provided a mechanism by which a growing desperation with conditions could be registered. The election proved to be a very effective means of registering a massive protest vote. Indeed, many later said they believed the Sandinistas would win anyway, so they voted for Violeta Chamorro's UNO just to let the Sandinista leadership know that their needs were not being met and that they felt they were being ignored. Given the conditions that existed, it is remarkable that the FSLN could still garner even 40.8 per cent of the vote. The fact that they did suggests the ambivalence many of the popular masses felt about their rule.

AFTER THE ELECTION

Many political observers celebrated the 1990 election as a return of true (Western, representative) democracy. In reality, it was an imposed regime that resulted from economic and military pressure from the United States and its allies and from pro-US conservative groups inside Nicaragua. During the election these forces employed a variety of tactics to induce a majority of the population to vote against the Sandinista government. As reflected in the strong pro-Sandinista vote in 1984, the revolutionary government was strongly supported until the Contra war, the embargo, other imposed measures,

and the leadership's own mistakes (which were also exacerbated by these pressures) started to take their toll. Initially, the
Sandinista leadership had been credited with ending the
Somoza dictatorship and sponsoring badly needed radical socioeconomic reform and cultural and educational renovation.
By stepping up pressure and exploiting Sandinista shortcomings in economics and management, those forces allied
against the government had created – with some help from
the Sandinista leaders themselves – a situation that was easily
manipulated by the US designed and supported Chamorro
campaign. Many Nicaraguan voters came to believe that the
only way things were going to improve was if they removed the
Sandinistas from office. The authoritarian decision-making
style of the government and the arrogance of many government and FSLN party leaders also convinced many other
voters to show their disapproval of the party in office the only
way they could – by voting for the only viable opposition,
UNO.

Before leaving office, the Sandinista government engaged
in what came to be a very controversial action. They rushed
legislation through the National Assembly that granted title to
confiscated property to those who had occupied it during the
Sandinista years. While this did give title to some peasants and
cooperatives and other small property owners, it also gave
quite a few Sandinista leaders title to expensive properties
they had used or been awarded as compensation for their
years of service and sacrifice. Known as the *piñata* (because of
all the 'treats' dispersed to those at the Sandinistas' 'going
away party'), it came to be regarded as a way for the Sandinista
leadership to enrich themselves before leaving office. As time
progressed and poverty among the masses increased, the
piñata bred increasing resentment, helped to erode support
for the Sandinistas, and seemed to confirm the growing
popular perception that government, while paid for by the
many, was by and for the few (Téfel 1995).

In retrospect, it would seem that the 1990 election marked
the beginning of a return to political decision-making by political and economic elites that was conducted far from institutions in which the masses could exercise any real power.
Indeed, the next six years saw the development of a political
system that was increasingly characterized by intense competi-

tion among political elites about issues that were ever more irrelevant to the daily lives of the Nicaraguan masses. As unemployment and poverty became more generalized and income
and wealth more concentrated, it became increasingly clear
that those aspects of economic democracy that had grown
during the earlier years of Sandinista rule were being severely
eroded by successive waves of neoliberal policies. But such was
the strong (and universally prescribed) medicine recom-
mended to combat any remaining socialist bacillus by the
international financial institutions and their capitalist backers.

The popular expectation was, however, quite different. It
was expected that the new government would heed the democratic mandate, utilize the bountiful aid and support that
(UNO voters believed) would surely be offered by the US government, and begin to listen to popular political demands and
respond to the masses' often desperate needs. In reality, it
seems that the real electors were not the majority who voted
for UNO, but the external and internal economic elites who
had engineered the Sandinistas' electoral demise. It would be
their demands – and not those of the *demos* – that would
receive that greatest attention.

What the majority who voted for UNO did not realize was
that Violeta Chamorro had been chosen as an electoral tool to
unseat the Sandinistas. Thus there would be strong pressure to
dismantle the type of state apparatus that had developed
under Sandinista rule, implement a conservative neoliberal
economic programme, and further reduce the power and size
of the mass organizations and the Sandinista Party. Nor would
the masses themselves be empowered in the new system. As
the new president began her term, she initially relied on the
now famous Mayorga plan[20] which was designed to revise the
structure of the Nicaraguan state and fully reintegrate
Nicaragua into the capitalist world economy on terms that
would be favourable to foreign investors and the dependent
Nicaraguan bourgeoisie.

This process continued over the next six years, but initially
it was tempered and at times blocked by the political power
that the FSLN had developed, by FSLN institutionalized power
in state structures like the Sandinista Army, and by sporadic
popular mobilizations. The mass mobilizations at the time of
the revolution and during the first years of Sandinista rule also

set the stage for an often tenacious popular resistance against many of the unpopular economic policies that the government tried to implement. As resistance was worn down, elements of the new policies were, however, gradually put in place.

Nor did the FSLN prove to be an adequate channel for popular resistance. The initial Sandinista commitment to participatory democracy was never reinstitutionalized in the party or in its ties to mass organizations.[21] Nonetheless, the electoral defeat sent profound shock waves through the entire party structure. One of the first responses was to convene a Sandinista Assembly in June 1990 to assess the party's errors and prepare for the future. The 300 delegates (most were elected by party militants) met in the town of El Crucero and passed several lengthy resolutions in which they confronted the party's errors and began to chart a new course (Resolution from El Crucero Assembly 1990).

The party's leaders were urged to 'restructure the FSLN through a democratic process so that grassroots support could contribute to the solution of the most urgent internal problems ...' (Resolution from El Crucero Assembly 1990). In acknowledging its authoritarianism and the autocratic nature of some (Stalinist) socialist influences, the party set the stage for its possible democratic restructuring (see Díaz Lacayo 1994). At the time it seemed for a while that the emphasis on the role of grassroots organization held out some hope that the initial participatory vision the Sandinistas had when they took power may not have been lost altogether after all.

Yet, an important party congress held in July 1991 revealed mixed interpretations of democracy and participation. The general delegates were elected through local assemblies and the National Directorate was to be elected for the first time. However, rather than voting for individual members of the National Directorate, the delegates could only cast their ballots for a pre-selected slate. In this way the very popular candidacy of Dora María Téllez never came to a vote before the congress and the National Directorate continued to be an elite, all-male club. The decision by the National Directorate to automatically include the votes of all members of the old (appointed) Sandinista Assembly also seemed to contradict the general democratization that was expected of the party. In the meantime, worker and peasant organizations became more radical in their mobilizations against the austere economic policies of the Chamorro government and made it known that they intended to focus the power of their mobilized constituencies on the problems that affected their daily lives. Several unions joined to form the Sandinista-affiliated National Workers' Front. Their street demonstrations, strikes and militancy forced the Chamorro government to temper its position and postpone the implementation of many aspects of Central Bank President Francisco Mayorga's austere economic plan.[22]

By 1991, it was becoming increasingly apparent that the Chamorro government was unable to solve basic economic problems for the common people. The fact that conditions actually deteriorated after the 1990 election did little to convince the masses of the ultimate utility of Western-style representative democracy. Nor were conflicts and centripetal forces limited to the Sandinista Party.

An uneasy alliance between Violeta Chamorro and her Vice-Presidential candidate Virgilio Godoy barely endured through the electoral victory. Godoy was rapidly eclipsed by Chamorro's son-in-law, Antonio Lacayo. Upon her inauguration, he assumed the office of Minister of the Presidency. Thereafter he operated as *de facto* head of government, performing most of the executive functions for the President (who was more head of state than head of government). This left Vice President Godoy not only outside the decision-making process, but literally outside the Presidential Palace. Further, the transition agreement that was negotiated between head of the Sandinista Army and President Ortega's brother, Humberto Ortega, for the Sandinistas, and Antonio Lacayo for the Chamorro administration, further alienated Godoy and his conservative following. Of particular concern to Godoy and the conservatives was the fact that the agreement provided for Sandinista control of the army and police and the continuation of Humberto Ortega as army head. Godoy finally resigned in October 1995 and was replaced by Julia Mena. Other rifts quickly developed in the UNO coalition. Eventually, the UNO members in the National Assembly divided into two often hostile camps: one group, led by conservative leader Miriam Arguello, was aligned with Godoy and the other, led by Alfredo César, was allied with the President. The National Assembly became a focal point for political competition and deal-making. While the economy continued to deteriorate political conflict increased.

> The feud between the administration and Chamorro's own political coalition, the National Opposition Union (UNO), boiled over in late 1992 when the president sided with the Sandinistas and a small group of UNO congressmen known as the Center Group to oust the majority faction from control of the National Assembly. (Millet 1994: 127)

This angered the other UNO delegates who questioned the legitimacy of the institution and began to boycott Assembly sessions. They believed that the understanding on which their coalition was based had been betrayed and further accused Chamorro and Lacayo of collaborating with the Sandinistas in a co-government. On the left, worker and peasant organizations, and the increasingly militant former Sandinista fighters (*recompas*) who had still not received land, accused the Sandinista leadership of collaborating with the government at their expense. Former Contras (*recontras*) who had likewise not received their promised land also became increasingly militant.

As the generalized political infighting continued, more and more Nicaraguans became disillusioned with the political process. By early 1993, 85 per cent of Nicaraguans indicated that they were not interested in the fights between the various political groupings. Indeed, 61 per cent said they had no faith in any political party. Many took matters into their own hands. Land takeovers continued and the armed *recompas* and *recontras* clashed with government forces. Hostages were taken and one group of rearmed ex-Sandinista fighters even occupied the city of Estelí until they were dislodged by a bloody army attack that left scores dead (Millett 1994: 128).

These events seemed to confirm earlier observations. 'By moving into the realm of secret, bartered pacts, the government surrendered the power of its overwhelming public mandate and unquestioned international legitimacy ...' (Uhlig 1991: 408 as cited in Colburn 1992: 73). Another student of Nicaraguan politics observed that the government seems 'to be continuing the long practice of exercising leader-ship by cutting deals in back rooms with ranking representa-tives of powerful political actors' (Colburn 1992: 73). He went on to note that such deals eroded faith in the government and opposition alike (Ibid.).

Responding to pressure from the United States and right-ist politicians in and outside UNO, Violeta Chamorro an-nounced in September 1993 that she was ousting Sandinista Lenin Cerna as head of the intelligence section of the Ministry of the Interior and that she was going to replace Humberto Ortega as head of the army in 1994. The strong resistance of Daniel Ortega to efforts to replace Humberto exacerbated tensions in the Sandinista Party. Several prom-inent Sandinistas thought that talks with the government might be more advisable than ultimatums. In the end, this led to negotiations and an agreement between most of UNO's congressional delegation, the Sandinistas and the Centre Group to initiate a series of constitutional reforms (Millett 1994: 128). Humberto Ortega was finally replaced as head of the army in 1995.

THE CRISIS

Many factors converged in 1994 to precipitate a crisis that shook the Nicaraguan state to its very foundations. Unemployment and underemployment were at horrendous levels (well over 50 per cent) and economic conditions gener-ally were approaching those of Haiti. But the political deterio-ration was equally bad. Coalitions and alliances that had been forged previously continued to unravel as the political setting became ever more contentious. The common vision and col-lective dedication that had characterized the uprising against Somoza and the first years of Sandinista rule were gone. Also forgotten by the leadership of the FSLN were how much of the revolutionary victory was owed to the masses' involvement in the insurrection or how important unity had been to their victory. Co-government had tied the FSLN to many govern-ment policies and the continuation of autocratic decision-making policies by the party leadership had angered many party loyalists. The perception that elements of the leadership

– and not the movement generally – had most benefited from the *piñata* added to the dissatisfaction.

Matters came to a head at the May 1994 party congress. Tensions had continued to mount between Daniel Ortega, Thomas Borge and the more orthodox party leadership on the one hand, and former Sandinista Vice President and acclaimed author Sergio Ramírez and a group of Sandinista representatives from the National Assembly, led by Dora María Telléz, on the other. The latter group sought to reform the party, but got short shrift in the party congress. Ramírez was even removed from his seat on the newly constituted National Directorate. Others associated with him were also removed from their party posts.

> The party lost an opportunity to discuss the basic differences between the currents and clear them up once and for all, to achieve the 'unity within diversity' it sought. The vote results were seen as the imposition of one current over the other and a punishment to those who proposed renovation. (Flakoll Alegría 1994: 4)

The way the congress was conducted and a subsequent nasty personal attack involving Ramírez' daughter (who was also a member of the National Assembly) and Dora María Téllez only exacerbated tensions and began an exodus from the party in the months that followed. Famed priest-poet and former Minister of Culture, Ernesto Cardenal, finally resigned his party membership, saying, 'The truth is that since the last congress, a small group led by Daniel Ortega has taken over the FSLN … they've kidnapped it. They've imposed an authoritarian, hierarchical structure on it and exalted party bosses …' (Cuadra and Coca 1994: 7). Ramírez, Dora María Téllez and quite a few prominent intellectuals left the party and eventually formed the Movimiento Renovadora Sandinista (MRS). They held their first party congress in May 1995 and vowed to run their own slate of candidates in the 1996 election. All but seven of the 39 Sandinista deputies in the National Assembly opted to form part of the Sandinista Renovation Movement (MRS) bench. Led by Dora María Téllez, this became one of the stronger blocks in the Assembly.

But the dissension within the Sandinista ranks was only part of a growing political crisis. Backed by the UNO Centre

Group, that part of the FSLN bench that eventually declared itself MRS, and Assembly speaker Luis Guzmán's Christian Democratic Union (UDC), there was a movement to reform the 1987 Constitution. Pushed by a coalition made up of parties and individuals who currently did not have easy access to power, it envisioned increasing the power of the National Assembly at the expense of the executive. The constitutional reforms would transfer some fiscal power from the executive to the legislature, prohibit nepotism, expand constitutional liberties, abolish the draft, clarify the right to private and other forms of property, reduce the presidential term from six to five years, and stipulate that a second round of voting would need to be held in those elections where the leading candidate did not receive at least 45 per cent of the vote. The net effect would have been to considerably strengthen the legislature at the expense of the presidency and (through the prohibition of nepotism) eliminate Antonio Lacayo from future governmental positions, including that of the presidency. Begun in 1993, this process gained momentum during 1994. It led to much heated discussion between the two branches of government, but to no consensus or compromise.

When the package of constitutional reforms was finally sent to the executive in January 1995, President Chamorro did not promulgate them (by publishing them in the official newspaper) in the required 15-day period and then announced in February that her government did not recognize them. The next day several national newspapers published the texts of the reforms as signed by President of the National Assembly Luis Humberto Guzmán, thus – it could be argued – promulgating them (IHCA 1995a: 5). This led to months of wrangling and mutual recrimination. For a while there were two constitutions, with each of the two branches declaring that theirs was the legal one. Nor could the two governmental institutions reach any compromise on how to move beyond the widening chasm. The situation worsened when the legislature would not accept Chamorro's recommendations for supreme court justices, and instead sent their own list back to the executive, who in turn refused to appoint them. This left the nation's highest court without a quorum.

The severity of the crisis was such that it took the combined effort of the major donor nations to convince the governmental institutions that cooperation was necessary to move beyond the breach. The impending June 1994 Paris meeting of donor nations acted as a catalyst. But the political immaturity of the institutions was so great that the US Embassy had to put pressure on both sides, and recourse to the good offices of the Cardinal Obando y Bravo was necessary to force both parties to resolve their differences. After Obando y Bravo presided over eight negotiating sessions lasting some 50 hours, a solution was finally reached. Most of the reforms were to be put into effect, but the nepotism law and a few others would be held in abeyance until January 1997. A political accord specifying the details was finally passed as Law 199 (Ley Marco de Implementación de las Reformas Constitucionales). It would remain in effect until 1 January 1997. The constitutional reforms and the implementation law were promulgated on 4 July 1995. Many saw this as a serious erosion of fledgling democratic political institutions, since it was necessary to go to extragovernmental actors and employ extralegal political deals to resolve the crisis. This further increased the general population's negative perception of the political class and weakened their confidence in Nicaraguan democracy (IHCA 1995b). By the end of this process, 'The majority of the population ... fed up with these duels by politicians brandishing cardboard swords, [was] gazing upon the outcome with consummate indifference' (IHCA 1995b: 3).

The participatory democracy that was developing in the mass organizations in the early eighties was weak indeed; the authoritarian, verticalist tendencies in the FSLN had won out over democratic reformist possibilities and the party had factionalized; and the US-modelled representative democracy that had been imposed on Nicaragua proved to be a totally inadequate means of governing. The people had been abandoned by the political elites who more and more turned to traditional struggles for power and influence and turned a deaf ear to popular needs.

As the 1996 elections approached, the orthodox Sandinista faction (the FSLN) began to ally itself with Antonio Lacayo's newly formed National Project. The Sandinista Renovation Movement (MRS) was making common cause with the Christian Democratic Union, Virgilio Godoy's Independent Liberal Party, Miriam Arguello's Popular Conservative

Alliance, the Nicaraguan Democratic Union (MDN), and the National Conservative Party (PNC). The strongest contender for the 1996 presidential election was Managua's conservative mayor, Arnoldo Alemán. Alemán was using his Constitutionalist Liberal Party (PLC) to gain control of the now factionalized old Liberal Party (including Liberal groups who were allied with Somoza).

Voter disillusionment was further increased when the government began to privatize public assets by selling them off to well-connected foreign and national buyers. The general population was increasingly wary of government manoeuvring and began to refer to the process as the second *piñata*. The November 1995 passage of a bill to sell off the national telecommunication system, TELCOR, greatly enraged TELCOR workers and served to further discredit the government and the politicians who backed the bill just as the first *piñata* had discredited the former Sandinista government.

And so it was that a population that was once mobilized to change their outdated, uncaring, exploitative and repressive system and challenge the international mechanisms and linkages that supported it, became disillusioned, cynical and unwilling to even vote, let alone engage in another campaign of mobilizations and militancy. One could easily blame this political degeneration on the lack of vision, integrity and understanding of the political leadership in Nicaragua. But before doing so, one should briefly contemplate the effect from the international capitalist economic system. What was once a nation mobilized and ready to take on almost any challenge that the US, its allies or quislings might hurl at it, had become as cowed and downtrodden as any in the Third World. Chamorro had even withdrawn Nicaragua's successful World Court case against the United States before a decision on the $17 billion damage claim could be made. Indeed, the people seemed resigned to try to endure whatever bitter new curative was foisted upon them by the IMF or the United States. Thus the symbolic treat posed by the revolutionary nation were neutralized. Nicaragua had been beaten and relegated to a very dependent position in the international system. It was back in its place. And, as though playing out their assigned roles, the political elites were squabbling among themselves so as to detract attention from the real issues and were very far from leading the masses in any new mobilizations.

But even burning the consciousness-provoking textbooks used during the revolutionary years and making education increasingly difficult to obtain for the masses (charging for public schools in an ever poorer land) could not totally stupefy a once mobilized and conscientized people. Given the fact that the Sandinistas and other parties were more involved in machinations than mobilizations, the people have done the best they could by opting for the strategy most often followed by the subjugated Latin American peoples when in prior centuries they received orders from the Spanish crown – 'obedezco pero no cumplo' (I obey but I take no action to carry out your orders). As suggested by the projected high rates of abstention, large numbers of the voting population were unwilling to participate in the empty electoral exercise that was being organized for 1996. In this way they denied the international capitalist system and its sponsor in Nicaragua (the US) what it needed most – popular legitimization of US inspired democratization.[23] And given the fractionalization of political leadership, that may be all they could do ... at least for the time being.

REFERENCES

Albert, Michael and Robin Hahn. 1990. *The Political Economy of Participatory Economics.* Princeton, NJ: Princeton University Press.
Alvarez Montalván, Emilio. [1995.] *Ensayo sobre los valores de la cultura política nicaraguense.* Managua: No publisher.
Barberena, Edgar S. 1995. '¡Abstencionismo a la vista!'. *El Nuevo Diario*, 24 June.
Booth, John. 1985. *The End and the Beginning: The Nicaraguan Revolution.* Boulder CO: Westview Press.
Colburn, Forrest. 1992. 'The Fading of the Revolutionary Era in Central America'. *Current History*, 91: 70–3, February.
Conroy, Michael. 1990. 'The Political Economy of the 1990 Elections'. Paper presented at the Coloquio sobre las Crises Económicas del Siglo XX, Madrid, Universidad Complutense de Madrid, April.
Cook, Mark. 1989. 'Unfit to Print about Nicaragua's Election'. *Extra* (A publication of Fairness and Accuracy in Reporting), 3 (1): 2–3, October/November.

Cronin, Thomas. 1989. *Direct Democracy, the Politics of Initiative, Referendum and Recall.* Cambridge, Mass: Harvard University Press.

Cuadra, Scarlet and Leonardo Coca. 1994. 'Gains and Losses'. *Barricada Internacional,* October/November.

Díaz Lacayo, Aldo. 1994. *El Frente Sandinista después de la Derrota Electoral.* Caracas: Ediciones Centauro.

Flakoll Alegría, Daniel. 1994. 'Navigating Between the Currents'. *Barricada Internacional,* June.

Gilbert, Dennis. 1988. *Sandinistas, The Party and the Revolution.* London: Blackwell.

IHCA (Central American Historical Institute). 1988a. 'The New Economic Package'. *Envío,* September.

IHCA. 1988b. *Update,* 12 July.

IHCA. 1990. 'After the Poll Wars – Explaining the Upset'. *Envío,* March/April.

IHCA. 1995a. 'The Foxes are Infighting; but the Hens Aren't Laughing'. *Envío,* April.

IHCA. 1995b. 'Not Yet to the Root of the Crisis'. *Envío,* August.

LASA (Latin American Studies Association). 1990. *Electoral Democracy Under International Pressure, The Report of the Latin American Studies Association Commission to Observe the 1990 Nicaraguan Election.* Pittsburgh: University of Pittsburgh Press.

McMichael, David. 1990. 'U.S. Plays Contra Card'. *The Nation,* 5 February.

Millett, Richard. 1994. 'Central America's Enduring Conflicts'. *Current History,* 93 (580): 124–8, February.

Newsweek. 1989. 'Washington Wants to Buy Nicaraguan Election'. *Newsweek,* 5 September and 9 October.

Norsworthy, Kent and Tom Barry. 1990. *Nicaragua: A Country Guide.* Albuquerque: Central American Resource Center.

El Programa Historico del FSLN. 1981. Managua: FSLN.

'Resolution from El Crucero Assembly'. 1990. *Barricada Internacional,* 14 July.

Ruchwarger, Gary. 1987. *People in Power.* Massachusetts: Bergin and Garvey.

Sklar, Holly. 1989. 'Washington Wants to Buy Nicaragua's Elections Again'. *Z Magazine,* December.

Téfel, Reinaldo Antonio. 1995. 'La mancha más fea: la Piñata'. *La Prensa,* 19 July.

Uhlig, Mark. 1991. 'Nicaragua's Permanent Crisis: Ruling from Above and Below'. *Survival,* 33 (5), September-October.

UNO. 1989. *Programa de Gobierno.*

Vanden, Harry E. 1990. 'Law, State Policy and Terrorism'. *New Political Science,* Fall/Winter: 55–75.

Vanden, Harry E. 1991. 'Foreign Relations'. In Thomas Walker (ed.), *Revolution and Counterrevolution in Nicaragua.* Boulder, CO: Westview Press.

Vanden, Harry E. and Thomas Walker. 1991. 'The Reimposition of U.S. Hegemony Over Nicaragua'. In Kenneth M. Coleman and George C. Herring (eds), *Understanding the Central American Crisis.* Wilmington: Scholarly Resources.

Vanden, Harry E. and Gary Prevost. 1993. *Democracy and Socialism in Sandinista Nicaragua*. New York: Praeger.

Vickers, George. 1990. 'A Spider's Web'. *NACLA Report on the Americas*. 30 (1), June.

Vilas, Carlos. 1990. 'What Went Wrong'. *NACLA Report on the Americas*. 30 (1), June.

Walker, Thomas (ed.). 1982. *Nicaragua in Revolution*. New York: Praeger.

NOTES

1. See Barberena (1995: 8). This article cites a survey by the M & R and the Fundación Centroamericana 2000 of 825 people in Managua and the other departamental capitals. In the survey 21.9 per cent said they will not vote and another 17.9 per cent said they are not sure if they will vote or not. The article also cited another survey of people in the streets of Managua conducted by *Esta Semana* which found even greater disillusionment. The quote is taken from this latter survey.

2. Interview with Emilio Alvarez Montalván, Managua, 21 July 1995.

3. See John Booth (1985).

4. Humberto Ortega as quoted in Ruchwarger (1987: 34).

5. Sergio Ramírez, as quoted in Ruchwarger (1987: 4).

6. See Denis Gilbert (1988), particularly Chapter 3, 'The Party in the State and Mass Organizations'.

7. See Vanden (1991), Vanden and Walker (1991), and Vanden (1990). See also Vanden and Prevost (1993).

8. By the late 1980s the Nicaraguan government was estimating direct damages from the Contras at some $12 billion. As the State of Nicaragua sought damages pursuant to the World Court decision, it also sought monetary compensation for victims of Contra attacks and their survivors and arrived at the figure of $17.8 billion dollars. See Norsworthy and Barry (1990).

9. Interview with Dr Mariano Fiallos, President, Supreme Electoral Council, Managua, 15 December 1987.

10. Interview with Dr Roberto Estevez, Managua, 24 February 1990. Dr Mariano Fiallos, the President of the Supreme Electoral Council indicated that it would be difficult to estimate the total cost of running the election but that his organization had a budget of $18 million. Interview, Managua, 20 February 1990.

11. Daniel Ortega Press Conference, Managua, 22 February 1990.

12. According to Wayne Smith, the Cuban government did not set up a specific administrative school or provide training in participatory administration or economics for its employees. Further, at one point in the eighties when it looked as though Cubans might be able to travel to the US for training, the Cuban government proposed that a group be sent to the Warton Business School at the University of Pennsylvania to get (business oriented) training in administration and

management. Wayne Smith, speech on 'Crisis in Cuba', University of
South Florida, Tampa, Florida, 18 October 1991.
13. See Albert and Hahn (1990). The authors argue that hierarchical production, inegalitarian consumption, central planning and market allo-
cations are incompatible with 'classlessness'. They also present an
alternative model of democratic workers' and consumers' councils operating in a decentralized, social planning procedure and suggest how
egalitarian consumption and job complexes in which all engage in
conceptual as well as executioner labour can be efficient.
14. These opinions were frequently being voiced to the chapter author
when he visited Nicaragua in 1987. They were widely discussed on a
second visit in early 1990.
15. 'Washington Wants to Buy Nicaraguan Election' *Newsweek*, 5
September 1989 and also 9 October 1989.
16. For an ample, if critical, discussion of these problems, see Vilas (1990)
and Vickers (1990).
17. The author was an observer to the 1990 election. As he informally surveyed people in and around Managua in the days before the voting,
he did find many who showed some inclination for the UNO coalition. Usually, their support for Chamorro and UNO seemed more
based on their disappointment with economic conditions or the draft
or reservations about the way the Sandinistas had been ruling. In few
instances did UNO support seem to flow from positive assessments of
Chamorro or UNO. See also Conroy (1990), especially page 32 – 'As
of mid-January 1990 the opposition candidacy of Violeta Chamorro
and the UNO coalition had not convinced a majority of Nicaraguans
that they offered a preferable solution to the nation's economic
problem.'
18. Greenberg-Lake/Itatani Research Center, 'Mid-January 1990 Poll', as
cited in Conroy (1990: 32–3).
19. Likewise, Univision's January 1990 poll showed the FSLN with an 18
point lead and the final Greenberg-Lake gave the Sandinistas a 27 per
cent lead (IHCA 1990: 30).
20. See Chapter 3 of this book.
21. See Chapter 5 of this book.
22. See Chapter 3 of this book.
23. Meanwhile, abstention rates in US elections were often higher than
the percentage of the eligible voters who bothered to go to the polls.
Thus it could be argued that the Nicaraguan electorate copied all too
well the model of US democracy they were given to emulate.

3 Structural Adjustment and Resistance: The Political Economy of Nicaragua under Chamorro
Richard Stahler-Sholk

Graffiti on the walls in Managua in the 1990s read, '¡Muerte al ESAF!' and 'La "priva" nos priva' – that is, 'Death to the Enhanced Structural Adjustment Facility' and 'Privatization deprives us'. Burning tyres and takeovers of farms and factories are reminders of the high levels of mobilization brought by the Nicaraguan revolution, yet structural adjustment seems a rather abstract concept to wave a machete at. What are its implications, and can it be resisted?

The ideology of the free market has long dominated the international economic system. Among the Bretton Woods institutions that regulate the post-WWII economic order, the International Monetary Fund (IMF) was established to provide finance to countries in balance-of-payments difficulty, to promote more free trade. Heavily influenced by monetarist doctrine, the IMF evolved a particular diagnosis and prescription for restoring economic balance. As a condition for providing finance, the IMF typically insisted on domestic demand restraint, for example through monetary policies such as restricting credit and raising interest rates, and fiscal measures such as cutting government spending and raising taxes or fees for public services. These prescriptions were supplemented by exchange-rate devaluation and price liberalization, supposedly to allow market forces to discourage imports and encourage exports.

Partly in response to objections that these policies overemphasized short-term goals of reducing inflation, the IMF began to extend the length of its financing in the late 1970s and encourage longer-term measures to promote exports. The World Bank, which had been established as a development lender, began in the 1980s to shift from project loans to sectoral and even broader 'structural adjustment' loans tied to reforms of macroeconomic policy. As the strategies of these two institutions began to converge, they also evolved a set of common prescriptions that included not only short-term stabilization through demand restraint, but also a sharp reduction in the size and role of the state in the economy, privatization of state enterprises and services, and liberalization, that is, removing regulations and restrictions on foreign trade and capital movements. The assumption was that developing countries had a 'comparative advantage' in raw materials and cheap labour, and that unrestrained market forces would allocate resources more efficiently and therefore better than states. This expanded prescription for market-oriented economic reforms came to be known as 'neoliberalism', and its proponents insisted that it simply represented sound economics rather than a political agenda.

In the wake of the Third World debt crisis of the 1980s, neoliberal orthodoxy acquired new force. International financial institutions expanded the use of 'conditionality', tying access to new loans to adoption of a standard set of policy reforms aimed at market liberalization. By one count, the IMF and World Bank made 566 such stabilization and structural adjustment loans to 89 countries from 1980–91 (Bello 1994: 130–2). In Central America, geopolitically motivated financial flows in the 1980s allowed some deviation, but by the late 1980s the entire region had undertaken some form of relatively orthodox adjustment programme (Timossi 1993). As the former Soviet Union and Eastern European countries also fell under the sway of structural adjustment in the 1990s, neoliberalism appeared to be a global trend.

Yet the apparent enthusiasm for what has been called the 'Washington consensus' on economic policy reform (Williamson 1990) is not universally shared beyond the beltway. Actual implementation of adjustment programmes around the world has been poor (Haggard 1986). Where implemented, austerity measures in Latin America have been regularly associated with 'IMF riots', social protests led by the poor who bear a disproportionate share of the burden (Walton 1989). Critics have long questioned the wisdom of indiscriminately applying a rigid set of policy prescriptions to widely varying economies. Since the 1950s, the structuralist critique (popularized by the UN Economic Commission for Latin America) highlighted external constraints, supply bottlenecks, and import inelasticities that often made market formulae inappropriate for developing countries. More recently, neostructuralists such as Lance Taylor have not only offered empirical evidence of those structural differences, but also advocated 'an alternative to orthodox stabilization programs in the interest of goals other than simply achieving sustainable external balance: goals such as economic growth, a more desirable distribution of income, and self-reliance' (Kahler 1990: 48).

Radical critics go a step further, suggesting that neoliberal programmes promoted by the IMF are a reflection of class conflicts at the national and international level:

> By providing the framework for an open trade system and by using conditionality ... the Fund helps secure the domination of labor by capital in various social formations ... This negative distributional impact is not simply due to the particular economic framework adopted by Fund missions. It is also because securing the cooperation of local elites in imposing economic stabilization often involves sparing them the costs of adjustment. (Pastor 1987: 31–2)

From this perspective, the IMF has become a kind of global capitalist planner. The radical critique suggests that a common set of interests, rather than a conspiracy, unites international financial institutions in responding to the kind of political and ideological challenges represented by the Nyerere government in Tanzania or the first Manley government in Jamaica (Pastor 1993: 293–7; Bello 1994).

A variety of sceptics of the neoliberal model have also questioned its political sustainability, noting the inherent tension between democratic access to political power and market-determined access to income (Przeworski 1992, 1995). The implementation of reforms that immediately lower the living standards of the poor seems to require an autocratic style of leadership by an insulated executive. Thus the short-term political dynamics of neoliberalism involve circumventing democratic processes and betraying the expectations of the electorate, in the hope that 'success' in lowering the inflation rate will eventually generate legitimacy (Roxborough 1992). Cardoso's ascent in Brazil suggests that controlling inflation can create its own political appeal, at least temporarily. Yet the examples of Menem in Argentina, Andrés Pérez in Venezuela, Fujimori in Peru, and Collor in Brazil all illustrate the political fragility of such strategies of economic policy-making by personal decree (Haggard and Kaufman 1995: 198–211). These new styles of allegedly depoliticized leadership, which Guillermo O'Donnell refers to as 'delegative democracy' and Carlos Vilas calls 'electoral *caudillos* of postmodernity', have not fully succeeded in bridging the gap between political democratization and socioeconomic wellbeing (Vilas 1995: 34). It remains to be seen whether a more participatory, consolidated form of democracy can survive the neoliberal onslaught in Latin America (Green 1995).

Defenders of the neoliberal faith are quick to blame any failure of adjustment measures on a lack of political will to apply the measures more strictly, or for a long enough period. However, such arguments verge on a tautological formulation (that is, neoliberalism works by definition, so any failure must be because of insufficient opening of the economy to the magic of the market). Rigorous evaluation is complicated by the difficulty of specifying the relevant counterfactuals, but the record of neoliberal policy implementation and outcomes by the mid-1990s remained mixed at best (Haggard and Kaufman 1995: 314–22). A more critical look at actually existing capitalism must acknowledge social and political opposition to the neoliberal agenda, and evaluate the results as part of this conflictual process.

The government of Violeta Chamorro in Nicaragua (1990–96) represents an interesting case in the complex dynamics of structural adjustment. The Sandinista government (1979–90) had attempted an expansionary and redistributive transformation of the economy, along with broad-based political mobilization. This effort was beset by war and other constraints, producing unusually large macroeconomic imbalances and hyperinflation. Stabilization packages introduced by the Sandinista government in 1985 and 1988 failed to restore economic equilibrium (Ocampo 1991; Ricciardi 1991), did not attract significant external finance, and eroded the Sandinistas' mobilized base of political support as living standards fell (Stahler-Sholk 1990; Vilas 1991). Polls pointed to the economy and the war as the main factors in the 1990 Chamorro victory over the FSLN (Conroy 1990; Castro and Prevost 1992).

The incoming Chamorro government moved swiftly to implement a more orthodox stabilization and adjustment programme, which brought financial support from the IMF, World Bank, IDB and AID. However, the Sandinista era had left a legacy of high levels of mobilization. Initially, this provided a base from which organized labour and other sectors could resist, forcing some modification of policy in 1990–91. Gradually, the organizational coherence of this resistance was eroded by the dynamic of economic adjustment itself; and by a combination of legitimacy problems and division within the Sandinista party, punctuated by the 1994 breakaway of the Sandinista Renovation Movement (MRS) led by Sergio Ramírez. The mass organizations, which still retained some disruptive power, struggled to define a more autonomous relationship vis-à-vis the 'orthodox' FSLN led by Daniel Ortega. The FSLN was politically crippled by the personal interests of some of its leaders, including the *piñata* in which state properties were appropriated by individuals during the government transition period. Meanwhile, the Chamorro government by the end of its six-year term was politically weak and economically dependent on external financing that was drying up. Inflation had been brought under control, but unemployment had soared, and there was serious doubt about the sustainability of a project that could not deliver economic growth or alleviate the poverty of the majority of the population.

POLITICAL MOBILIZATION AND ECONOMIC DISEQUILIBRIA IN THE 1980S

The Sandinista economic model proposed an alternative to the old agroexport model, in which economic growth was passively determined by world-market prices and profitability depended on cheap labour (Gibson 1987). The revolution brought state control of some 40 per cent of the economy, along with nationalization of banks and foreign trade. The Sandinista mixed economy model called for the state sector to become the 'centre of accumulation', based on the thesis that agricultural and agroindustrial modernization (rather than intensified exploitation) would increase productivity and improve Nicaragua's position in the world market. Structural transformation was supposed to take place through major state-directed investment, as well as redistribution which would broaden the domestic market.

This model, which might be conceived as a kind of long-term expansionary adjustment, assumed that foreign loans would be available during the period of transformation. It also assumed that exports could be sustained both by channelling more resources to state enterprises, and by creating the conditions for the simple reproduction of the capitalist sector, which controlled 59 per cent of agroexport production.[1] Finally, it assumed that workers and peasants could be politically organized in support of a state-centred model of accumulation. These and other assumptions proved problematical.

From the start, an ambivalent relationship developed between the FSLN as governing party and the mass organizations (Haugaard 1991; Serra 1991, 1993). On the one hand, mass mobilization was an important Sandinista political resource against the competing project of the non-Somoza bourgeoisie. On the other hand, the empowerment of the mass organizations unleashed demand pressures that strained the Sandinista government's short-term capacity to respond, especially as external constraints tightened (Vanden and Prevost 1993: Chapter 3). The resulting disequilibria were reflected in widening public-sector deficits, hyperinflation, and a multitude of economic irrationalities (Stahler-Sholk 1990).

While rejecting orthodox stabilization, the FSLN leadership in 1983 reactivated an 'economic cell' of cadre who were assigned to develop alternative measures for dealing with the looming macroeconomic imbalances and accelerating inflation (Martínez Cuenca 1992: 65–6). In the midst of the group's discussions, however, the decision to institute a military draft (SMP) sent defence spending soaring and limited the possibility of bringing the fiscal deficit under control. Only years later was it revealed that planning for a 'shock' adjustment and monetary reform continued in 1983–84. In fact, technical preparations were in place in 1984 – with a new currency printed up and the banknotes dated 1985 – but the timing was judged politically inconvenient, and the measures put off.[2]

Postponing adjustment until after the November 1984 election, the FSLN won with 67 per cent of the vote. In February 1985, the government announced a stabilization package aimed at correcting some of the serious distortions in the economy and reactivating production. This included major currency devaluations, along with some cutbacks in credit and public spending. Price subsidies were to be phased out and replaced with regular salary increases (Ricciardi 1991). However, the devaluations and partial price liberalization unleashed accelerating inflation, and real wages fell (see Table 3.1).

The failure to follow through on the 1985 adjustment, as well as the escalating cost of defence and the rigidities of the public investment programme in the 1985–87 period, all contributed to a worsening of economic disequilibria. These were aggravated by external constraints, including the May 1985 US trade embargo, the suspension of Mexican petroleum credits, and a decline in credits from the Soviet Union and Eastern Europe after 1985. By mid-1987, the Nicaraguan economy was experiencing hyperinflation, with monthly inflation rates exceeding 50 per cent. By the end of 1987, inflation stood at 1347 per cent, the market exchange rate was 500 times the official rate, and the banking system only collected five real *córdobas* out of every 100 it loaned. Real wages had dropped 85 per cent from their 1985 average (Arana *et al.* 1987). Between late 1987 and 1988, a coalition of 14 opposition parties of the left and right had formed, appealing to middle sectors and the working class mainly on the basis of economic issues. This alliance, formed with US support, was the forerunner of the National Opposition Union (UNO) that defeated the FSLN in the 1990 election.

The severity of the economic disequilibria, and the political cost of an economy that was perceived as out of control, led to an evolving policy consensus in favour of a major adjustment package (CIERA 1988, 1989). The Esquipulas peace accords of August 1987 appeared to hold out the prospect of an eventual reduction in military activity and its associated economic

Table 3.1 Nicaragua: Basic Economic Indicators, 1985–94

	1985	1986	1987	1988	1989	1990	1991	1992	1993	1994*
Percentages										
GDP growth	-4.1	-1.0	-0.7	-12.4	-1.7	-0.1	-0.1	0.4	-0.4	3.2
GDP growth per capita	-6.7	-3.5	-4.0	-15.4	-4.9	-3.4	-3.3	-2.8	-3.5	0.0
Inflation (Dec.–Dec.)	334.3	747.4	1 347.3	33 657.3	1 689.1	13 490.3	865.6	3.5	19.5	12.4
Fiscal deficit/GDP	23.4	18.0	16.4	26.6	6.7	17.1	7.5	7.6	7.3	9.7
Unemployment	23.1	25.7	28.9	32.5	39.4	44.3	52.3	50.3	50.1	53.6
Open unemployment	3.2	4.7	5.8	6.0	8.4	11.1	14.2	17.8	21.8	20.7
Unemployment-equivalent	19.9	21.0	23.1	19.2	31.0	33.2	38.1	32.5	28.3	32.9
Debt service/Exports	19.8	11.1	7.7	4.0	3.5	4.4	14.0	55.0	54.5	55.3
Indices (1980=100)										
GDP	103.2	102.2	101.4	87.7	86.2	86.1	85.9	86.3	85.9	88.7
GDP per capita	89.6	86.5	83.8	70.7	67.7	65.7	63.3	61.5	59.4	59.4
Real wages	48.5	20.3	8.2	4.7	7.8	12.6	13.0	15.5	15.0	15.3
Millions of US $										
Trade balance	-579	-549	-570	-583	-326	-290	-486	-610	-449	-428
Exports (FOB)	344	287	325	273	341	392	338	309	367	445
Imports (FOB)	924	837	895	856	667	682	824	919	816	873
Foreign debt	4 936	5 760	6 270	7 220	9 741	10 616	10 312	10 806	10 987	11 695

Source. United Nations Economic Commission for Latin America & the Caribbean (ECLAC).
*1994 figures are preliminary.

cost, raising hopes that the economy could be brought under control before the 1990 Nicaraguan election.

The Sandinista government launched two successive 'shock' economic packages in February and June 1988, involving massive devaluations coupled with more serious fiscal and monetary austerity. These stabilization measures provoked considerable debate within Sandinista ranks. When the February package was followed in June 1988 by another maxidevaluation, wage-price liberalization, and interest rate indexation, the measures were harshly criticized for their anti-popular impact (IHCA 1988). Some critics suggested that the measures consolidated a tilt in the ambiguous class orientation of the Sandinista government, away from the popular classes and in favour of the interests of technocrats and professionals and their allies in the conservative bourgeoisie (Vilas 1991; Vilas 1992: 329–37).

Even as the adjustment programme took on an increasingly orthodox character, the Sandinista government attempted to maintain some social compensations. Credit restrictions imposed in February 1988 were eased in May to prevent a collapse in production. Interest rates were not actually indexed to the Consumer Price Index, but rather were adjusted according to complex and shifting formulas yielding an annual interest rate that remained negative in real terms, though less so than before (Spoor 1995: 132–43). The government also reintroduced a much more limited and selective basic food subsidy in July 1988 for 160 000 public employees in the health, education, and defence sectors. The monthly subsidized package (consisting of ten pounds each of rice and beans and five pounds of sugar, and referred to by the Spanish acronym for those products, 'AFA') was intended to compensate for the fact that state salaries remained controlled at low levels.

The huge devaluations of 1988 fuelled an increase in inflation to over 33 000 per cent, while real wages fell to less than 5 per cent of their 1980 value and production contracted 12 per cent. By the end of 1988, it was clear that inflation could only be reduced by imposing even more drastic demand restraint, which would inevitably prolong the recessionary impact of the reforms. Faced with this dilemma, the Sandinista government took the calculated political risk in 1989 of proceeding with further austerity measures, appealing to Western European bilateral lenders for an extraordinary package of liquid foreign exchange in support of economic stabilization. In direct response to policy 'suggestions' from an economic mission led by MIT economist Lance Taylor and sponsored by Sweden (acting as coordinator for the European donor group), the government put forward a four-phase programme for 1989, beginning in January with severe fiscal and credit austerity and a commitment to real 'mididevaluations' (Taylor *et al.* 1989: 31–6). The policies also included a new initiative towards *concertación* (social pact or conciliation) with the private sector. Based on this programme, the government made a formal proposal to a special Stockholm conference of Western European donors in May 1989, calling for $250 million in support, complete with monitoring of compliance every trimester by an independent commission of experts.

Despite the orthodoxy of the economic package which one observer suggested might have earned IMF endorsement if not for political factors (Taylor *et al.* 1989: 2–3), little international finance was forthcoming. The Stockholm meeting in May 1989 produced only modest financial commitments, and US pressure succeeded in postponing a second donors' conference until after the Nicaraguan election (Martínez Cuenca 1992: 19–20). Despite a series of Sandinista political concessions – including advancing elections from November to February 1990 and allowing foreign campaign contributions – in exchange for the August 1989 Tela agreement of Central American presidents calling for Contra demobilization, the US government and the Contras refused to suspend military hostilities. With the unexpectedly harsh external financial and military circumstances, economic growth fell in 1989 for the sixth consecutive year. Participation in mass organizations declined, as individual survival became the watchword.

For the popular sectors in general, the 1988–89 austerity measures brought further slippage in welfare to critical new lows. Salaried workers and small producers of basic grains lost out in the realignment of relative prices, while the public sector cutbacks affected social services and employment (Stahler-Sholk and Spoor 1989). Per capita consumption of basic foodstuffs, already in general decline after 1983, fell below minimum nutritional requirements by 1988 (Utting 1991: 45–6). By 1989, real per capita income had dropped by one-third from the level of 1980. With elections scheduled for February 1990, the timing of the economic crisis and potential recovery were politically crucial. As the military dimension of the war diminished (but refused to disappear), popular expectations for improved living standards outpaced the more lengthy process of economic adjustment and obtaining financing for post-war reconstruction (Conroy 1990). There were some indications of technical 'progress' towards stabilization, but few prospects for quick recovery. The fiscal deficit was reduced from 26.6 per cent of GDP in 1988 to 6.7 per cent in 1989. A real devaluation was achieved for the first time in the Sandinista era, with the real effective exchange rate reduced over 60 per cent between the second and fourth quarters of 1988, and exports rose 23 per cent. Inflation began to fall, from the peak of 33 657 per cent in 1988 to 1 689 per cent in 1989 (IMF 1991: 4–6, 44). However, production of basic grains fell, unemployment approached 40 per cent, and the accumulated deterioration of living standards finally took a toll on Sandinista support. Electoral options for 1990 were constrained, since '*sandinismo* without war and embargo' did not appear on the ballot. With the US government openly backing both the electoral and armed opposition, and Yale-educated UNO economic adviser Francisco Mayorga claiming to have a plan for 'an accelerated process of economic recovery and simultaneously eliminating inflation in a few weeks',[3] many voters apparently opted for relief.

THE 'MAYORGAZO': ORTHODOXY WITH A VENGEANCE

Upon assuming office in April 1990, Violeta Chamorro turned economic policy over to Francisco Mayorga, appointing him President of the Central Bank. 'Plan Mayorga', as outlined during the electoral campaign and in the early months of the new administration (UNO 1990; Nicaragua 1990b), called for a strictly orthodox programme. The first stabilization phase was supposed to bring inflation to zero within 100 days through drastic austerity, combined with the anchor of a new 'strong currency' fixed at parity with the US dollar. This was to be followed by structural adjustment and privatization, which were supposed to generate agroexport-based growth rates of 10 per cent a year for the next five to six years (UNO 1990: 8). In practice, the first phase of Plan Mayorga was applied with even greater orthodoxy and rigidity than the written outline had called for. The plan provoked massive social unrest, and failed to win crucial external financial support or eliminate inflation within 100 days as Mayorga had pledged. The centrepiece of Plan Mayorga was the introduction of a new currency, the 'gold *córdoba*' (*córdoba oro,* or CO). A series of large devaluations was intended to make the old currency become worthless while the new currency, fixed at parity with the dollar, was phased into circulation. However, workers would be paid in the old 'pigsty' *córdobas* (*chanchero*), while utility bills and other prices would be set in the new dollarized currency.

The original Plan Mayorga had promised social compensations such as emergency credit to small producers, special social security programmes, and job creation (UNO 1990: 4–6). Instead, the plan was launched with massive lay-offs and salary lags in the public sector, in an apparent attempt to disarticulate one of the bastions of Sandinista union strength (Neira and Acevedo 1992: 53–5). A series of maxidevaluations totalled 116 per cent for May 1990, while wages of public employees were only scheduled to be adjusted 60 per cent. When the public employees' union UNE organized a march to the Presidency demanding a 200 per cent wage increase, government ministers refused to meet with labour representatives. Instead, the government took a step toward rule by decree, issuing the unprecedented Decree 8–90 which suspended the Civil Service Law and annulled public sector collective bargaining agreements. This cleared the way for unilateral dismissals and elimination of protections such as the 'AFA' subsidy package for public employees, which had cushioned stabilization measures in the Sandinista period.

In response, UNE called a strike in May 1990, which was declared illegal by the Ministry of Labour. Workers occupied their offices, paralysing government operations, and police were called in as the conflict escalated. Other pro-Sandinista unions formed a new coalition called the National Workers' Front (FNT), which joined in support. In a major setback to the Mayorga strategy, the government had to back down, negotiating a compromise that effectively granted a 100 per cent wage adjustment and indexed wages to a basket of basic consumer goods.

Almost as soon as the May strike was settled, the FNT began to complain that the government was reneging on its commitments. Moreover, the broader dimensions of the adjustment programme became clearer as the government raised utility rates and bus fares, implemented credit and fiscal tightening that triggered massive lay-offs in industry, and pressed forward with privatization via Decrees 10–90 and 11–90 which returned state agricultural enterprises to former owners. When the government suspended negotiations in late June, the FNT called for a general strike. This time, strike supporters erected barricades in the barrios in early July, reminiscent of the insurrection against the Somoza regime. The far right of UNO organized its own violent response, encouraged by Vice President Virgilio Godoy's calls for a movement for the 'salvation of democracy' (O'Kane 1995: 187–8).

The July 1990 general strike, which brought the country to the brink of civil war, proved to be a watershed. The more pragmatic sectors within the Chamorro government were finally convinced that a confrontational approach to stabilization was not viable, and that some form of cooperation would have to be worked out with organized social forces. The strike was defused when FSLN General Secretary Daniel Ortega met with Minister of the Presidency Antonio Lacayo, and the FNT was brought in to ratify an agreement ending the strike on 11 July 1990.[4]

With this precedent established, a round of negotiations began in September to draw up a basic pact on social and economic principles (*concertación*). The FNT initially boycotted in protest over government non-compliance with previous accords, but intense negotiating between the FSLN leadership and Lacayo-led government pragmatists eventually brought the Sandinista unions back into the talks. These consultations produced a first pact (*Concertación I*) on 26 October 1990, in which labour accepted the need for a 'realistic' stabilization plan and agreed to 'exhaust the mechanisms of negotiation and dialogue' before resorting to strikes; while the government agreed to prioritize the reactivation of production, respect property transfers that had occurred before

Chamorro took office, and allow workers an unspecified participation in the property of any privatized enterprises (Nicaragua 1990a). The umbrella organization of business associations, COSEP, refused to sign in protest over the compromise on the issue of privatization.

The Chamorro government's first attempt at economic stabilization was a noisy failure, as 1990 closed with inflation over 13 000 per cent, an increased fiscal deficit, and stagnant GDP. It was also clear that external financial support would depend on securing a minimum of social peace, and in fact the FNT spelled out its terms directly to the IMF and World Bank (FNT 1991). By this time the UNO coalition had split, with the far right pushing for more confrontation, while the Lacayo faction sought to negotiate with the FSLN leadership to win space for a more gradual stabilization and adjustment programme. Before the end of 1990, a new economic package was prepared (Montealegre *et al.* 1990) and Mayorga was replaced by more moderate technocrats.

'PLAN LACAYO': GETTING DOWN TO BUSINESS

The new 'Plan Lacayo' (named after Antonio Lacayo, Minister of the Presidency and de facto head of government) was formally announced on 3 March 1991. It represented a continuation of the basic neoliberal programme, but with a somewhat less confrontational style that proved better suited to negotiating domestic social pacts and securing international finance. After losing a year to Plan Mayorga, the first phase of the UNO economic programme still called for stabilization, that is, short-term measures aimed at correcting macroeconomic imbalances. These included major devaluations, fiscal austerity, and credit tightening. This first phase was not qualitatively different from the Sandinista package of June 1988 (Neira and Acevedo 1992), but differed in intensity. However, the full UNO programme went much further, calling for wholesale liberalization and privatization (Nicaragua 1992).

Having negotiated a labour truce, Plan Lacayo implemented a 400 per cent devaluation in March 1991, coupled with more demand restraint. In contrast to the Mayorga approach, the new plan deliberately scheduled the 1991 wage adjustments for the beginning of the year, following IMF advice to 'forestall a prolonged dispute with the strong labor unions', although inflation was projected to overtake the wage increase by year's end (IMF 1991: 10–13). The plan also offered some modest social compensations, and it came at a time when there was little popular support for the idea of yet another general strike. The Sandinista unions were also struggling to define a newly autonomous position, which seemed to be undercut by the intervention of the FSLN leadership in negotiating an end to the 1990 strikes (Stahler-Sholk 1995).

By mid-1991, the government was also moving forward with its privatization project. In a second round of negotiations (*Concertación* II) in May–August 1991, the unions decided to settle for a share of worker ownership in what seemed to be the inevitable privatization of state enterprises. With this second agreement in hand and a demonstrated commitment to fiscal austerity, the government obtained a long-sought IMF standby loan in September 1991 that paved the way for a series of new loans and debt renegotiations. With a significant flow of external resources, the government was able to hold down the fiscal deficit and reduce inflation to a mere 3.5 per cent in 1992.

One price of this success in stabilization was an increase in unemployment. The Sandinista programme of 1988–89 had already resulted in the elimination (*compactación*) of 20 000 public sector jobs, including 8300 central government positions (IMF 1989: 9). Under the UNO adjustment programme, another 30 000 public sector jobs were eliminated by 1993 (about 25 per cent of the total), along with 83 000 military personnel; with plans to eliminate another 13 569 public sector jobs in 1994–96 (IMF 1994a: 3, 21). Another 73 700 jobs were eliminated in the privatization of former state enterprises in the 1990–94 period (MCE 1995: 11). Underutilization of the workforce (including open unemployment and underemployment) rose from 32.5 per cent in 1988 to 53.6 per cent in 1994.

To offset this staggering unemployment, Plan Lacayo included several programmes designed to forestall the kinds of social eruptions that met Plan Mayorga in 1990. One was the Emergency Social Investment Fund (FISE), established under Decree 59–90 in February 1991. By June 1992, FISE had received $22.4 million from USAID, and created 21 000 person-months of short-term jobs (USAID 1992). However, FISE was more politically expedient than economically meaningful. One study calculated that direct employment created by FISE in 1993 represented only 4.2 per cent of the total under- and unemployment; and survey respondents employed in FISE projects were contracted for an average of one to three months, at salaries equivalent to one-third the cost of a basic food basket (Renzi *et al.* 1994: 41–2, 54). The programme also provided a source of patronage for the municipal governments, which were controlled mainly by the far right faction of UNO (Enríquez *et al.* 1991: 9; Vickers and Spence 1992).

In addition to FISE, a Fund for Assistance to Oppressed Sectors (FASO) was set up in early 1991, with US funding to resettle Nicaraguans returning from abroad. A third employment programme was the Occupational Conversion Plan, which received $47.5 million from USAID between 1990 and June 1992. This programme offered state employees several months' severance pay if they 'voluntarily' left their jobs and renounced public employment for at least four years. By mid-1992, over 23 000 employees had been induced to leave the sector under this programme (USAID 1992). While neoliberal enthusiasts cited the public sector lay-offs as evidence of greater efficiency, critics noted that those who took the job buyout tended to be the more skilled people who knew they could get work elsewhere, leaving public services both quantitatively and qualitatively deteriorated.[5]

Many of those who accepted 'occupational conversion' lay-offs hoped to use their severance payments as start-up capital for small businesses. Indeed, UNO government policies favoured an explosion of commerce based on imported consumer goods for the upper and middle classes. USAID provided $243 million in import financing from 1990–92, allowing the government to maintain the exchange rate and sell dollars cheaply to importers (USAID 1992; Neira and Acevedo 1992: 74–80). However, with tens of thousands of new ex-state employees aspiring to be small shopkeepers, the commercial sector quickly became saturated. Studies showed that the capacity of the urban informal sector to absorb the unemployed had long since been exhausted (IHCA 1991c: 36–44), so the main beneficiaries of trade liberalization were big commercial capitalists.

Drastic trade liberalization had other adverse consequences for production. The average nominal tariff protection was slashed from 43 per cent in 1990 to 15 per cent in 1992, comparable to levels in neighbouring countries (World Bank 1993a: 14). Combined with credit restrictions and large devaluations, these policies devastated the industrial sector, where Plan Lacayo caused an estimated loss of 5083 jobs in medium and large industry, or 26 per cent of the workforce in that sector in 1991 (Neira and Acevedo 1992: 93). This trend continued, as total employment in industry fell from 188 000 workers in 1991 to 171 000 in 1994 (ECLAC 1995: 25).

In the agricultural sector, the government launched an assault on the Sandinista-era agrarian reform, much of which had never been formalized with new property titles. The resulting conflict and confusion over property rights was a major factor inhibiting investment and reactivation of production (IDB/IBRD/FAO 1992). The Lacayo reforms also eliminated the state monopoly on grain trading represented by the ENABAS agency. Instead of encouraging competition and efficiency, however, the withdrawal of ENABAS – together with major grain imports and restriction of agricultural credit – had the effect of depressing prices for peasant producers and re-establishing private monopolies in rural commerce (Spoor 1995: 204–7; UNDP 1994: 15). When a Sandinista nongovernmental organization attempted to import 1800 tons of donated rice in 1995, the government blocked the imported donation on the grounds that it would depress rice prices. However, officials at the Augusto César Sandino Foundation (FACS) noted that existing supplies of rice covered only 60 per cent of demand, and argued that government policy was aimed at benefiting large commercial importers.[6]

Overall, the credit cutback reduced the agricultural area financed from 560 500 manzanas (1 mz = 0.7 hectares) in the 1990/91 agricultural cycle to 214 800 in 1994/95 (BCN 1995: A–6). Credit restrictions fell particularly hard on the rural poor. For example, the number of *campesino* families attended by the National Development Bank, BANADES, had expanded from 16 000 in 1978 to a peak of 102 200 in 1988 under the Sandinista government. This coverage was contracted to

31 700 families in 1991, which included 6700 ex-Contra and 1200 UN-assisted repatriated refugees and demobilized Contras (Baumeister 1995: 259); and was further reduced to 12 000 by 1995.[7] The shift in credit away from small producers was partly a reflection of the altered class orientation of the new government. It was also reinforced by the partial privatization of the financial system. With seven new private banks operating in 1992, BANADES had its staff cut by 61 per cent and its number of branch offices reduced by 46 per cent (World Bank 1993a: 8), making it more difficult to attend thousands of dispersed small producers. Though small and medium producers accounted for 60 per cent of agricultural production, their share of credit fell from 56 per cent in 1990 to 23 per cent in 1993 (Acevedo 1994: 17). Even USAID was critical of the Chamorro government's failure to provide titles and credit to the country's small and medium farmers, who it noted 'have the greatest potential to work with market interest rates of credit, to repay their loans, and to generate the greatest amounts of savings' (USAID 1995: 40).

Another impact of adjustment on the agricultural sector was the decline in agricultural wages, which dropped to 65 per cent of the national average (ECLAC 1994: 47). The government's vision of structural adjustment, in a throwback to the Somoza era, called for reducing wage costs as a way to promote agroexports. When the exchange rate for the new *córdoba oro* was devalued by a factor of five in March 1991, wages were adjusted by a factor of only two, and outstanding debts of traditional agroexporters were revalued only 3.4 times. Wages for coffee and cotton pickers were set at US$0.97 a day, only 60 per cent of the rural minimum wage in Guatemala, where basic consumer goods were cheaper (Neira and Acevedo 1992: 63, 97). A 1992 USAID consultancy (Edwards 1992), noting that the currency was still overvalued but that a devaluation would trigger inflation, called for further reducing wages to make agricultural exports more competitive. A revealing World Bank memo to the Consultative Group of lenders, citing low productivity in Nicaraguan agriculture, recommended 'necessary realignments in the relative price of labor to compensate for lower productivity' (World Bank 1993a : 19). In contrast to this rather one-dimensional view which seemed to prevail within the government, another international mission emphasized that reactivation of agricultural production would require investment to raise productivity levels, a political solution to land tenancy conflicts, and a special credit programme to finance small and medium producers (IDB/IBRD/FAO 1992: 3–6).

Part of the low-wage strategy for creating additional incentives to capital included labour market 'flexibilization'. As part of the conditions for obtaining an Economic Recovery Credit from the World Bank's International Development Association (IDA), the government submitted a 'letter on labour policy' in April 1994. In accordance with the new policy, draft legislation was introduced in the National Assembly to allow more temporary labour contracts, reduce severance pay, ban workplace takeovers by strikers, and expand Ministry of Labour (MITRAB) powers to declare strikes illegal (IMF 1994c: 13). Proposed new Labour Code reforms would restrict public sector workers' right to strike, limit collective bargaining agreements, and eliminate MITRAB's power to obligate management to negotiate with unions.

New fiscal incentives were granted to the Las Mercedes 'free zone' in the industrial belt on the outskirts of Managua near the airport, where labour leaders claimed there was an unwritten ban on unionization. In the Taiwanese-owned textile firm FORTEX, where the owner had reportedly kicked a woman worker and threatened another with a pistol, MITRAB failed to back the incipient union in a 1993–94 labour dispute, leading to the resignation of 150 workers and the end of the union.[8] By July 1995, not a single union had successfully formed among some 6000 workers in 14 firms in the free zone (11 of them textile/clothing firms). One Nicaraguan business leader noted that the free-zone firms were given 'tax and labour exemptions to do things that a Nicaraguan could not', and suggested that foreign capital was beginning to come to Nicaragua because of AFL-CIO pressure over labour practices in free zones in El Salvador and Costa Rica.[9]

Exports from the free zone grew from $6.3 million in 1993 to $27.7 million in 1994 (MEDE 1995: 17); but it was not clear from official figures how much if any of that represented net exports, or whether there was any reinvestment after foreign owners repatriated profits. Government economic plans described the free zone programme as a 'success', noting cheerily that 80 per cent of the workers were women between the ages of 18 and 23, and that Nicaragua had a comparative advantage in cheap labour and low-rent industrial space (Nicaragua 1995: 50–1). The plan called for expansion to include four more free zones in other regions of the country, which would employ 20 000 workers by 1999.

Despite significant changes in the regime of capital accumulation, there was relatively little reactivation of investment and production. While USAID noted 'significant progress in opening Nicaragua to foreign investment' – including a new Foreign Investment Law allowing 100 per cent profit remittances, and repatriation of original capital after three years – the total stock of US direct investment in Nicaragua at the end of 1993 was only about $110 million, compared to $385 million in Costa Rica (USAID 1995: 15–16). Public investment, which had increased from an average 7 per cent of GDP in 1973–78 to 16.4 per cent in 1979–89, fell to 8.6 per cent in the 1990–94 period; while Nicaraguan private investment, which had fallen from 10.2 per cent in 1973–78 to 2.8 per cent in the Sandinista decade, only inched up to 5.9 per cent in 1990–94 (Martínez Cuenca 1994: 15; BCN 1995: B-2), and the largest category of private investment was in commerce and services (MEDE 1995: 27). Moreover, public and private sector national savings were both negative in the 1990–94 period, so even these modest levels of investment were only possible due to flows of external savings averaging $848 million/year, not counting donations (Avendaño 1994: 9).

Among the factors dampening investment were political instability, uncertainty over property disputes, credit restrictions, and the limited domestic market (especially with half the population unemployed). Traditional business elites, represented by COSEP, felt excluded from economic policies formulated in consultation between the Ministry of the Presidency and the international financial institutions, and they remained sceptical of the government's capacity to overcome political resistance on property and other key issues.[10]

One of the persistent weaknesses of the Chamorro government's adjustment programme was in the external sector. From 1990–92, despite trade and exchange rate liberalization and a reorientation of credit away from peasant producers, exports fell by $107 million; and an estimated 40 per cent of that drop was due to declining terms of trade (World Bank 1993a: 7). An unexpected upturn in coffee prices in 1994/95 due to the Brazilian frost generated a $100 million windfall that boosted economic growth to 3.2 per cent in 1994 (ECLAC 1995: 1–2), but coffee prices soon fell again. Although this was the highest economic growth rate in ten years, it still was not enough to represent growth in per capita terms. A potentially promising exception to the generally poor export performance was in the area of nontraditional exports. A new export promotion law (Decree 22–92 of March 1992) granted special import-duty and sales-tax exemptions to exporters, as well as income-tax exemptions for nontraditional exporters. Exports of nontraditionals rose from $82.9 million in 1990 to $133.3 million in 1994 (BCN 1995: A–14).

The policy of maintaining a stable exchange rate as an anchor for price stabilization made it difficult to use the exchange rate to improve the trade balance. Despite a 20 per cent devaluation in January 1993 and the shift to a crawling-peg exchange rate, the *córdoba oro* remained overvalued by at least 50 per cent by 1994 (ECLAC 1994: 41). Imports continued to rise due to the reduction of tariffs and large flows of external aid, but most of the increase was in consumer goods rather than capital goods for investment. The share of consumer goods in total imports rose from 18.3 per cent in 1988 to 35 per cent in 1992, while capital goods fell from 33 per cent to 23.2 per cent of total imports in the same period (IMF 1994b: 94). The unsustainability of this pattern was highlighted by projections that international grants and loans would drop from $712 million in 1992 to a projected $550 million or less by 1996 (World Bank 1993b: 21).

Nicaragua's foreign debt, which reached $11.5 billion by the end of 1994, was the highest per capita debt in the world. Debt service indicators were far worse than the standard used by the World Bank to classify a 'severely indebted low-income country' (SILIC), the most critical category. Despite a series of renegotiations, annual debt service obligations for 1994–2000 were projected to average $622 million – almost twice the level of exports – plus another $220 million in interest arrears (Dumazert and Neira 1994: 1–2). Obviously this amount was unpayable, but even debt service payments actually made came to $221.2 million, equivalent to 64 per cent of

Nicaragua's exports of goods in 1994 (MCE 1995: 5). Under the terms of the 1994 ESAF signed with the IMF, Nicaragua would have to continue to make payments averaging $280.7 million a year during 1995–97 (Avendaño 1994: 16–20). Meanwhile, external financing commitments during that period, reaffirmed at the Consultative Group meeting of donor countries in Paris in June 1995, would average only $170 million a year in liquid foreign exchange and $350 million a year in tied credits (IHCA 1995: 15). This means the net flow of liquid external resources (that is, excluding tied credit lines) would remain negative, as it had been since 1993. In the context of severe austerity, the idea of indefinite belt-tightening to make large payments to foreign creditors was not likely to be politically popular.

Another kind of limit to adjustment was represented by the failure of the programme to improve the living standard of the poorest. A new Living Standards Measurement Survey (LSMS) conducted in 1993 revealed that 50.3 per cent of the Nicaraguan population was below the poverty line (US$428.94), while 19.4 per cent lived in extreme poverty. The LSMS showed that only 54 per cent of the population had access to potable water, the second-lowest figure in Central America; while 40 per cent of all infant mortality was caused by easily preventable diarrhoeal diseases, and 28 per cent of all children under five suffered from malnutrition (World Bank 1993c). The wealthiest 20 per cent of the population received 65 per cent of national income, while the poorest 20 per cent lived on 3 per cent of income, putting Nicaraguan income distribution among the worst in the world (UNDP 1994: 1).

Some of this polarization was aggravated by the Chamorro government's fiscal policies, which also hurt future productivity by affecting human capital. The reintroduction of fees for health and education made these social services inaccessible to many Nicaraguans. For example, with the average Nicaraguan's amount of schooling already low at 4.5 years, the cost to parents of 'public' primary-school education per student was equivalent to one-sixth of per capita income (World Bank 1993c: 8, 27). While Health Ministry officials spoke euphemistically about decentralization and a shift to 'self-responsibility for health care',[11] medical consultations per capita fell 21 per cent from 1990 to 1994 (BCN 1995: C–1).

Government spending on health and education by 1993 had fallen 35 per cent in real terms since the mid-1980s (Evans 1995: 208). The tax structure was also made much more regressive, as the maximum income tax was cut from 60 per cent in 1989 to 30 per cent in 1992 (Evans 1995: 210). The share of tax revenues from regressive indirect taxes (such as sales tax) increased from 75 per cent in 1989 to 89 per cent in 1994 (Acevedo 1994: 5).

Typically with orthodox adjustment, the distributive impact fell heavily on women (Pérez-Alemán 1992). For example, 60 per cent of central government employees were female (Evans 1995: 197), so cutbacks in public-sector employment particularly affected women. Recession tended to force more women out of participation in the salaried workforce and into the urban informal sector. Since men had a larger share of formal-sector jobs, open unemployment rates were higher for males; but surveys in 1992 and 1993 showed a higher (and rising) rate of underemployment for women (Renzi and Agurto 1993: 116).

Moreover, social-service cutbacks placed a particular burden on women due to the gendered division of labour in society. Although studies showed that men averaged 47 hours a week at paid work compared to 37 hours for women, once unpaid domestic tasks were added in, the total was 77 hours for women versus 55 hours for men. Not surprisingly, then, women reported that economic austerity had a greater impact on their domestic workload (Renzi and Agurto 1993: 65, 103). The number of female-headed households rose from 24 per cent in 1985 to 28 per cent in 1993, and the incidence of poverty was higher in these households (Renzi and Agurto 1993: 154–61). The gender impact of structural adjustment was no longer invisible: banners draped around Managua in June 1995 said 'No to the feminization of poverty'. Women's organizations, which reflected increased diversity and autonomy from the FSLN in the 1990s, were among the most dynamic of the popular organizations. Among the new, independent initiatives were a variety of groups working on issues of women's health, participation in development, and a movement of unemployed women. Women's organizations also demanded that the government publicly release its 1995 National Development Plan (presented to the Consultative

Group in Paris, but not to Nicaraguans) for discussion in grassroots assemblies.[12]

The long-term structural impact of the adjustment programme remained somewhat ambiguous, but the tendency seemed to favour modernizing capitalists, and particularly the financial and commercial elites. This produced some interesting political realignments. For example, some of the traditional agrarian capitalists represented in the entrepreneurial association COSEP were uncomfortable with the economic reforms; while newer groups like the Association of Nicaraguan Non-Traditional Export Producers, APENN, moved into the spotlight (Spalding 1994: 180–7). The FSLN and UNO, representing left and right opposition parties respectively, issued an unusual joint statement in which they agreed that:

(a) The Government's economic plan has failed, and a new comprehensive plan is therefore needed to stimulate production, promote investment, facilitate credit and create jobs … ; (b) in order for the new plan to be successful, there must be political stability … ; (c) any agreement with international lending agencies that would lead to higher unemployment and/or a reduction of social services or business loans is not a viable option … (quoted in ECLAC 1994: 8)

Lacayo's close adherence to conditions imposed by the international financial institutions had made him a clear favourite in those circles, but the government suffered from the lack of an organized political base in Nicaragua. This was a technocratic government par excellence: none of the top officials had a political party background, and virtually all of them were lawyers or engineers. The FSLN, on the other hand, which did have an organized base, suffered from (among other problems) indecisiveness over whether to accept the parameters of economic adjustment in the interest of national stability and keeping out the far right.

Politically, the broad support for change that had brought the government to office narrowed considerably over the course of Chamorro's term. In response to polls asking 'Do you feel that your interests are represented by the government of Violeta Barrios de Chamorro?', the proportion of negative respondents rose from 47 per cent in 1991 to 72 per cent in 1992,

76 per cent in 1993, and 87 per cent in 1994. When asked 'How do you consider your economic situation after X years of the government's term?', those answering 'worse' rose from 35 per cent in 1991 to 60 per cent in 1992, 67 per cent in 1993, and 72 per cent in 1994 (IEN 1994: 28, 34; IEN 1995: 6–7). This discontent seemed to cut across traditional lines. In polls conducted at the end of 1994, the leading candidate for president was 'nobody' with 31.2 per cent, followed by Arnoldo Alemán with 22.8 per cent, Daniel Ortega with 15.8 per cent, 'don't know/don't respond' with 11.5 per cent, Violeta Barrios de Chamorro with 4.1 per cent, and First Son-in-Law Antonio Lacayo only 1.9 per cent (IEN 1995: 15). With the FSLN bitterly divided on the eve of the 1996 election, the biggest beneficiary appeared to be the right-wing populist mayor of Managua and presidential aspirant, Arnoldo Alemán.

ADJUSTMENT IN THE ADJUSTMENT?

Some of the problems in the Nicaraguan economy in the mid-1990s seemed to reflect not so much structural adjustment as the lack thereof, if adjustment is understood to mean changes in the productive structure that might sustain an improvement in the balance of payments. Much of the thrust of economic policy was aimed at reversing the redistributive policies of the Sandinista years, as USAID noted:

> The primary reason for hyperinflation was the creation of money to finance excessive Government spending on the war, for resource transfers (credit), and on social programs. 'Structural Adjustment' in Nicaragua has thus principally meant reducing government spending. (USAID 1995: 13)

Aside from stabilization measures which brought down inflation, there was a modest increase in nontraditional agricultural exports and free trade zone production. There was structural change in the institutional framework of the economy, but with little productive response from investors. Perhaps the main structural reform was the transfer of property ownership towards the private sector, a contentious process which at least in the short run had a disruptive effect on production.

The struggles over privatization led to one of the more interesting modifications in the Chamorro government's original neoliberal project. Along with the negotiated social pact or *concertación* approach which was forced by grassroots resistance, the principle of worker participation in ownership of privatized enterprises was a potentially significant variation from the neoliberal model (Stahler-Sholk 1994).

Pressure for privatization came partly from former owners who saw an opportunity to reverse the Sandinista confiscations, partly from other capitalists who wanted to pick up cheap assets, and partly from the need to redistribute land to ex-combatants on both sides to defuse social tension. Also, while there was little interest from foreign investors, there were other pressures from external actors. The international financial institutions coordinating the structural adjustment programme specifically demanded privatization (IMF 1991: 15–16; IDB 1991: 5; World Bank 1992: 3). USAID tended to favour rapid privatization, consistent with its broader strategy of promoting a reconstitution of the dominant role of the entrepreneurial class in Nicaragua (USAID 1991; Saldomando 1992: 54–73). Government officials confirmed this component of 'conditionality', as well as pressure from the US Embassy for return of property to US citizens.[13]

The property issue contributed to the US Congress suspending over $100 million in USAID funds in mid-1992. Another US aid suspension loomed in 1995 when Senator Jesse Helms continued to press the case as chair of the Foreign Relations Committee, even though many of the complainants were actually Nicaraguans who had acquired US citizenship after the confiscations. The US Embassy actually set up a 'US Citizen Property Office' to pursue these claims, which had become one of the main US foreign policy issues with Nicaragua.[14] By June 1995, 522 such disputed claims had been resolved, with another 1154 'US citizen' properties still in dispute. This obsessive focus of US policy was strange not only because ex-post-facto citizenship rights had no basis in international law or practice, but also because US aid levels had dropped sharply from $270 million in fiscal year 1990 to a proposed $19 million in FY 1995. Since Nicaragua was no longer a Washington priority and US foreign policy had generally shifted to a 'hands-off' approach to Central America, the

Clinton administration appeared torn between placating
Senator Helms and contributing to post-conflict reconstruction in Nicaragua. On 31 July 1995, the Clinton administration issued a waiver to allow a continuation of aid to
Nicaragua, citing progress towards resolving property claims
as well as a national security interest in promoting stability as
Nicaragua's 1996 elections approached.

The Chamorro government launched its privatization drive
with Decrees 10–90 and 11–90 in May 1990, which provided
for the immediate rental and return of state lands that had
been 'unjustly' confiscated from private owners. Workers
affiliated with the pro-Sandinista Association of Rural Workers
(ATC) responded by taking over state enterprises to block privatization, crippling production at the start of the 1990/91
agricultural cycle. A war of attrition ensued, with outbreaks of
violence as the police and army, former landowners, and even
demobilized combatants who had been promised land,
clashed with occupying workers.

When the FNT staged its general strike in July 1990, the
demands included revocation of the privatization decrees.
These demands stemmed in part from the fact that the privatizations were often followed by large-scale lay-offs, with union
activists among the first to be fired (Stahler-Sholk 1994). The
state holding company overseeing privatization, CORNAP, calculated a 40.5 per cent reduction in the workforce of the enterprises that had been privatized, which it attributed to 'the
new economic reality' (CORNAP 1992: 12).

Eventually the union position evolved from outright rejection of privatization to negotiation for a worker share of the
property. The government first proposed a 15 per cent
worker share, and the two sides finally compromised in the
concertación II accord of 15 August 1991, accepting the principle of 25 per cent worker ownership. Some of the first property transfers to the 'workers' property area' (APT) were
negotiated in agriculture. Sectoral negotiations gave workers
30 per cent of the former state cattle properties, 33 per cent
in coffee, 32 per cent in cotton, and a 25 per cent share in
the banana corporation.[15] In the industrial sector, which was
operating below capacity and which featured a number of
mixed enterprises, the precise mix of ownership and mode
of privatization was determined in practice through a pro-

longed process of conflict and negotiation by enterprise and branch.

Officially, the government declared the main objectives of privatization to be first, to reactivate the economy by attracting private national and foreign investment and improving efficiency of management; second, to improve the national budgetary balance; and third, to diversify property in order to give 'all sectors the opportunity to participate' (CORNAP 1995: 5). One close observer of the process commented that the real motives seemed to be first, to respond to pressures from the international financial institutions; second, to improve macroeconomic balances, though in practice the privatization failed to generate fiscal resources; and third, to break the union movement, which had a strong base in the state-owned enterprises.[16]

Of the 351 state enterprises representing 30 per cent of GDP in 1990, the state had disposed of 160 by the end of March 1992 (CORNAP 1992: 3–6), with the rest scheduled for privatization by the end of 1993. Due to resistance, the process dragged on, and the government failed to meet its commitment under the ESAF to dispose of the remaining enterprises by the end of 1994. As of June 1995, CORNAP had privatized 98 per cent of its enterprises, with only five or six pending (DeFranco 1995: 14). About 52 per cent of the privatized enterprises were acquired by capitalists (mainly Nicaraguan), 23 per cent were transferred to workers, and 16 per cent to ex-combatants (CORNAP 1995: 24).

Of the privatization transactions, some 44 per cent were simply returned to private owners, with little effort to collect on state investments that had been made over the previous decade (since many of the firms had initially been confiscated for decapitalization). Former owners whose properties were not returned received $200 million in indemnization bonds, to be paid over 15 years at 3–5 per cent interest, with the first two years of interest to be capitalized. The first $6 million in interest would fall due in 1995, another strain on macroeconomic balances (ECLAC 1995: 6). Of the 46 per cent of CORNAP holdings put up for sale, the government grossed $48.5 million, of which only $16.5 million was in legal tender. The rest was paid in the form of indemnization bonds, which the owners were allowed to use at face value to purchase new property. Since the bonds were trading on the secondary market at only 17–20 per cent of their face value, that meant capitalists (but not workers) could acquire property at fire-sale prices (DeFranco 1995: 26). The state in the end earned nothing (after deducting administrative costs and funds used to retire compensation bonds) on the privatization of 351 enterprises that had represented 30 per cent of GDP! By one calculation, the value of this giveaway could be as much as $600 million; and meanwhile the state would have to pay out on some $102 million in outstanding bonds (DeFranco 1995: 28–33).

While the exact figures might be debated, it was clear that the privatization involved a significant transfer from the state to capitalists. In addition to the 351 firms, the government also committed itself under the ESAF to privatize 40 per cent of the profitable operations of the telecommunications agency, TELCOR, by the end of 1994. One motive for doing so would be to generate revenues to back the indemnization bonds, including the $200 million outstanding and a similar amount which it was estimated would be required to resolve other pending property claims (ECLAC 1995: 6). However, the proposed privatization of TELCOR provoked stiff opposition from the Sandinista union as well as generalized nationalist opposition, and the project was stalled in the National Assembly through early 1995.

Further impetus to privatize TELCOR came in July 1995 when a conference on property conflicts was held in the seaside resort of Montelimar, starring former US President Jimmy Carter (Dye *et al.* 1995: 31). At that meeting the government agreed in principle to uphold Laws 85 and 86, which recognized the property rights of smallholders who had benefited from past urban and rural redistribution, in exchange for the FSLN dropping its opposition to the privatization of TELCOR. In the wake of this pact, which would only heighten tensions within Sandinista sectors, the legislature moved forward with the first stage of legislation to privatize TELCOR and bidding was opened in December 1995. The law allowed sale of 40 per cent to a foreign investor and 11 per cent to the workers; with 80 per cent of proceeds earmarked for redeeming compensation bonds held by former owners of confiscated property.

Another component of privatization was the banking system. While cutting back severely on credit through the state banks, the government circumvented constitutional prohibitions and authorized the opening of private banks, of which there were nine functioning and two more authorized by mid-1995. The international financial institutions continued to press for further privatization of the banking system (World Bank 1993a: 17). As with the rest of the privatization process, however, this represented more of a transfer of wealth than a structural adjustment that might actually stimulate productive efficiency. The new private banks limited their lending mainly to the commercial and financial sectors, and took advantage of the overvalued exchange rate to move their depositors' money to offshore banks.[17]

In response to the partial privatization of banking, UNAG created its own Banco del Campo, with 45 per cent capital from European sources. This new bank loaned mainly to agricultural producers, with a 'special credit' programme offering lower interest rates to small producers. However, this effort did not make up for the drastic reduction in the state National Development Bank, and the credit squeeze was one reason the number of agricultural cooperatives had fallen from 3000 to 1400 by 1995.[18]

The issue of modifying privatization plans in particular, and defining alternatives to the neoliberal project in general, produced considerable ambivalence and division among the popular sectors once mobilized by the FSLN. The role the FSLN had assumed as mediator in the 1990 strikes generated some concern among the FNT that labour mobilization was being used as a bargaining chip to further narrow interests among the FSLN party leadership. The FSLN attempted to position itself after 1990 as the defender of the property rights of the poor, and especially of the beneficiaries of the agrarian reform and urban property redistribution of the previous decade. However, the credibility of these efforts was seriously undermined by the 'spontaneous privatization' or *piñata*, which had involved a significant transfer of state property to individual FSLN leaders in the lame-duck period between the February 1990 election and the April inauguration of the Chamorro government. This continued to be a major political liability as the 1996 election approached; even if, as one union activist argued, the Sandinista *piñata* was minor compared to what he called the 'capitalist *piñata*' represented by the CORNAP privatization process.[19]

The notion of 'privatization to the workers' carried a number of risks, ranging from bankruptcy to cooptation. With 25 per cent ownership and little independent access to capital, workers might not effectively wield control. By 1995, the experience of the new Area of Workers' Property (APT) was mixed at best. In general, the APT enterprises that were in best shape were those that were 100 per cent worker-owned, in potentially profitable sectors where the worker-owners had the capacity to quickly pay off the purchase price of the firm, and that had a unified union. Even in the best of cases, however, problems remained. For example, in the cereals processing plant El Caracol, government delays in completing the transfer of legal ownership made it more difficult to get credit.[20] This meant the coffee beans and grains could not be purchased when they were cheapest, and aging machinery was in need of replacement. The director of the worker-owned firm was also the head of the union, creating some tension when the firm laid off 35 workers and cut benefits by 50 per cent in an effort to remain solvent.

An even more problematical case was the match factory, La Fosforera, where the union was divided and workers owned only 50 per cent. The capitalist partner with the largest share began buying off workers and manoeuvreing to bankrupt the enterprise, and the Ministry of Labour refused to intervene, arguing that the workers were not legally entitled to union recognition if they were also owners. Through a combination of political work on the shop floor and a takeover of the installations, the workers were able to regain the upper hand in July 1995. One union activist concluded that:

> Nobody is enchanted with privatization anymore, because they see that it's a double-edged sword. And this government only calls out the riot police when people come out to protest.[21]

Besides the contest that pitted workers against capitalists and the state, there was also the battle within. To the extent that workers became owners, where would their interests lie? It remained unclear whether the new Area of Workers' Property

(APT) could form the nucleus of a progressive alternative (IHCA 1991b: 12–30; Núñez Soto 1992) against a competing project, promoted by the state, which favoured big capital (IHCA 1991a, 1991c). Dissidents within the ATC wondered whether the worker-owned enterprises would mean real workplace democracy, or simply be run like corporations with the same old directors. In June 1995, thousands of ATC-organized agricultural workers set up a protest encampment in Managua to demand land titles and credit. What might have been a dramatic symbol of resistance was undermined, however, by doubts about its real purpose. Though the issues were real, cynics wondered whether the sit-in was orchestrated to bolster the sagging grassroots credentials of the FSLN party leadership.

Similar questions faced the small farmers' association, UNAG, which had historically carved out more autonomy from the FSLN than other mass organizations (Luciak 1995). Given the wholesale dismantling of credit and marketing agencies that had protected peasant production, UNAG was torn between integrating fully into the new model and taking a direct role in commerce, agroindustry and banking, or defending the smaller producers who were most vulnerable to the impact of adjustment (Baumeister 1995: 260). Yet UNAG showed flexibility in reaching out to ex-Contras on common issues of land security, and positioning itself as an interlocutor between the government and agricultural producers.

The question of autonomy of the mass organizations (Haugaard 1991; Quandt 1995) became particularly critical in defining responses to structural adjustment. Critics of the neoliberal agenda differed in their interpretations (IHCA 1991a; CRIES 1992; Ruíz and Téllez 1992), and the discussion of alternatives tended to be either sectorally specific or excessively abstract (UNAG 1993; Asamblea Sandinista 1993). The mass organizations may find a new vitality by defining their interests independently of party leadership. However, the impact of adjustment tends to disarticulate the bases for organized opposition, for example by lay offs that weaken unions and credit restrictions that destroy cooperatives. In this context, the division of the FSLN – formalized by the breakaway of Sergio Ramírez' MRS after the May 1994 party congress – undermined the prospects for formulating a broad national alternative to the neoliberal project.

A number of economic proposals began to circulate in anticipation of the 1996 election, ranging from a group of advisers to Alemán (Ramírez *et al.* 1995) to the various currents of the once-unified Sandinistas (FSLN 1995; MRS 1995; Ruíz *et al.* 1994). These 'alternative' proposals, however, tended to be mainly diagnostic or vague or both. One of the problems plaguing the FSLN was the apparent inconsistency of a strategy involving on the one hand confrontational mobilizations at the grassroots, and on the other hand pacts negotiated between the FSLN leadership and the Lacayo group. As one observer put it,

> If *sandinismo* does not permit it, there is no structural adjustment in this country. They permitted it, on the basis of the 1990 *concertación* [pact].[22]

This point was made more bluntly and publicly by dissident Sandinista leader Henry Ruíz, who still remained on the FSLN National Directorate, in 1995:

> Here they stage sit-ins and take over the National Assembly denouncing economic repression, and the same week they go holding hands with the government [to the Consultative Group meeting in Paris] to pawn the nation. The only thing that is coherent and clear, is that the FSLN has turned into the principal ally of the government of Antonio Lacayo and everything that that neoliberal government signifies for this country. (Ruíz 1995: 16)

The more general lesson here is that neoliberal adjustment programmes tend to fracture traditional lines of organization, which may be why they so often open political space for right-wing populists who claim to represent a national interest that is above partisan politics. Popular organizations, which have to respond to immediate needs, are faced with the real dilemma of whether to try to lick them or join them. If they make compromises in order to deliver some short-term results (for example, partial worker ownership or peasant credits), they seem coopted by the state; if they refuse to compromise, they seem to be placing party politics above the interests of their sectors.

Neoliberalism tends to weaken some of the traditional spaces for class-based organization, such as unions (particularly in the public sector). Successful resistance depends on the previously developed capacity of popular organizations to respond before they are dismantled, and on their ability to forge alliances. The negotiation of social pacts does not have a predetermined outcome; but if *concertación* is well coordinated with the disruptive power of a broad-based social movement, it may counteract the effort of a technocratic government to carve out a depoliticized space for top-down economic adjustment (Munck 1994). In the Nicaraguan case, the legacy of the revolution could be measured in terms of the continued vitality and resiliency of the popular movement. During the Chamorro/Lacayo administration of 1990–96, the FSLN did not succeed in establishing the kind of creative new relationship with its mobilized social base that was implied by Daniel Ortega's 1990 promise, that the electorally defeated Sandinistas would 'govern from below'. In this respect, the Nicaraguan case highlighted the general need to rethink party/social movement dynamics in response to structural adjustment. Challenging the neoliberal agenda requires mobilization from below, but it also requires a coherent strategy and organization that can formulate alternatives.

REFERENCES

Acevedo Vogl, Adolfo. 1994. *Algunas implicaciones de los acuerdos con el FMI y el Banco Mundial (ESAF y el ERC-II) para el país y la sociedad nicaragüense.* Documento de Trabajo, 94(3). Managua: CRIES, March.

Arana, Mario, Richard Stahler-Sholk, Gerardo Timossi and Carmen López. 1987. 'Deuda, estabilización y ajuste: La transformación en Nicaragua, 1979–1986'. *Cuadernos de Pensamiento Propio*, Serie Ensayos No. 15. Managua: CRIES, November.

Asamblea Sandinista. 1993. 'Propuesta: Para una salida nacional a la crisis'. El Crucero: 27–8 March.

Avendaño, Nestor. 1994. *La economía de Nicaragua: El año 2000 y las posibilidades de crecimiento.* Managua: Nitlapán/CRIES, 7 November.

Baumeister, Eduardo. 1995. 'Farmers' Organizations and Agrarian Transformation in Nicaragua'. In Minor Sinclair (ed.), *The New Politics of Survival: Grassroots Movements in Central America.* New York: Monthly Review/EPICA.

BCN (Banco Central de Nicaragua). 1995. *Indicadores Económicos*, 1(4), April.

Bello, Walden. 1994. *Dark Victory: The United States, Structural Adjustment and Global Poverty.* Oakland, CA: Institute for Food and Development Policy.

Castro, Vanessa and Gary Prevost (eds). 1992. *The 1990 Elections in Nicaragua and their Aftermath.* Lanham, MD: Rowman and Littlefield.

CIERA (Centro de Investigaciones y Estudios de la Reforma Agraria). 1988. *El debate sobre la reforma económica.* Managua: CIERA.

——. 1989. *Política económica y transformación social.* Managua: CIERA.

Conroy, Michael E. 1990. 'The Political Economy of the 1990 Nicaraguan Elections'. *International Journal of Political Economy*, 20(3), Fall.

CORNAP (Corporaciones Nacionales del Sector Público). 1992. *Proceso de privatización de empresas: Evaluación del impacto económico y social.* Managua, May.

——. 1995. *Avance del proceso de privatización al 31 de diciembre de 1994.* Managua, March.

CRIES (Coordinadora Regional de Investigaciones Económicas y Sociales)/Equipo de Investigadores. 1992. 'La farsa del neoliberalismo'. *La Avispa*, 9, April–June.

DeFranco, Mario. 1995. 'Nicaragua: Experiencia de privatización de empresas públicas'. Seminario Nacional sobre Privatizaciones organizado por CEPAL/ASDI y PNUD. Managua, 12 June.

Dumazert, Patrick and Oscar Neira. 1994. *From Debt Burden to the Search for Development Alternatives: Could the Debt Be an Opportunity to Overcome the National Crisis in Nicaragua?* Managua: Nitlapán/CRIES, August.

Dye, David R. *et al.* 1995. *Contesting Everything, Winning Nothing: The Search for Consensus in Nicaragua, 1990–1995.* Cambridge, MA: Hemisphere Initiatives, November.

ECLAC (UN Economic Commission for Latin America and the Caribbean). 1994. 'Nicaragua: An Economy in Transition'. LC/MEX/R. 458. Mexico, 31 May.

——. 1995. 'Nicaragua: Evolución económica durante 1994'. LC/MEX/R. 519. Mexico, 8 May.

Edwards, Sebastian. 1992. 'Real Exchange Rates, Competitiveness and Macroeconomic Adjustment in Nicaragua: A Progress Report'. AID consultancy report. Managua, 20 February.

Enríquez, Laura J. *et al.* 1991. *Nicaragua: Reconciliation Awaiting Recovery. Politics, the Economy and U.S. Aid under the Chamorro Government.* Washington, DC: Washington Office on Latin America, April.

Evans, Trevor. 1995. 'Ajuste estructural y sector público en Nicaragua'. In Trevor Evans (ed.), *La transformación neoliberal del sector público: Ajuste estructural y sector público en Centroamérica y el Caribe.* Managua: CRIES/Latino Editores.

FNT (Frente Nacional de los Trabajadores). 1991. 'Posición del FNT ante el FMI y BM'. Managua: 12 January.

FSLN (Frente Sandinista de Liberación Nacional). 1995. *Propuesta del FSLN para debatir la orientación de la economía nicaragüense.* Managua, May.

Gibson, Bill. 1987. 'A Structural Overview of the Nicaraguan Economy'. In Rose J. Spalding (ed.), *The Political Economy of Revolutionary Nicaragua.* Boston: Allen and Unwin.

Green, Duncan. 1995. *Silent Revolution: The Rise of Market Economics in Latin America.* London: Latin American Bureau.

Haggard, Stephan. 1986. 'The Politics of Adjustment: Lessons from the IMF's Extended Fund Facility'. In Miles Kahler (ed.), *The Politics of International Debt*. Ithaca, NY: Cornell University Press.

Haggard, Stephan and Robert R. Kaufman. 1995. *The Political Economy of Democratic Transitions*. Princeton, NJ: Princeton University Press.

Haugaard, Lisa. 1991. 'In and Out of Power: Dilemmas for Grassroots Organizing in Nicaragua'. *Socialism and Democracy*, 7 (3), Fall.

IDB (Inter-American Development Bank). 1991. *Nicaragua Trade and Finance Adjustment Loan (NI-0012)*. Washington, DC, 20 September.

IDB/IBRD/FAO (Inter-American Development Bank/International Bank for Reconstruction and Development/Food and Agriculture Organization). 1992. *Nicaragua: Misión de identificación sectorial agropecuaria. Ayuda memoria*. Managua, 16 March.

IEN (Instituto de Estudios Nicaragüenses). 1994. 'La gobernabilidad y la democracia local en Nicaragua: Investigación sobre la opinión pública nacional'. [Poll sponsored by UNDP.] Managua, 31 January.

——. 1995. 'La gobernabilidad y el acuerdo nacional en Nicaragua: Investigación sobre la opinión pública nacional'. Managua, 3 January.

IHCA (Instituto Histórico Centroamericano). 1988. 'El pueblo de Nicaragua: Por la paz y por un modelo económico más popular'. *Envío*, 7 (85), July-August.

——. 1991a 'Los pies de barro del plan económico'. *Envío*, 10 (121), November.

——. 1991b 'Privatización: Tres puntos de vista'. *Envío*, 10 (120), October.

——. 1991c ¿Qué esperar del plan económico: Reactivación o recesión? *Envío*, 10 (117), July.

——. 1995. 'En París, desfile de imágenes'. *Envío*, 14 (160), July.

IMF (International Monetary Fund). 1989. *Nicaragua: Staff Report for the 1989 Article IV Consultation*. Washington, DC, 2 November.

——. 1991. *Nicaragua – Request for Stand-By Arrangement*. Washington, DC, 12 September.

——. 1994a. *Enhanced Structural Adjustment Facility, Policy Framework Paper, 1994–97*. Washington, DC, 2 June.

——. 1994b. *Nicaragua: Recent Economic Developments*. Washington, DC, 13 June.

——. 1994c. *Nicaragua: Staff Report for the 1994 Article IV Consultation and Request for Arrangements Under the Enhanced Structural Adjustment Facility*. Washington, DC, 2 June.

Kahler, Miles. 1990. 'Orthodoxy and Its Alternatives: Explaining Approaches to Stabilization and Adjustment'. In Joan M. Nelson (ed.), *Economic Crisis and Policy Choice: The Politics of Adjustment in the Third World*. Princeton: Princeton University Press.

Luciak, Ilya A. 1995. *The Sandinista Legacy: Lessons from a Political Economy in Transition*. Gainesville: University Press of Florida.

Martínez Cuenca, Alejandro. 1992. *Sandinista Economics in Practice: An Insider's Critical Reflections*. Boston: South End Press.

——. 1994. *El comportamiento inversionista en Nicaragua*. Materiales de Estudio y Trabajo No. 13. Managua: Fundación Friedrich Ebert, February.

MCE (Ministerio de Cooperación Externa). 1995. 'Nicaragua: Situación y perspectivas económicas 1994–1995 (Versión preliminar)'. Managua, January.

110   *The Undermining of the Sandinista Revolution*

MEDE (Ministerio de Economía y Desarrollo). 1995. *La economía nicaragüense 1994*. Managua: MEDE.
Montealegre, Haroldo, *et al.* 1990. 'Programa de estabilización y ajuste estructural para Nicaragua 1990–1993'. Propuesta de la Comisión del Plan Económico. Managua, 17 September.
MRS (Movimiento Renovador Sandinista). 1995. *Estatutos, principios y programa*. Managua, 21 May.
Munck, Ronaldo. 1994. 'Workers, Structural Adjustment, and *Concertación Social* in Latin America'. *Latin American Perspectives*, 21 (3), Summer.
Neira Cuadra, Oscar, and Adolfo Acevedo. 1992. *Nicaragua: Hiperinflación y desestabilización. Análisis de la política económica 1988 a 1991*. Managua: Cuadernos CRIES, Serie Ensayos No. 21.
Nicaragua, República de. 1990a. 'Acuerdos de la concertación económica y social y la política exterior del Gobierno de Nicaragua'. Managua, 26 October.
——. 1990b. 'Documento presentado por el Gobierno de Nicaragua ante la conferencia de donantes en Roma'. Rome, June.
——. 1992. *Nicaragua: Medium-Term Development Strategy 1992–1996*. Document presented by the Government of Nicaragua at the Consultative Group Meeting. Washington, DC, 26 March.
——. 1995. *Plan Nacional de Desarrollo (Borrador preliminar para discusión en el comité técnico)*. Managua, 31 March.
Núñez Soto, Orlando. 1992. 'La agenda de la revolución: Los nuevos sujetos económicos'. *La Avispa*, 9, April–June.
Ocampo, José Antonio. 1991. 'Collapse and (Incomplete) Stabilization of the Nicaraguan Economy'. In Dornbusch, Rudiger and Sebastian Edwards (eds), *The Macroeconomics of Populism in Latin America*. Chicago: University of Chicago Press.
O'Kane, Trish. 1995. 'New Autonomy, New Struggle: Labor Unions in Nicaragua'. In Minor Sinclair (ed.), *The New Politics of Survival: Grassroots Movements in Central America*. New York: Monthly Review/EPICA.
Pastor, Manuel. 1987. *The International Monetary Fund and Latin America: Economic Stabilization and Class Conflict*. Boulder, CO: Westview Press.
——. 1993. 'Managing the Latin American Debt Crisis: The International Monetary Fund and Beyond'. In Gerald Epstein, Julie Graham and Jessica Nembhard (eds), *Creating a New World Economy: Forces of Change and Plans for Action*. Philadelphia: Temple University Press.
Pérez-Alemán, Paola. 1992. 'Economic Crisis and Women in Nicaragua'. In Lourdes Benería and Shelley Feldman (eds), *Unequal Burden: Economic Crises, Persistent Poverty, and Women's Work*. Boulder, CO: Westview Press.
Przeworski, Adam. 1992. 'The Neoliberal Fallacy'. *Journal of Democracy*, 3 (3), July.
——. 1995. *Sustainable Democracy*. Cambridge: Cambridge University Press.
Quandt, Midge. 1995. 'Unbinding the Ties That Bind: The FSLN and the Popular Organizations'. In Minor Sinclair (ed.), *The New Politics of Survival: Grassroots Movements in Central America*. New York: Monthly Review/EPICA.
Ramírez, Noël, *et al.* 1995. *Nicaragua: La nueva estrategia económica 1997–2001*. Managua, n.d.

Renzi, María Rosa and Sonia Agurto. 1993. *¿Qué hace la mujer nicaragüense ante la crisis económica?* Managua: FIDEG.

Renzi, María Rosa with Mario J. Cangiani and Sonia Agurto. 1994. *Impacto de los proyectos FISE en las condiciones de vida de los nicaragüenses.* Managua: FIDEG.

Ricciardi, Joseph. 1991. 'Economic Policy'. In Thomas W. Walker (ed.), *Revolution and Counterrevolution in Nicaragua.* Boulder, CO: Westview Press.

Roxborough, Ian. 1992. 'Neo-liberalism in Latin America: Limits and Alternatives'. *Third World Quarterly,* 13 (3).

Ruíz, Henry. 1995. 'Henry Ruíz rompe el silencio'. [Interview by Jorge Katín with Cmdte. Henry Ruíz.] *Semanario,* 29 June – 5 July.

Ruíz, Henry and Dora María Téllez. 1992. '¿Apoya el FSLN el neoliberalismo en Nicaragua?' *La Avispa,* 9, April–June.

Ruíz, Henry *et al.* 1994. *Para una salida nacional a la crisis.* Managua: INPASA, November.

Saldomando, Angel. 1992. *El retorno de la AID: El caso de Nicaragua; condicionalidad y reestructuración conservadora.* Managua: CRIES.

Serra, Luis. 1991. 'The Grass-Roots Organizations'. In Thomas W. Walker (ed.), *Revolution and Counterrevolution in Nicaragua.* Boulder, CO: Westview Press.

———. 1993. 'Democracy in Times of War and Socialist Crisis: Reflections Stemming from the Sandinista Revolution'. *Latin American Perspectives,* 20 (2), Spring.

Spalding, Rose J. 1994. *Capitalists and Revolution in Nicaragua: Opposition and Accommodation, 1979–1993.* Chapel Hill: University of North Carolina Press.

Spoor, Max. 1995. *The State and Domestic Agriculture Markets in Nicaragua: From Interventionism to Neo-Liberalism.* New York: St. Martin's Press.

Stahler-Sholk, Richard. 1990. 'Stabilization, Destabilization, and the Popular Classes in Nicaragua, 1979–1988'. *Latin American Research Review,* 25 (3), Fall.

———. 1994. 'El ajuste neoliberal y sus opciones: La respuesta del movimiento sindical nicaragüense'. *Revista Mexicana de Sociología,* 56 (3), July–September.

———. 1995. 'The Dog that Didn't Bark: Labor Autonomy and Economic Adjustment in Nicaragua Under the Sandinista and UNO Governments'. *Comparative Politics,* 28(1), October.

Stahler-Sholk, Richard and Max Spoor. 1989. 'Nicaragua: Las políticas macroeconómicas y sus efectos en la agricultura y la seguridad alimentaria'. Report of consultancy for PAN/CADESCA/EEC. Managua, July.

Taylor, Lance *et al.* 1989. *Report of an Economic Mission to the Government of Nicaragua.* Managua: Swedish International Development Authority, April.

Timossi Dolinsky, Gerardo. 1993. 'Crisis y reestructuración: El balance centroamericano de los años ochenta'. In Carlos M. Vilas (ed.), *Democracia emergente en Centroamérica.* Mexico: UNAM.

UNAG (Unión Nacional de Agricultores y Ganaderos). 1993. 'La estrategia de desarrollo agropecuario en Nicaragua: Una visión desde la UNAG'. Foro sobre una Estrategia de Desarrollo Agropecuario en Nicaragua. Managua, 23 February.

112   *The Undermining of the Sandinista Revolution*

UNDP (United Nations Development Programme). 1994. 'Statement for the Consultative Group Meeting on Nicaragua'. Paris, 16–17 June.

UNO (Unión Nacional Opositora). 1990. 'Agenda para el rescate de la economía nacional'. Managua, February.

USAID (United States Agency for International Development)/Nicaragua. 1991. *Country Development Strategy Statement, USAID/Nicaragua 1991–1996.* Managua, 14 June.

——. 1992. 'USAID Programs in Nicaragua: A Brief Description and Current Status'. Managua: USAID, 10 June.

——. 1995. *Nicaragua 2000: Challenges for Developing a Stable, Democratic, Prospering Society.* Managua: USAID, March.

Utting, Peter. 1991. *Economic Adjustment under the Sandinistas: Policy Reform, Food Security and Livelihood in Nicaragua.* Geneva: UNRISD.

Vanden, Harry E. and Gary Prevost. 1993. *Democracy and Socialism in Sandinista Nicaragua.* Boulder, CO: Lynne Rienner.

Vickers, George and Jack Spence. 1992. 'Nicaragua Two Years After the Fall'. *World Policy Journal,* 9 (3), Summer: 533–62.

Vilas, Carlos M. 1991. 'The Revolution that Fell from the Grace of the People'. *Socialist Register 1991.* London.

——. 1992. 'Family Affairs: Class, Lineage and Politics in Contemporary Nicaragua'. *Journal of Latin American Studies,* 24 (2), May.

——. 1995. 'Entre la democracia y el neoliberalismo: Los caudillos electorales de la posmodernidad'. *Socialismo y Participación* (Lima, Peru), 69. March.

Walton, John. 1989. 'Debt, Protest, and the State in Latin America'. In Susan Eckstein (ed.), *Power and Popular Protest: Latin American Social Movements.* Berkeley: University of California.

Williamson, John. 1990. 'What Washington Means by Policy Reform'. In John Williamson (ed.), *Latin American Adjustment: How Much Has Happened?* Washington, DC: Institute for International Economics.

World Bank. 1992. *Nicaragua: Managing the Transition from Stabilization to Sustained Economic Growth.* Washington, DC, 26 March.

——. 1993a. *Nicaragua – Stabilization and Adjustment: Enabling Private Sector-Led Growth.* Consultative Group Meeting for Nicaragua. Paris, 2 April.

——. 1993b. *Nicaragua: Opciones de política económica en el marco de perspectivas de ayuda extranjera decreciente.* Background document prepared for economic seminar. Managua, 7–8 October.

——. 1993c. *The Who, What and Where of Poverty in Nicaragua.* Washington, DC, 24 November.

NOTES

1. 'Lunes socio-económico', *Barricada,* 28 November 1983.
2. 'Operación "Bertha"', *Barricada,* 1–3 March 1988.
3. 'Puedo terminar con la inflación en cuestión de semanas', *La Crónica,* 3–10 January 1990.
4. 'Acuerdo entre el Gobierno y el FNT', *Barricada,* 11 July 1990.
5. Interview with Trevor Evans, economist at CRIES, 22 June 1995.

6. Interview with Comandante Henry Ruíz, member of FSLN National Directorate, 22 June 1995.
7. Interview with Amílcar Navarro, member of the national board of directors of UNAG, 29 June 1995.
8. Interviews with Dámaso Vargas, CST leader, 5 July 1995; and Carlos Borge, CST leader, 7 July 1995.
9. Interview with Roger Cerda, General Manager of the Nicaraguan Chamber of Commerce, 6 July 1995.
10. Interview with Gilberto Cuadra, President of the Superior Council of Private Enterprise (COSEP), 29 June 1995.
11. Interview with Julio Norori, Director of Policy and Development for the Ministry of Health, 26 June 1995.
12. Interview with María Teresa Blandón, 'La Malinche' feminist collective, 22 June 1995.
13. Interview with Iván Saballos, General Director of Privatization, National Corporations of the Public Sector (CORNAP), 10 July 1992.
14. Interview with Western diplomatic source in Managua, 27 June 1995.
15. Interviews with Salvador Ramírez, Secretary of Employment and Land, and José Adán Rivera, Secretary of Organization of the ATC, 7 and 13 July 1992.
16. Interview with an economist working for a nongovernmental organization in Nicaragua, 3 July 1995.
17. Interview with Roger Cerda, General Manager of the Chamber of Commerce, 6 July 1995.
18. Interview with Amílcar Navarro, national board of directors of UNAG, 29 June 1995.
19. Interview with Carlos Borge, national board of directors of the Sandinista urban union, CST.
20. Interview with Ronaldo Rodríguez, President of the board of directors of the worker-owned firm El Caracol and Secretary-General of the firm's CST union, 5 July 1995.
21. Interview with Sonia Silva, labour leader from the Communist Party union CAUS at La Fosforera match factory, 3 July 1995.
22. Interview with foreign consultant to an international organization in Nicaragua, 24 June 1995.

4 Nicaragua's Transition of State Power: Through Feminist Lenses

Cynthia Chavez Metoyer

Following ten years of internal conflict and US-sponsored aggression, Nicaragua's external debt totalled $11 695 million in 1990 (CEPAL 1994). The Chamorro government inherited a very fragile political and economic system. Chamorro, however, had neither a well-elaborated strategy for Nicaragua's political and economic development nor a well-defined social programme when she took office in March 1990. Rather, the economic programme was a response to external pressure and elite insecurity.[1] As time progressed it became evident that the Chamorro government was formulating a neoliberal development strategy for the agrarian sector that favours private agroexport production at the expense of both internal market development and the reformed sector, the sector created by the agrarian reform land redistributions during the Sandinista revolution (Escoto and Amador 1990). For example, Central Bank figures show that credit for agricultural production decreased by 43 per cent in 1992, with loan preferences given to large producers (FIDEG 1994: 8).

The Chamorro government unleashed a neoliberal programme of stabilization and structural adjustment policies to restore economic stability that relies on privatization, credit restriction, and massive cutbacks in state personnel.[2] Hyperinflation was reduced from monthly rates that exceeded 50 per cent in early 1991 to below 1 per cent from January to May 1992 (FIDEG 1994: 5). In 1994, Nicaragua's growth was estimated at 3.2 per cent (BCN 1994), largely due to an unexpected rise in coffee prices following the Brazilian frost. Yet, as Chamorro nears the end of this presidential term, her neoliberal economic programme has not resulted in widespread improvement. Instead, unemployment, inflation, rural conflict, undernourishment and malnutrition rates have been

114

1. The Revolution fades.

2. Sandinista militants keep the faith despite deteriorating conditions (July 1995).

3. *(above)* End of FSLN rally, 19 July 1995.

4. *(below)* National Assembly often shows more interest in its own needs than in those of the public.

5. *(above)* Nicaraguan scavenges for food outside the National Assembly.

6. *(below)* Dissatisfaction with governmental policies often erupts in street demonstrations, as in this one. Burning tyres are used to stop traffic.

7. *(above)* The move to privatize TELCOR generated great animosity among workers and in the society

8. *(below)* Worker protest against privatization of TELCOR, the national postal and telecommunication systems.

rising over the last five years, while social services such as health care, education and housing facilities have been dwindling.

Slightly more than half of Nicaragua's population is estimated to live below the defined poverty line, with nearly 20 per cent below the extreme poverty line (World Bank 1993). An estimated 63 per cent of total poverty in Nicaragua is concentrated in the rural sector (World Bank 1993). Information reported in *Envío* reveals that average wages covered 92 per cent of the basic needs in 1990 but two years later covered only 72 per cent (*Envío* 1995: 7). One study conducted by Renzi and Agurto (1994) shows that the average monthly cost of living was 734 *córdobas* in 1993, approximately $104. Yet 42 per cent of households earned less than 700 *córdobas* ($100) of which 20 per cent earned less than 300 *córdobas* ($43) a month. Finally, total unemployment was reported at 53.6 per cent in 1994 (CEPAL 1994).

There is a general consensus among academics and policymakers that economic reactivation in Nicaragua is far off. For example, Aguilar and Stenman (1994: 51) point out that since Nicaragua's longterm economic development depends on agricultural production, property insecurity and technological deterioration must be reversed before Nicaragua's economy can be reactivated. But if rising disputes over these issues are any indication, reversal will not occur soon. Moreover, Vanderlaan (1993: 80) contends that Nicaragua's economic reactivation will be aggravated further by Chamorro's 'Northern-prescribed' economic reforms which waste time and political capital essential to processes of political development.

While these and other studies are useful for understanding the problems of Chamorro's economic programme, the implications for women have not been explored sufficiently. However, given that feminist studies have long documented the fact that men and women experience state polices differently and differentially, it is unlikely that the outcomes of Nicaragua's transition of state power can be understood without studying the gendered outcomes.

The amassing global data reveals the extent and pattern of gender inequality: women everywhere have less access to political power and economic resources and less control over processes that reproduce this systemic inequality. Moreover, our knowledge of the world of men and the politics they create is incomplete and inaccurate without knowing how men's activities, including their politics, are related to, even dependent upon, what women are doing and why. (Peterson and Runyan 1993: 12)

Notwithstanding, male-centred understanding and experiences of state and class have traditionally been presented as the 'true' understanding and experience. As a result, women's understandings and experiences that do not fit into this male-defined pattern are ignored and the validity of women's understandings and experiences are denied.

While feminist scholars have only recently begun to analyse the complex web of relationships between states and women, they have already carved out a path towards more comprehensive social science understanding by insisting that analysis begin with state–women relationships. In fact, Hartsock (1983b) argues that all science should begin with women who have a privileged epistemological vantage point by virtue of their experience, resulting in a 'universalistic' understanding of reality. Hartsock explains that women are better knowers because they are able to identify and express truth to which the traditional cultural and political hegemons are blinded. Though perhaps Hartsock makes too large a claim, her feminist perspective reverses the epistemological primacy that conventional state theories have given themselves through their neglect of gender analysis. Harding notes, 'a standpoint is not simply an interested position (interpreted as bias) but is interested in the sense of being engaged' (Harding and Hintikka 1983: 285). As such, women are central in feminist standpoint analysis where women's experiences are taken seriously rather than simply 'added' into our social science explanations; *what* we know is transformed through *how* we know.

Many feminist scholars argue that states' action is male-biased, resulting in policies and spending patterns which may not coincidentally benefit men more than women (Enloe 1989; Parpart and Staudt 1989). For example, the ability to develop one's land or to diversify into marketing or retail trade typically depends on access to credit in agricultural *societies.* Access to credit, in turn, depends on whether the prospective creditor, be it woman or man, has property collateral. Perhaps at first glance this loan criteria appears to be gender-neutral. However, evidence shows that in an overwhelming majority of cases, states have issued land title deeds in the sole names of men, with the result that fewer women than men are legal landowners (Boserup 1970; Parpart and Staudt 1989; Tinker 1990).

For example, the Nicaraguan case reveals that 63 per cent of the families who benefited from the 1990 land assignments were demobilized Contra soldiers (RN), 32 per cent were traditional land claimants, that is, *campesinos*, and 5 per cent were repatriated citizens (CIPRES 1992: 77), while only 6 per cent were women (CIPRES 1992: 123).

It is particularly interesting that male-biased policy persists in Nicaragua where Chamorro, one of the world's few women heads of state, holds executive office. Yet as feminist scholars point out, male-biased policy is not simply the result of individual action, but of structural and institutional discrimination as well. Therefore, it is not likely that male-biased policy will be reversed by individual action alone. Moreover, it cannot be assumed that women leaders will pursue a feminist agenda simply because they are female.

Furthermore, the criteria established for Chamorro's privatization process give preference to those workers to receive land from the state property sector who were honourably discharged from the army. However, insofar as historical structures of discrimination in Nicaragua dictate that women typically enter the military in smaller numbers than men, Chamorro's redistribution of state property mainly benefited men. By 1992, only 1221 (24 per cent) of the 5000 APT associates that existed were women; of the 772 honourably discharged army personnel who received land assignments during 1990–91, only 55 were women (7 per cent); and of the 370 912 manzanas of land assigned to 10 493 ex-Contra officers and repatriated citizens, only 630 were women (6 per cent) (CIPRES 1992: 123).

In short, women are less likely to meet ownership and other criteria necessary to secure loans and, therefore, are unable to develop their land. Eventually an agricultural production pattern is created where women produce low-income-generating subsistence crops while men produce profitable cash crops, creating an income gap between women and men. Thus, 'gender-neutral' loan criteria actually have gender-specific results or gendered outcomes.

Given what we have learned from feminist scholars, the effects of the transition of state power on Nicaragua and on the revolutionary programme are better understood when analysis begins with an understanding that Nicaragua's transition has resulted in uneven gendered outcomes. A feminist framework that makes women central to analysis is particularly useful for at least four important reasons. First, women potentially provide less distorted interpretations of reality; as marginalized people who do not generally wield societal power, wealth, and/or status, women not only experience life in a particular way, but they also experience the lives of the dominant group which is imposed upon them (Mohanty 1991).

Second, making women the central focus of analysis is symbolically important for eradicating women's oppression because the epistemological primacy of conventional social science that disregards women is reversed. Hence, women's experiences can be recovered from the hidden peripheries of theory. Third, a feminist framework is necessary for understanding Nicaragua's transition of state power because women are at the heart of the Nicaraguan revolutionary experience. Women engaged in revolutionary warfare in unprecedented numbers, constituting 25 to 30 per cent of the insurrectionary forces that deposed Somoza, achieved legal status on a par with their male counterparts as a constitutional right, and made significant material gains during the Sandinista revolutionary era (Chinchilla 1990; Chuchryk 1991).

Fourth, a feminist approach is useful in the study of Nicaragua's transition of state power because it moves away from conventional Western social science that relies heavily on quantitative data such as gross national product, un/employment rates, and inflation percentages to also rely on local knowledge, women's experiences, and other nontraditional indicators. This is not to suggest that 'objective' indicators are useless and unnecessary, only that they are incapable of exhausting the meaning of daily life, including daily life for women. The remainder of this chapter is organized in two main sections. State policy during the Sandinista and Chamorro governments is reviewed in the first section, to evaluate policy outcomes. However, since this data is unable to tell the experiences of the people who may or may not share the 'meanings' of the objective measures, interviews with *campesinas* are assessed in the second section. The interviews are important to the study as they provide real-life accounts of people whose experiences are often overlooked by conventional social science approaches yet have distinct vantage points as 'knowers'.

THE SANDINISTAS: AN EXPERIMENT IN REVOLUTIONARY CHANGE

Following the overthrow of Somoza in 1979, the Sandinista revolutionaries proceeded to implement changes in social, political, economic and foreign policy that were both shaped and limited by a revolutionary philosophy. The Somocista structure of domination was most apparent in the countryside where much of the country's land resources were concentrated in the hands of Somoza and Somocistas. Somocistas were supporters of the Somoza family, and included the National Guard militia, large business owners, many of the traditional elite, and US business people and government officials. Initially the Sandinistas estimated that Somoza and Somocista landholdings constituted approximately 50 per cent of Nicaragua's total arable land, but later calculations revealed that the total was closer to 20 to 30 per cent (Baumeister 1991; Baumeister and Cuadra 1986; Ricciardi 1991). At any rate, all Somoza and Somocista properties were seized and an agrarian reform programme was initiated.

The FSLN's economic plan to steer the national economy was designed to bring about economic recovery through redistributive policies, a plan that involved major social welfare spending. It is widely recognized that during the Sandinista period, concrete social conditions were improved significantly from the Somoza era, including health, housing, education and basic provisions (Molyneux 1985; Walker 1991; Williams 1991). As in

Cuba, whose women were identified as essential components of the revolution, the Sandinistas made the eradication of sexual inequalities a revolutionary objective. This led to the enactment of several unprecedented legal and economic reforms, including gender-sensitive policies. For example, the Law of Cooperatives provided the legal grounds for women's incorporation and leadership in production cooperatives under the same conditions as their male counterparts.

Women's material conditions were improved via legislation that reduced the workday, improved health and safety provisions, and granted four weeks' paid leave before childbirth and eight weeks' paid leave following childbirth. The Law of Relations between Mothers, Fathers, and Children (1981) 'remove[d] men's special privileges over custody in divorce settlements ... and recognized the legal rights of illegitimate children' (Molyneux 1985: 154). The Provision Law of 1982 attempted to redefine family responsibilities, making all adult family members legally liable to contribute to the maintenance of their family. Gender-sensitive laws were also passed to prohibit advertisers from portraying women as sexual objects and from promoting baby formula. Finally, other policies granted women the right to adopt children and made children born out of *situaciones conyugales* (unmarried living arrangements) the legal responsibility of both parents (Chuchryk 1991).

The Sandinistas' revolutionary triumph sparked a series of structural transformations that involved sweeping social reform that significantly affected the domestic sphere. Women had most to gain from the Sandinista revolutionary programmes because the sexual division of labour made women disproportionately responsible for 'domestic' labour, such as childcare and household maintenance (Molyneux 1985; Wheelock 1984; Williams 1991). Molyneux summarizes the effects of the reform on women:

> They [women] gained more access to health, education training, and housing; their basic provisions, although rationed, were until 1984 heavily subsidized. These benefits, a direct product of the priorities and policies of the state, had a particular significance for women, who by virtue of their place within the sexual division of labor, were dispropor-

tionately responsible for the provision of basic needs. (Molyneux 1985: 160)

The extensive and extended involvement of men in the war created a labour shortage that left primarily women responsible for agricultural production. In general, Nicaraguan women moved increasingly into areas of 'formal' employment that had previously been dominated by male labour and began to receive public recognition for the important contribution their labour force made to Nicaragua's economy during the revolution. Nicaraguan women organized in great numbers during the revolution. AMNLAE, an official organization of the FSLN, was the mass organization that showed the greatest promise in representing women's interests at the time of the 1979 Sandinista triumph. By 1981, AMNLAE boasted a membership of 25 000 women (Criquillon 1989: 166), and in 1985, 40 000 women attended AMNLAE's second National Assembly 'to generate proposals and discuss ideas around sexuality' (Chinchilla 1990: 385). However, AMNLAE continued to incorporate women into general revolutionary programmes such as the literacy and health brigades, rather than address needs such as domestic violence, reproductive issues, and childcare. Eventually women earned the 'legitimate right' to publicly voice their demands, and in 1987, the *Proclama de la Mujer* was enacted by the FSLN, making women's demands and problems an official priority. However, AMNLAE's lack of autonomy and separate discourse from the FSLN led to splits within AMNLAE's leadership by the late 1980s. Some AMNLAE leaders maintained that women's emancipation would result from party participation in the revolutionary struggle, while others believed it was necessary to develop a feminist discourse autonomously from the FSLN.[3]

Policy outcomes did not always match the policy intentions of the Sandinista administration. For example, despite legislation that made women direct beneficiaries of the 1981 Agrarian Reform and Cooperative Laws, an early study on women's participation in cooperatives revealed that it was extremely limited, constituting 6 per cent of total membership in 1982 (CIERA 1984). A more recent study by CIERA reported that approximately 1976 cooperatives were formed in the first three years following the revolutionary triumph, nearly doubling to 3600 cooperatives by 1990 (CIERA 1990: 206). Yet while the cooperative movement gained momentum in the early years following the implementation of the laws, women were not incorporated in large numbers. A study by Pérez Alemán, *Organización, Identidad, y Cambio*, indicates that female membership only increased to 12 per cent between 1984 and 1990 (Pérez 1990: 90). Why did there remain a gap between the laws and practices of gender equality throughout the Sandinista era? Molyneux (1982) argues that while Sandinista state policy encouraged women to enter the formal economy and politics and granted them the legal right to participate in cooperatives, it did so without actually shifting some household responsibilities to men. Table 4.1 reveals a feminization of the workforce in Nicaragua, a trend that is evident throughout Latin America.[4] Case study findings reported in Table 4.2 show that rural women continued to perform a disproportionate amount of household maintenance. Thus, while women gained economic and political responsibilities, they remained primarily responsible for household production and reproduction. Therefore, the improved legal rights and increased economic activity of women that occurred during the Sandinista era should not be exaggerated. Rather than a substantial redefinition of the

Table 4.1   Evolution of economic participation, according to sex (economically active population, 10 years and older, percentages)

	1977		1980		1988		1990	
	(a)	*(b)*	*(a)*	*(b)*	*(a)*	*(b)*	*(a)*	*(b)*
Total	43.7	48.4	43.8	49.3	44.6	50.3	44.8	50.3
Men	68.8	68.8	68.4	68.4	67.0	67.9	67.8	67.8
Women	19.2	28.6	19.7	29.5	22.1	32.5	22.7	33.3

(a) Estimations from CELADE; (b) Data from ESDENIC.
Sources: CELADE (Bulletin 35), 1985; CELADE (Bulletin 36), 1985; INEC, CELADE (Nicaragua: 1950–2025), 1983; OEDEC (ESDENIC 1976–1978), 1979; INEC, (ESDENIC-85), 1989; President of the Republic (Declaration, 1 November 1989).

Table 4.2   Time allocation of one day in the life of a rural woman
(in hours)

	Women	Daughters	Husband/Sons
Household maintenance	9 hrs 38 min. (53.5 per cent)	6 hrs 39 min.	50 min.
Cooking/ dishwashing	6 hrs 43 min.	2 hrs 2 min.	–
Collect water	35 min.	5 min.	–
Fetch wood	–	20 min.	35 min.
Cleaning	5 min.	7 min.	–
Sewing	10 min.	2 hrs 35 min.	–
Errands	–	55 min.	–
Childcare	2 hrs 5 min.	35 min.	15 min.
Total	19 hrs 16 min.	13 hrs 18 min.	1 hr 40 min.

Source: Martha Luz Padilla and Nyurka Perez, 'La Mujer Semi-Proletaria', CIERA, 1981.

social relations between the sexes, Molyneux points out that 'to the traditional roles of housewife and mother have been added those of full-time wage worker and political activist, while the provision of childcare facilities remains inadequate' (Molyneux 1985: 280).

Padilla *et al.* (1987) attribute the gap in policy outcomes and policy intentions to a *machista* ideology that justifies denying women their right to participate in cooperatives based on assumptions that women's economic contributions are not valuable and that women are incapable of making agricultural decisions. The scholars note, 'ideological values such as these are reinforced by state functionaries responsible for supporting and promoting cooperatives and often are voiced by rural women themselves' (Padilla *et al.* 1987: 129). In short, the outcomes of the Sandinista agrarian reform failed to accomplish the original intentions to integrate women into the cooperative movement because structural and ideological barriers such as the subvaluation of women's work, the 'double day' workload, and historically constructed norms of the gender division of labour were not eliminated.

FROM TRIUMPH TO TRANSITION: CHAMORRO COMES
TO POWER

The advent of the Chamorro government's neoliberal economic
programme in 1990 struck a debilitating blow to the Sandinista
revolutionary experiment. In March 1991, the Lacayo Plan replaced the original Mayorga Plan. The Lacayo Plan included
some of the Sandinistas' demands to address social needs but
was basically a continuation of Chamorro's neoliberal programme. An IMF report summarized the Lacayo Plan:

> The cornerstone of the economic program is the elimina-
> tion of the public sector's need for domestic financing ...
> Structural policies are being pursued in the context of an
> increased reliance on market forces and the re-establish-
> ment of relations with external creditors ... For successful
> achievement of the objectives of the program there is no
> room for slippage, especially in the implementation of the
> fiscal measures. It is particularly important, in this regard, to
> exercise close control over public sector wage adjustments
> and to insure that the reduction in the size of the public
> sector takes place as planned. (IMF 1991a. 12, 28–9)

Over the past five years, the Chamorro government's neoliberal economic model 'has whittled away at the transformations
of the 1980s – in health, agriculture, education, industry – and
challenged the FSLN conception of the government's relationship to the market' (Vickers and Spence 1992: 542). One
major problem with the application of Chamorro's neoliberal
programme is that the policies of stabilization and structural
adjustment assume free competition, not exclusively but as a
determinant, for production in a perfect market of free
market forces.

However, class, gender, and race inequalities that give form
to most, if not all, social structures make it unlikely that free
competition is a reality for most economies. For example, stabilization and structural adjustment policies tend to assume
that people in all class levels have the same opportunities in
the supply and demand of factors of production in the
market. Yet policy results contradict this assumption. Central
Bank data (see Table 4.3) show that rural credit was reduced
by 80 per cent between 1990 and 1993.

Table 4.3   Short-term rural credit structure in percentages by property type

	1990	1991	1992
Small & medium producers	56.0	40.0	29.0
Large private land	31.0	56.0	71.0
Popular Public Area (APP)	13.0	4.0	0.0
Total	100.0	100.0	100.0

Source: Banco Central de Nicaragua, 1994.

With respect to gender, the Chamorro government's neoliberal programme has resulted in similar marginalizing effects for women. In the short term, women do not receive the benefits of stabilization and structural adjustment policies on a par with their male counterparts, while the structures of male domination that have relegated women to a marginal position tend to be reinforced in the long term. One notable example of a gendered outcome was mentioned earlier: biased criteria established for Chamorro's privatization policy gives preference to military personnel, which primarily benefits men.

While on the surface the Chamorro government's stabilization and structural adjustment policies appear to be void of gender-specific content, they are not necessarily gender-neutral. For example, the government attributes the cause of the economic crisis to market inefficiency, and therefore relies on neoliberal measures such as massive personnel cutbacks and state spending reduction to correct the economic crisis and to bring about market 'efficiency'. When neoliberal measures have been applied elsewhere in Latin America, however, they have resulted in disparate outcomes for women and men. Women constitute more than one-half of total Nicaraguan unemployment. Some 56 per cent of the unemployed and underemployed are women (Ministry of Labour 1994). Moreover, women are generally first to lose their jobs in personnel cutbacks because historically constructed social norms have falsely determined firstly that women are less apt to develop the work norms necessary to generate economic revenue; secondly, that men are more capable of being efficient and effective in the workplace; and thirdly, that men's economic contributions are essential for their families' survival while women's economic contributions are elective.

The Chamorro government's neoliberal measures to correct market inefficiency through drastic personnel reductions have resulted in a prioritized masculine workforce in which women are believed to be dispensable workers. Women workers were also the victims of massive dismissals in 1988 under the Sandinista administration. Yet adverse impacts of stabilization and structural adjustment policies are notable under the Chamorro government because selection criteria for dismissal to reduce personnel in state enterprises not only prioritize a masculine workforce, but actively pursue stabilization and structural adjustment policies.

In addition to measures of massive personnel reduction and privatization policies, women tend to be disproportionately disadvantaged by other neoliberal policies such as credit restriction and production efficiency that are also driven by historically constructed social norms that are gender-laden. The most noted of these norms is the sexual division of labour. It is widely accepted among scholars that a sexual division of labour operates in both the market and in subsistence production and reproduction. Men are typically protected from most domestic responsibilities because sexual divisions of labour, combined with other socially constructed hierarchies, make domestic reproduction and production biological extensions of women.

> Thus, women's household and child-care work are seen as an extension of their physiology, of the fact that they give birth to children, of the fact that 'nature' has provided them with a uterus. All the labour that goes into the production of life, including the labour of giving birth to a child, is not seen as a conscious interaction of a human being *with* nature, that is, a truly human activity, but rather as an activity *of* nature, which produces plants and animals unconsciously and has no control over this process. (Mies 1986: 45)

I am not suggesting that divisions of labour by sex are inherently exploitative. Yet they become so when they establish hierarchies of responsibilities that value 'masculine work' over 'feminine work'.[5] Exploitation becomes imminent when these unequal relations between the sexes are accepted as part of the 'natural' order. Eventually patterns and ideologies based on this presumed natural order are institutionalized, placing them beyond the scope of social change.

EXPLORING THE TRANSITION THROUGH FEMINIST LENSES

My gender-sensitive analysis of Nicaragua and the revolutionary programme since the 1990 transition of state power is focused by two related questions. First, what policy gains were made during the Sandinista period that increased women's opportunities to challenge and/or articulate their claims to the state? Early on, the Sandinistas were successful in improving material conditions that particularly benefited women. More specifically, the Sandinistas established a universal health system that increased popular access to medical care, built more schools (particularly in rural areas), and reduced illiteracy from 52 per cent to 13 per cent (Serra 1991). In addition, progress was made in the area of legislative reform for women. The 1987 Constitution established an ideological and structural framework within which women could individually and collectively press for the eradication of sexual inequality. Laws were enacted that abolished sexual discrimination in the family and at work. 'Although they did not wage a campaign against sexism, or develop a comprehensive challenge to traditional gender roles, the Sandinistas did at least provide an ideological framework to support those who did' (Chuchryk 1991: 159).

Second, what has become of the revolutionary gains since the 1990 transition of state power? When quantitative indicators on current unemployment, land tenancy patterns, and income rates are disaggregated by gender, it appears that gains made during the Sandinista period have been diminishing since 1990. As a result, opportunities for women to participate individually and collectively in 'public' life are being reduced. In particular, Chamorro's neoliberal programme calls for austerity measures that include cutbacks in social service and social welfare spending, reduction in public personnel, privatization of state property, and increasingly stringent credit policy, which have greater negative effects for women than men. Furthermore, where the FSLN made the eradication of sexual inequality a revolutionary objective and actively 'courted'[6] women, the Chamorro government has addressed issues of class and gender from a conservative agenda. To explore these questions, I interviewed rural women from 14 agricultural cooperatives[7] in the department of Masaya, Region IV. Initially *campesinas* were asked to comment on their daily living conditions during the Somoza era. Invariably they reported substandard living conditions that were characterized by economic hardships, poor infrastructure, and political repression. Without exception, the *campesinas* and their families were involved in subsistence crop production and at least one member of their family worked for a large landowner to earn income. Following the revolutionary triumph in 1979, *campesinas* generally described economic improvement:

> We received our own land. (*Campesina* from Roger Cano)

> Production and revenue increased. (*Campesina* from Mario Brenes)

> Credit was easier to get, and resources and technical assistance were more readily available after the triumph. (*Campesina* from Panamá)

When asked to compare their present situation with their living conditions during the Sandinista era, *campesinas* commonly reported economic deterioration in their living conditions. In fact, not one *campesina* indicated that her economic situation was currently more stable than under the Sandinista administration.

> UNO favors capitalists. FSLN defended small farmers. (*Campesina* from Los Pocitos)

> During the counterrevolution, Nicaragua faced the economic blockade from the U.S., and we were forced to concentrate resources on the country's defense. Now the UNO government faces economic crisis, but they are not solving

the problem in the interest of the poor masses. (*Campesina* from Panamá)

There was economic hardship during the Sandinistas and there is hardship now ... still then was better than now because at least basic needs were met. (*Campesina* from Roger Cano)

With the FSLN, cooperatives generated revenue. But with UNO, we make no profit because the devaluation of the *córdoba*, inflation, and debt eat our profits. (*Campesina* from Diniosio Méndes Laríos)

Our economic situation is still the same. With the FSLN there were financial constraints due to the war, and with UNO there are financial constraints because of their imperialist policies. (*Campesina* from Mirazul)

Credit restrictions, resource availability and property insecurity were repeatedly noted as current problems. Combined with low market prices for domestic crops, these problems have made it nearly impossible for cooperativists to produce enough basic foodstuffs for household subsistence much less to earn a profit. According to one *campesina* from Vista Alegre cooperative, banks now lend a maximum of 25 per cent of the cooperative's need as opposed to the 80 per cent maximum that was lent under the Sandinista administration.

We are economically stagnant. (*Campesina* from Manuel Sánchez García)

With UNO there is finally an adequate supply of inputs such as fertilizer, seeds, and food. But now we have no money to purchase them. (*Campesina* from Héroes y Mártires)

Most *campesinas* were critical of the Chamorro government for its failure to keep campaign promises to develop the rural sector.

UNO invests in projects that benefit only a handful. (*Campesina* from Mirazul)

For example, one *campesina* noted that a recent government project to add hard dirt to the roads has done little to help the community.

What we need is credit and food to feed. Improved roads
don't feed our families. (*Campesina* from Manuel Sánchez
García)

During the transitional period between February and April
1990, the Sandinistas carried out a massive and hurried process
to distribute a significant amount of land. A campaign led by
ultra conservative UNO leaders accused the Sandinistas of
abusing agrarian reform land and property titling for personal
gain, a scandal that came to be known as *la piñata*. This scandal
resulted in a political liability for the FSLN, which claimed to
defend property rights of the poor, yet failed to conduct a
serious ethics investigation of its own. Moreover, much of the
land distributed by the Sandinista agrarian reform was never
officially registered nor were legal titles given to the
beneficiaries. As a result, the insecure legal status of land made
it possible for former property owners to reclaim their land
from *campesinos*.[8] Although the Sandinista administration re-
spected the land assignments, the transition of state power
made it apparent (albeit belatedly) that legal title and registry
were essential, but not sufficient, to provide land security.

Shortly after taking office, the Chamorro government initiated a campaign to provide legal titles and registry to
Sandinista agrarian reform beneficiaries. The campaign aimed
at providing legal titles for 1 011 500 manzanas of land that
would benefit 34 661 families. The estimated cost of the campaign was $9 450 110 over a three-year time period (Cofré
1992: 3). Some *campesinas* commended the Chamorro government for its efforts to bring about land security. Others dis-
agreed, arguing that the Chamorro government has created
land insecurity by enabling former landowners to reclaim
land, by offering ex-Contra and EPS soldiers property in exchange for the 1990 cease-fire, and by failing to respect land
assignments made under the Sandinista agrarian reform.

What UNO wants is for us to lose our land. (*Campesina* from
Vista Alegre)

UNO doesn't care whether we lose our land or not. All
they're concerned about is if we produce. And if we don't,
it's better [from UNO's perspective] that we lose the land.
(*Campesina* from Vista Alegre)

Another *campesina* pointed out the merits of one government project to secure legal land.

> With Chamorro, the land tenancy issue was resolved and that's a good thing because it enables farmers to get credit against [their] property. (*Campesina* from Dionisio Méndes Sánchez)

But another *campesina* quickly responded with,

> Big deal. Having a secure title allows us to risk losing our farms ... and that's exactly what happens because tough credit restrictions and economic crisis make profitability impossible. (*Campesina* from Dionisio Méndes Sánchez)

It is unlikely that the motivation behind the government's project to legalize land titles is ultimately aimed at providing agrarian reform beneficiaries with land security. Rather, by providing secure land title and registry to property, land becomes a tangible asset that cooperativists can use to buy, sell, borrow against, and/or invest, to compete in the free market. Many *campesinas* did not consider possession of legal land title to be meaningful.

> The ability to sell the cooperative is only the ability to lose it. (*Campesina* from mario Brenes)

> Look. To compete with large land owners is burdensome. We can hardly survive. But according to the Chamorro government, if small farmers cannot generate revenue, that is, if large land owners can produce more, we should sell our farms. (*Campesina* from Los Pocitos)

> It's true that large producers are able to produce more and with more efficiency. UNO would like to see that they [large landowners] take over our property. For UNO it's purely a money matter. But our survival is in farming. (*Campesina* from Los Pocitos)

When asked to describe daily household chores for their families during the Somoza, Sandinista and Chamorro governments, *campesinas* repeatedly described a division of labour based on sex and age. Household chores, childcare, buying and selling at the market, and working the fields during peak time are primarily the responsibility of women and children; farming and cattle raising are the main responsibility of men. There appeared to be no significant change in domestic duties between governments, and it was commonly noted that women bear the disproportionate burden of domestic chores.

> Chores in the home are the same ... they haven't changed. (*Campesina* from Génaro Tapia)

> Women still do everything. (*Campesina* from Mario Brenes)

This unequal sexual division of labour, however, was not regarded as problematic. It is not surprising that the sexual division of labour has remained constant in spite of the revolutionary transition of state power in Nicaragua. After all, a revolution in the social means of production is not necessarily a revolution in social consciousness from which gender consciousness[9] ensues. Nicaraguan scholar Pérez Alemán (1990) argues that it is unreasonable to expect to find women 'naturally' (that is, automatically) and increasingly questioning gender subordination; women cannot be expected to instinctively recognize that their conditions of subordination are somehow related to other women who share in these conditions based on their common gender. Moreover, gender consciousness implies that women recognize that there are alternatives and that it is possible to construct new egalitarian relations between men and women. Gender consciousness also assumes that there is a search for and development of collective actions that confront hegemonic relations necessary to change life conditions.

In my interaction with *campesinas*, however, they did not appear to have a gender consciousness. This is not to say that Nicaraguan women do not or have not historically resisted gender subordination, nor that they have not somehow rejected the system of dominant values that is linked to gender questions. It is more likely the case, however, that women 'move into known spaces to gain concrete things; they develop forms of struggle that are different, less heroic and risky, and more immediate and self-serving' (Vargas 1989: 100). Furthermore, the Sandinista administration did not create the mechanisms necessary to foster gender consciousness despite its pro-women agenda.

When asked to describe the type of benefits received and/or the gains made under the early years of the Sandinistas (1979–85), benefits were first noted in terms of social goods: food rations, health services, and education for children and adults. Economic benefits were subsequently mentioned: land assignments, the availability of credit and other resources, technical assistance, and training. It is interesting to note that legal gains were not mentioned among those benefits received. This is particularly noteworthy given that women clearly gained most in legislative reform. For example, no mention was made of the laws that were established to abolish gender discrimination in the workplace and in the family. Neither was reference made to the laws that prohibited the sexual objectification of women in the media. Perhaps this reflects the gap between the theory of sexual equality and the actual practice of eliminating sexual inequality.

Many *campesinas* noted that benefits such as seeds and fertilizers were increasingly limited after 1985 and that health care facilities and services were eventually cut back, yet they reported overall satisfaction with the benefits they received.

The FSLN was broader in their policies in general. (*Campesina* from Vista Alegre)

Schools used to be free for children. But now there's a charge of five *córdobas* a month here in Avaluz. That's a lot of money if you're poor. Books and uniforms are also costly, and the money could be used to buy food. So, most children in our cooperative do not attend school. (*Campesina* from Avaluz)

Adult education was available under the FSLN for a small charge, and nutrition and health was free. Now these are restricted. Health care is almost nonexistent in the countryside. (*Campesina* from La Curva)

Credit is now difficult to get because it favours large production. That doesn't help us because we only produce basic crops. (*Campesina* from Panamá)

With the UNO government we no longer receive technical assistance, except from the PRODETEC project. (*Campesina* from Mario Brenes)

134   *The Undermining of the Sandinista Revolution*

Yet while those interviewed expressed contentment with the FSLN, election poll data indicates otherwise. More specifically, support for the FSLN declined from 65.12 per cent of the rural vote in 1984 to 36.4 per cent in 1990 (Castro 1992: 130–1).

CONCLUSION

What has happened to Nicaragua since the electoral victory in 1990 that substituted the Chamorro for the Sandinista government? Despite promises that Chamorro's neoliberal programme would bring about economic reactivation, conventional data show that over the last five years, Nicaragua has experienced a retreat from the redistributive process initiated by the Sandinista administration in 1979. Moreover, the Chamorro government's efforts to manage the economy with stabilization and structural adjustment measures have not translated into the positive results that Chamorro and her supporters had hoped for but has instead had adverse effects for Nicaragua's poor majority, including women. Total unemployment is 53.6 per cent of Nicaragua's economically active population (EAP) and external debt looms at $11 695 million (CEPAL 1994). With export production shortfalls, Nicaragua continues to spend more on imports than it earns on exports, forcing government leaders to seek foreign loans and donations to offset the trade deficit (CIA 1994).

While conventional analysis reveals that Nicaragua's economy continues to experience economic crisis, it tends to separate quantitative data from the human element. Who are the people affected by state policy and what are they saying about their current situations? Conventional analysis treats knowledge as individualistic rather than relational, telling little if anything about the actual experiences of many people, especially women. However, as Mohanty points out, 'while such descriptive information is useful and necessary, these presumably objective indicators by no means exhaust the meaning of women's day-to-day lives' (Mohanty 1991: 6). Thus, I have utilized a feminist standpoint approach in which the testimonies of people whose experiences have historically been invalidated by conventional approaches are integral sources of information for answering the research questions.

The interviews reveal outcomes for some people who are directly harmed by the policies. Two important points stemmed from the interviews. One, *campesinas* indicated that the daily survival of the Nicaraguan *campesinado* is particularly threatened under the Chamorro government because access to basic goods is further restricted by its policies. Two, the interviews suggest that the lack of warfare has not meant peace for the rural sectors of Nicaragua where soaring unemployment, land insecurity and reduced access to seeds, fertilizer, credit and technology make daily living difficult.

While stabilization and structural adjustment policies have proved effective in some industrialized countries, data show that steady and productive development has been limited in the case of Nicaragua and the interviews with *campesinas* cast doubt on whether neoliberalism is the best development model for Nicaragua to follow. The negative outcomes of Chamorro's stabilization and structural adjustment programme have contributed to a sharper visibility of the need to redefine women's economic contributions, including economic activities outside the formal market. This is a difficult task as women perform multiple activities, many of which are noneconomic or considered to be natural activity. Major obstacles in redefining women's economic activity also include gender-based stereotypes, measuring nonpaid work, and accounting for informal and rural sector activities.

With all its tensions and contradictions, it might appear as though neoliberalism is doomed in Nicaragua. But just as the Sandinistas' mixed economy experiment was not destined to fail but was destroyed by interrelated external and internal influences that undermined the potential effectiveness of policies, neither is Chamorro's neoliberal programme automatically doomed. It would be a serious error to underestimate the Chamorro government's ability to draw on the support of the Nicaraguan right and the US government to protect the neoliberal programme, whatever the costs. At least in the short term, Chamorro's neoliberal programme is likely to continue as an economic project. However, in the longer term, few winners, many losers, and serious strains and tensions will result; it is likely that women will be the most adversely affected.

Thus, Nicaragua's transition of state power to the Chamorro government beckons the question, at whose expense will neoliberalism persist in Nicaragua? It is likely to be those who have carried the disproportionate burden of stabilization and adjustment policies thus far, the poor majority, that is, women. The success of the Chamorro government's neoliberal programme depends not only on its ability to maintain investor confidence that will endure market volatility and avoid capital flight. The government must also successfully deal with popular expectations to prevent the development of serious political challenges to its neoliberal programme. Thus it is also necessary for the Chamorro government to take up women's issues.

Why women's issues? As I noted earlier, women's contributions to Nicaragua's political and economic development were increasingly recognized during the decade-long struggle for social justice and material improvement. And while US aggression ultimately forced policy makers to divert resources and attention towards national defence efforts that reduced the state's capacity and autonomy, women's issues were nonetheless introduced into political discussions at local and national levels, increasing the ability of women to articulate their claims.

It is likely therefore that gender will become an additional and vitally important constraint on the state, that reduces the state's capacity and autonomy to pursue neoliberal politics without women's support. Ironically, although women are most adversely affected by stabilization and structural adjustment programmes, they may simultaneously be in a pivotal position to challenge the Chamorro government's actions if they mobilize and take advantage of the political openings that have been created since the revolution. This remains to be seen as the political situation in Nicaragua unfolds. However, my study shows that the effects of Nicaragua's transition of state power cannot be understood apart from analysing the effects on women in rural Nicaragua.

REFERENCES

Aguilar, Renata and Äsa Stenman. 1994. *Nicaragua 1994: Back into the Ranks.* Gothenburg, Sweden: Department of Economic University of Gothenburg.

Alvarez, Sonia E. 1990. *Engendering Democracy in Brazil.* Princeton, NJ: Princeton University Press.

Banco Central de Nicaragua. 1994. Report. Managua.

Baumeister, Eduardo. 1991. 'Agrarian Reform', in Thomas W. Walker (ed.), *Revolution and Counterrevolution in Nicaragua.* Boulder, CO: Westview Press: 229–47.

Baumeister, Eduardo and Oscar Neira Cuadra. 1986. 'The Making of a Mixed Economy: Class Struggle and State Policy in the Nicaraguan Transition', in Richard R. Fagen, Carmen Diana Deere and José Luis Coraggio (eds), *Transition and Development: Problems of Third World Socialism.* New York: Monthly Review Press and Center for the Study of the Americas: 171–91.

Boserup, Ester. 1970. *Women's Role in Economic Development.* New York: St. Martin's Press.

Brydon, Lynne and Sylvia Chant. 1989. *Women in the Third World.* New Jersey: Rutgers University Press.

Castro, Vanessa. 1992. 'Electoral Results in the Rural Sector', in Vanessa Castro and Gary Prevost (eds), *The 1990 Elections in Nicaragua and their Aftermath.* Lanham, MD: Rowman and Littlefield Publishers, Inc.: 129–47.

Castro, Vanessa and Gary Prevost (eds), *The 1990 Elections in Nicaragua and their Aftermath.* Lanham, MD: Rowman and Littlefield Publishers, Inc.

CEPAL. 1994. United Nations Economic Commission for Latin America. *Economic Panorama of Latin America.* Santiago, Chile: United Nations.

Chinchilla, Norma. 1990. 'Revolutionary Popular Feminism in Nicaragua: Articulating Class, Gender, and National Sovereignty'. *Gender and Society,* 4 (3), September: 370–97.

Chuchryk, Patricia. 1991. 'Women in the Revolution'. In Thomas W. Walker (ed.), *Revolution and Counterrevolution in Nicaragua.* Boulder, CO: Westview Press: 143–66.

CIA (Central Intelligence Agency). 1994. *World Fact Book 1994.* Washington, DC: Central Intelligence Agency.

CIERA (Centro de Investigaciones y Estudios de Reforma Agraria). 1984. *Las Mujeres en Cooperativas Agropecuarias en Nicaragua.* Managua: CIERA.

CIERA. 1990. 'Tough Row to Hoe: Women in Nicaragua's Agricultural co-operatives', in Kathleen Staudt (ed.), *Women, International Development and Politics: The Bureaucratic Mire.* Philadelphia: Temple University Press, 181–201.

CIPRES (Centro para la Investigación, la Promoción, y el Desarrollo Rural y Social). 1990. 'La instabilidad política y su impacto socioeconómico en el campo'. Managua: CIPRES, October.

———. 1992. *El Acceso de la Mujer a la Tierra en Nicaragua.* San José, Costa Rica: Fundación Arias Para la Paz y el Progreso Humano, CIPRES.

Cofré, Jaime. 1992. 'La Titulación Asegura la Tenencia de la Tierra'. *Teosintle.* 11–12, December: 3–5.

Criquillon, Ana. 1989. 'La rebeldía de las mujeres nicaragüenses: semillero de una nueva democracia', in *Construccíon de la Democracia en Nicaragua,* Escuela de Sociología de la Universidad Centroamericana. Managua, Nicaragua.

138   *The Undermining of the Sandinista Revolution*

Enloe, Cynthia. 1989. *Bananas, Bases and Beaches*. Berkeley, CA: University of California Press.

Escoto, René and Freddy Amador. 1990. *El Contexto Macroeconómico de la Reforma Agraria*. Managua: Departamento Economía Agrícola de la Facultad de Ciencias Económicas, Universidad Nacional Autónoma de Nicaragua.

FIDEG. 1994. 'EI Observador Económica'. Nicaragua.

Harding, Sandra and Merrill Hintikka (eds). 1983. *Discovering Reality: Feminist Perspectives on Epistemology, Metaphysics, Methodology and Philosophy of Science*. Dordrecht: Reidel.

Hartsock, Nancy C. M. 1983a. *Money, Sex, and Power: Toward a Feminist Historical Materialism*. New York: Longman.

Hartsock, Nancy C. M. 1983b. 'The Nature of Standpoint'. In Sandra Harding and Merrill Hintikka (eds). *Discovering Reality: Feminist Perspectives on Epistemology, Metaphysics, Methodology and Philosophy of Science*. Dordrecht: Reidel: 283–310.

IMF (International Monetary Fund) 1991a. Report cited in *Envío*, 12: 28–9.

Joekes, Susan. 1987. *Women and the World Economy*. New York: Oxford University Press.

Mies, Maria. 1986. *Patriarchy and Accumulation on a World Scale*. New Jersey: Zed Books.

Ministry of Labour. 1994. 'La Situación del Empleo Urbano en Nicaragua: Resumen Global de ocho ciudades'. Mimeograph. Managua: Ministry of Labour.

Mohanty, Chandra (ed). 1991. *Third World Women and the Politics of Feminism*. Indiana: Indiana University Press.

Molyneux, Maxine. 1982 'Mobilization Without Emancipation? Women's Interests, State, and Revolution.' In Richard R. Fagen *et al.* (eds), *Transition and Development: Problems of Third World Socialism*. New York: Monthly Review Press and Center for the Study of the Americas: 280–302.

Molyneux, Maxine. 1985. 'Women'. In Thomas W. Walker (ed.), *Nicaragua: The First Five Years*. New York: Praeger: 145–162.

Padilla, Martha Luz and Nyurka Pérez. 1981. 'La Mujer Semi-Proletaria'. CIERA.

Padilla, Martha Luz, Clara Marguialday and Ana Criquillon (eds). 1987. 'Impact of the Sandinista Agrarian Reform on Rural Women's Subordination', in Carmen Diana Deere and Magdalena León (eds). *Rural Women and State Policy*. Boulder, CO: Westview.

Parpart, Jane and Kathleen A. Staudt (eds). 1989. *Women and the State in Africa*. Boulder, CO: Lynne Rienner.

Pérez Alemán, Paola. 1990. *Organización, Identidad y Cambio: Las Campesinas en Nicaragua*. Managua: Centro de Investigación Acción para la Promoción de los Derechos de la Mujer. Nicaragua: CIAM.

Peterson, V. Spike and Anne Sisson Runyon. 1993. *Global Gender Issues*. Boulder, CO. Westview Press.

Renzi, María Rosa and Sonia Agurto. 1994. *¿Qué Hace la Mujer Nicaragüense ante la Crisis Económica?* Managua: Fundación Internacional para el Dasafío Económico Global.

Ricciardi, Joseph. 1991. 'Economic Policy'. In Thomas W. Walker (ed.), *Revolution and Counterrevolution*. Boulder, CO: Westview Press: 247–74.

Schrieberg, David. 1992. 'Nicaragua: After the Sandinistas'. *The Atlantic*, 270 (1), 1 July: 24.
Serra, Luis Hector. 1991. 'The Grass-Roots Organizations'. In Thomas W. Walker, (ed.), *Revolution and Counterrevolution in Nicaragua.* Boulder, CO. Westview Press: 49–76.
Spalding, Rose J. 1995. 'Economic Elites: The Chamorro years'. Paper presented at the Latin American Studies Association Meetings, Washington, DC.
Standing, Guy. 1989. 'Global Feminization through Flexible Labor', *World Development*, 17, 7 1077–95.
Tinker, Irene (ed.). 1990. *Persistent Inequalities.* New York and Oxford: Oxford University Press.
United Nations Development Programme (UNDP). 1992. *Human Development Report.* New York: Oxford Press for the UNDP.
Vargas, Virginia. 1989. *El Aporte de la Rebeldía de Las Mujeres.* Santo Domingo: CIPAF.
Vickers, George R. and Jack Spence. 1992. 'Nicaragua: Two Years After the Fall'. *World Policy Journal*, 9 (3): 533–62.
Walker, Thomas W. (ed.). 1991 *Revolution and Counterrevolution in Nicaragua.* Boulder, CO: Westview Press.
Williams, Harvey. 1991. 'Social Reforms'. In Thomas W. Walker (ed.), *Revolution and Counterrevolution in Nicaragua.* Boulder: Westview Press: 187–212.
Witness for Peace. 1995. 'Structural Adjustment in Nicaragua'. Managua: Witness for Peace.

NOTES

1. Rose J. Spalding (1995) points out that Nicaragua's traditional economic elite have been characterized by a lack of unity, representing competing interests. Thus, it follows that causes of elite insecurity are multidimensional.

2. Just as it is difficult to evaluate Sandinista policy outcomes without understanding the impacts of prolonged counterrevolutionary war, economic blockades, and US-sponsored aggression, it is difficult to assess policy outcomes for Chamorro's neoliberal programme without considering the effects of Sandinista efforts at earlier adjustment.

3. Other mass organizations, independent of the FSLN, attempted to advance women's interests during the revolution, including the Farmworkers' Union (ATC) and the Farmers and Ranchers' Union (UNAG). The ATC and UNAG confronted different types of limitations to women's direct access to land such as women's exclusive responsibility for the domestic sphere. Initially the ATC and UNAG tended to ignore more women-specific demands, fighting exclusively for the general recovery of the rural sector (Chuchryk 1991: 50).

140   *The Undermining of the Sandinista Revolution*

However, in 1984 the ATC established a women's section to address women-specific demands, and UNAG followed suit four years later.

4. Case studies from various Latin American countries show the growing importance of female employment in nontraditional manufacturing activities in both the formal and informal sectors. See Susan Joekes, *Women and the World Economy* (New York: Oxford University Press, 1987); Lynne Brydon and Sylvia Chant, *Women in the Third World* (New Jersey: Rutgers University Press, 1989); and Guy Standing, 'Global Feminization through Flexible Labor', *World Development*, 17, 7, (1989), 1077–95. Export-oriented manufacturing employs more women than men in many developing states, making it likely that employment opportunities for women will expand. However, import liberalization, central to structural adjustment programmes, often leads to a contraction in female employment in other sectors of the economy. Thus, the expansion of female labour in export-manufacturing is often offset by the contraction of female labour elsewhere in the economy. Moreover, women are generally not paid the premium wages.

5. Feminine and masculine work are not concretely or universally definable. Rather, they are shifting concepts, informed by gender, familial, cultural, historical, generational, political and economic factors. Maria Mies notes, 'the organic differences between men and women are differently interpreted and valued, according to the dominant form of appropriation of natural matter for the satisfaction of human needs' (Mies 1986: 53).

6. Sonia Alvarez (1990) uses this term to refer to the active pursuit of women's support.

7. The names of the cooperatives interviewed are Avaluz, Dionisio Méndes Laríos, EI Crucero, Génaro Tapia, Héroes y Mártires, La Curva, Las Crucitas, Los Pocitos, Manuel Sánchez García, Mario Brenes, Mirazul, Panamá, Roger Cano and Vista Alegre.

8. A University of Wisconsin Land Tenure Center study reveals that approximately 172 000 families in rural Nicaragua have property that is threatened due to its insecure legal status (*Envío* 1993e: 47).

9. Gender consciousness is understood as a process that first proposes to contradict the dominant social values in which there exist codes and norms of daily life for men and women that are reproduced and reinforced throughout society.

5 The Evolution of the Popular Organizations in Nicaragua

Pierre M. LaRamée and Erica G. Polakoff[1]

INTRODUCTION

The aims and aspirations of the Sandinistas in the domain of political practice were perhaps best and most succinctly addressed, in July 1983, by Sergio Ramírez, then Vice President of Nicaragua:

> For us, the efficiency of a political model depends on its capacity to resolve the problems of democracy and justice. Effective democracy, like we intend to practice in Nicaragua, consists of ample popular participation – a permanent dynamic of the people's participation in a variety of political and social tasks: the people who give their opinions and are listened to; the people who suggest, construct and direct; [the people who] organize themselves [and] attend to community, neighborhood, and national problems; the people who are active in the sovereignty and the defense of that sovereignty, and [who] also teach and give vaccinations; [in other words] a daily democracy and not one that takes place every four years ... [But] when formal elections take place, the people ... consciously elect the best candidate [via] a vote freely made and not manipulated by an advertising agency ... For us democracy is not merely a formal model but a continual process capable of giving the people that elect and participate in it the real possibility of transforming their living conditions, a democracy which establishes justice and ends exploitation. (Quoted in Ruchwarger 1987: 4)

It is ironic that even as this comprehensive conception of democracy and popular participation was presented as a

141

matter of party and national policy, Ronald Reagan justified funding and arming the counter-revolution by describing Nicaragua as 'a totalitarian dungeon'. While the Nicaraguan revolution may not have achieved its ambitious goals or realized in full many of its aspirations, it certainly embodied a serious and credible attempt to build a genuinely representative, participatory, and popular democracy.[2] Indeed, both the virulence of Reagan's rhetoric and the viciousness of his attack on the revolution, may be ascribed to what Ernesto Cardenal called the 'threat of the good example' – the sincerity of the attempt to construct a democratic socialism and its real potential for success.

This chapter focuses specifically on the attempt by the FSLN to create a broadly participatory political process as the foundation for a new Nicaraguan democracy via the creation of popular/mass organizations. We explore the relative successes and failures of that attempt by considering the trajectories of two organizations – the women's organization (AMNLAE) and the neighbourhood associations (CDS) – tracing their historical roots, their development and transformation under Sandinista leadership, and their more recent incarnations in the aftermath of the electoral defeat of the FSLN and the imposition of a neoliberal state by the Chamorro/UNO government. The principal driving force behind our analysis is the intention to address the question, 'what difference did the revolution make?' In order to do justice to this question, however, we must begin by examining the FSLN's conception of democracy – its ideological and theoretical underpinnings – as well as the Frente's revolutionary praxis.

THEORETICAL PARAMETERS: REVOLUTION AND DEMOCRACY

Sergio Ramírez' conception of democracy encapsulated a model which emerged gradually over time, was fashioned from diverse, and sometimes contradictory, elements, and was forged in the furnace of historical experience. The main theoretical and ideological components of the Sandinista model had their roots in such diverse sources as: the wider Marxist tradition; the Marxism-Leninism of the Bolshevik revolution; the communist internationals; Sandino's popular anti-imperialism with its elements of anarcho-syndicalism and revolutionary communism; the 'Latin American' Marxism of Mariátegui; the evolving Cuban revolutionary model; Maoism; European and North American neoMarxist currents (such as dependency theory); the liberation theology of Vatican II and Medellín; European parliamentary and social democracy; and the US federal-presidential system.

Although many of these ideological fountainheads contained significant components of a viable democratic theory, such as that sketched out by Ramírez, the Sandinistas had no viable large-scale or national-level model of democracy – with a genuine participatory element – to draw on. Capitalist democracies more or less limit participation to periodic voting exercises between (mostly) ideologically similar parties. Their governments vary only marginally in terms of their degree of representativity, and they tend to reduce competition for power to contests between factions of what C. Wright Mills called the 'power elite'. Civil society is reduced to participation in the marketplace and membership in voluntary associations.

The 'really existing socialist' regimes were authoritarian, highly centralized and bureaucratic party-states. Communist parties operated on the Marxist-Leninist principle of democratic centralism which concentrated power in the hands of Djilas' 'new class' of party cadre and state managers. The legitimacy of their rule was based on their claim to represent the interests of the majority on the strength of having eliminated class-based exploitation and oppression. Thus, the problem of representation was effectively defined out of existence, while participation was reduced to obedience to the dictates of the party.

These historical deformations are, of course, related to underlying political theories in much the same way that the 'holy inquisition' represents an accurate reflection of Christianity. Both the liberal and Marxist traditions contain varied and rich prescriptions for high levels of direct participation in social governance but these have been defeated or rejected in favour of more restrictive, elitist, and authoritarian formulations. In the United States, for example, the Jeffersonian approach was superseded by Madisonian federalism. In the USSR, soviets and communes were supplanted by state enterprises.

It is ironic that the former 'socialist' states suffered most from these distortions of theory since they held out the greatest promise of emancipation – economic as well as political. But Marx was much more prescriptive than programmatic in his conception of democracy – he admired the Paris Commune, came to see potential in the Russian village commune, and predicted that with the advent of communism, the state would wither away. Unlike liberal theorists, who proposed clear-cut mechanisms such as the franchise, however, Marx was generally vague with respect to purely political issues. Lenin developed theoretical notions such as the vanguard party and democratic centralism in response to specific conjunctural challenges related to seizing and maintaining revolutionary power. Moreover, like all revolutions, the Russian Revolution confronted massive external opposition while trying to resolve internal conflicts and opposition. As the Sandinistas were to learn in their turn, such conditions – external aggression, civil war, and the need for rapid development – do not lend themselves well to libertarian social experiments.[3]

Revolution requires the mobilization of a wide majority of a given population to make possible the overthrow of an oppressive regime. But that is only the beginning.[4] To be successful, a revolution must also contain the basis for organizing and orienting the participation of the popular majority in the revolutionary project. Although the mobilization of the people is generally coordinated by a disciplined revolutionary party/movement such as the FSLN, the revolutionary overthrow of the old regime can be accomplished only where there is also a high level of autonomy and spontaneity at the grassroots (see Ruchwarger 1987: Introduction). As Humberto Ortega said of the relationship between the FSLN and the people:

> The truth is that we always took the masses into account, but more in terms of their supporting the guerrillas, so that the guerrillas as such could defeat the National Guard. This isn't what actually happened. What happened was that it was the guerrillas who provided support for the masses so that they could defeat the enemy by means of insurrection. (Quoted in Ruchwarger 1987: 2)

What makes a revolution possible to begin with and ultimately successful, then, is the ongoing complementarity between legitimate leadership and genuine grassroots participation. The leadership of the revolution derives its legitimacy from the consolidation of revolutionary power, which means above all the creation of new structures and institutions which allow the people themselves to continue the process of social transformation begun in the struggle. The revolutionary government is legitimate and revolutionary to the extent that it can foment genuinely popular policies that lead to real improvements in the lives of the majority (Coraggio 1985: 4–5). For this dynamic to occur, the nurturing of a new popular social consciousness as a revolutionary priority is essential. In other words,

> ... the crucial political element is the systematic search for and implementation of paths for making it possible for the increasingly more organized people to become the *revolutionary subject*, thus losing their condition as a 'mass' of atomized citizens without identity who are summoned together but who lack autonomy. (Coraggio 1985: 4–5, emphasis added)

Indeed, the transition from an oppressive existence under the old regime to the promise of a better life under the new one actually marks the beginning of the revolution. From that point on, rapidly growing levels of participation and commitment to the process are required. Social, economic, and political life must be reorganized in a very short time, and an effective new order must be established to realize the goals of the revolution.[5]

In an initial post-triumphal context of resource scarcity and disorganization, such as existed in Nicaragua after the overthrow of Somoza, grassroots mobilization and participation must meet the immediate needs of the people, and thereby legitimate the emerging state. The emphasis in this early stage is on empowerment and meeting needs through small-scale, labour-intensive, low input, and low-cost investments, none of which can happen without meaningful democratic participation.[6] Popular organizations such as the CDS operate for a time essentially as a proto-state, especially at the micro level, and within them, key questions of class, development and democracy are inextricably bound together.[7] Thus, out of both ideology and need, the new revolutionary regime must encourage the growth of popular organizations and the proliferation of their activities. But the emerging party and state eventually find themselves compelled to shape these popular organizations for greater efficiency and control, creating over time an apparent and growing contradiction between grassroots mobilization and the institutionalization of the revolution.

This contradiction arises because immediately after coming to power, the revolutionary government must begin to devise and administer policies that will get the economy back on its feet, satisfy immediate and long-term needs, deal effectively with foreign-sponsored subversion, and resist counter-revolution. The imperative to plan and control, a 'natural' tendency of the revolutionary process (Lowy 1986: 267) which derives from this urgent agenda, generally materializes in the form of centralized, hierarchical organizations and institutions, and large-scale, capital-intensive development programmes emphasizing authority and efficiency. Initially, a revolutionary party such as the FSLN emerges as the country's most powerful and cohesive political force, seemingly undifferentiated from the nascent state. That is, party structures and state institutions function as parallel, and sometimes identical, entities. But even as they become more differentiated, the emerging symbiosis between party and state leaves the grassroots organizations in a relatively weaker position.[8]

THE EMERGENCE OF A GRASSROOTS DEMOCRACY IN THE NICARAGUAN REVOLUTION

At its founding in 1961, the FSLN became one of many new revolutionary organizations in Latin America to take up the torch of revolution through guerrilla struggle. But the Frente, even by its very name, became linked with the legacy of Sandino and a peculiarly Nicaraguan history of mass mobilization and armed struggle. When the Cuban 'foco' strategy of mobilization via armed struggle resulted in disastrous military debacles for the Sandinistas, they began to move towards Sandino's model of mobilization prior to, and in support of, the armed struggle. During the period between 1967, the year of the deadly massacre at Pancasán, and 1978, the beginning of the massive popular insurrection against the Somoza dictatorship, the FSLN engaged in the serious and laborious task of building up its forces and its mass base of support in both urban and rural areas.

Severe repression of the Sandinista rural base by Somoza's National Guard led to the 'accumulation of forces in silence' through work carried out via intermediate or 'front' organizations (Vanden and Prevost 1993: 43). But even prior to 1967, the Sandinistas were actively organizing rural and urban workers, and establishing student 'cells.' Subsequently, they intensified these efforts in working-class *barrios* and factories establishing the foundation for a trade union movement. Organizing efforts in the universities picked up with the reviving of the Revolutionary Student Front (FER), through which many cadre were recruited. Eventually, such painstaking organizing work resulted in the formation of the women's organization (AMPRONAC) in 1977 and the Rural Workers' Association (ATC) in 1978 (Ruchwarger 1985: 90–2).

In December 1974, the Sandinistas returned to openly confrontational tactics by staging a daring hostage-taking at the house of a prominent Somocista during a party for the US Ambassador. The subsequent renewal of severe repression and growing differences of opinion on ideology and tactics, led to a split within the FSLN. The previously two-pronged strategy of urban and rural organization and mobilization evolved into two separate tendencies within the movement: the 'Prolonged People's War' (GPP), drawing its inspiration from the Chinese Revolution and Maoist thought, which focused on organizing a peasant base of support and recruitment; and the 'Proletarian Tendency' which focused its energies mainly on organizing the embryonic Nicaraguan working class, but also established itself in the schools and universities.

Two critical developments broke the stalemate. The first was the emergence of liberation theology and Christian base communities as a bridge between the Marxism–Leninism of the FSLN and a potentially wider base of support among the general population. Liberation theology and the growing popular church also functioned as a major force behind the diversification of the Frente itself. The second was the emergence of a mediating third tendency within the Frente – the Insurrectionalists (or Terceristas) including Daniel and Humberto Ortega and Sergio Ramírez. This new tendency proposed a strategy of broad alliances incorporating all possible sectors of Nicaraguan society in the struggle to overthrow Somoza, and it further assumed that conditions were ripe for a massive, mainly urban insurrection, coordinated by the FSLN, to topple the dictator. This strategy required unity between the tendencies, the creation of a broad popular front (eventually the United People's Movement or MPU), and the willingness to disband guerrilla columns in favour of leading a mass movement.[9]

Formed in June 1978, the MPU included 23 popular organizations of all kinds, each of which had been carefully developed and cultivated by the Sandinistas and their supporters in all walks of life. By August, the MPU had created a network of neighbourhood-level underground cells called Civil Defence Committees (CDCs).

> During the last year of the war against Somoza, these cells provided urban residents with an autonomous power structure. Activists in the CDCs (which subsequently became the Comités de Defensa Sandinista (CDS)) carried out many tasks: they organized the stockpiling of food, medicine and weapons; built air-raid shelters; and trained people in first aid, military strategy, barricade-building and the use of weapons. After FSLN military forces had liberated a city, the CDCs met the emergency needs of the population. (Ruchwarger 1985: 92)

It would be fair to say that of all the popular organizations, the CDC/CDS was the brainchild of the Terceristas since their approach to revolution involved the mobilization of the entire population both politically and militarily. After the triumph, the CDS represented, perhaps more than any other popular organization, the aspirations of both the people and the Frente for a truly broad-based and participatory democracy – the 'people who are active in the sovereignty and the defense of that sovereignty'.

To make sense of how the CDS and the other popular/mass organizations developed during the decade of Sandinista rule, it is important to understand the wider context within which they operated. The key components of this framework were the FSLN as a self-styled vanguard party; the broad-based nature of the alliance that brought the Frente to power; the attempt to design and create a political system combining features of both participatory and representative democracy; and finally, the relentless opposition of the United States towards the Nicaraguan revolution.

Vanden and Prevost (1993: 19–20) argued that three models of democracy came uneasily to coexist in Nicaragua from the moment of the Sandinista triumph: the democratic centralism of the vanguard party, direct participatory democracy at the grassroots, and the representative democracy demanded by the international community and expected by the traditional political parties and their (largely) middle-class base of support.

> Indeed, it could be argued that the particular forms that democracy took in Nicaragua were related to the specific (and very diverse) nature of the class coalition that overthrew the Somoza dictatorship and to the way in which the FSLN's political leadership conceived and interpreted those classes and their role in the continuing revolutionary process. Likewise, external pressures from the United States and other actors would also condition the ways in which democracy would develop during Sandinista rule. (Vanden and Prevost 1993: 49)

In the aftermath of the triumph against Somoza, the FSLN could lay claim to the support of the popular sectors in Nicaragua, and therefore, of the vast majority of the population. They could also claim effective leadership of the Sandinista movement which they had led to victory. And, since the FSLN had led the struggle to overthrow Somoza, not to establish bourgeois democracy, but rather to create a genuine democratic socialism, they could also claim a mandate to create a new system of popular democracy. The popular organizations which had provided the basis for the revolutionary struggle declared their support for the Frente and became the new Sandinista 'mass organizations'. These organizations all experienced rapid growth immediately after the triumph, and they were called upon to play a key role in the transition from the old system to the new.

It is generally agreed that there were six major popular/mass organizations: the Sandinista Defence Committees (CDS), the Sandinista Workers' Federation (CST), the Luisa Amanda Espinosa Nicaraguan Women's Association (AMNLAE), the Sandinista Youth (JS), the Rural Workers' Association (ATC) and its 1981 spin-off the National Union of Farmers and Ranchers (UNAG). The principal tasks of the mass organizations were in three basic areas: socioeconomic development, overall defence, and the development of a democratic political system (Serra 1985: 65ff.). Socioeconomic development functions included promoting production, supplying basic consumer goods to the population, educational and cultural development, promoting public health, and community development. Building a democratic political system, at the heart of the mass organization's *raison d'être*, included serving as 'schools for democracy' by building the capacity of the population at large to participate in the decision-making process and acting as effective pressure groups to promote the interests of the popular majority vis-à-vis state and party. Indeed:

> These new mass organizations were to become the primary mechanism for popular empowerment and for the political education and guidance that the masses would need from the FSLN until they ... had achieved full political consciousness. These organizations were also to be the direct communication link between the masses and the political leadership. They would inform the people of new political directions and channel popular demands through the party to the National Directorate [of the FSLN]. (Vanden and Prevost 1993: 51)

The concept of a 'mass organization' is inextricably linked to the idea of the revolutionary vanguard party. The Leninist notion of the vanguard incorporates the idea of an ideologically pure elite whose members devote themselves to leading – while serving their needs and interests – a less enlightened population. The goal is not to dominate, but rather to empower the 'masses' by mobilizing them, and making them the masters of their destiny as a conscious collective subject. But, as previously noted, there is an inherent tension between mobilization and institutionalization in the revolutionary project. In other words:

Mass organizations are implicit in the idea of a revolutionary vanguard: they are the vanguard's necessary link with those it would instruct and lead ... The vanguard wants to liberate and empower the opressed and, at the same time, to control and transform them. The Sandinista popular organizations were created to represent their constituencies, but also to mobilize them behind a program prescribed from above. (Gilbert 1988: 77)

The Sandinista mass organizations thus became the foundation of revolutionary governance, but this created a dilemma for the FSLN. Although intent on empowering the masses and leading the country down the road to democratic socialism, the FSLN wanted to do so on the basis of the same broad alliance that brought down Somoza. In fact, the Sandinistas wanted to build a mixed economy with the full participation of the 'patriotic sector' of the business class.[10] The pluralistic nature of the revolutionary alliance, the Sandinistas' commitment to that pluralism, and finally, the balance of social forces in the revolution led to an interesting, but ultimately unworkable, experiment in the institutionalization of this new democracy. This was the Council of State which acted as a legislature until promised national elections were held in 1984. The Council of State was an appointed corporatist assembly consisting of the designated representatives of both the political parties and the major organizations representing the diversity of interests in civil society.

The distribution of seats in the Council was based on roughly the proportion of the population represented by each party or organization. This resulted in an overwhelming majority for the Sandinistas and the organizations most strongly supporting them. Of the eventual 51 seats in the Council, the FSLN had six, while the other six parties had only one each; private sector organizations had five, while popular and labour organizations had 23; guilds, professional groups and other social organizations had ten seats. Of the 23 seats occupied by popular and labour organizations, 16 were held by the principle Sandinista popular organizations: the CDS held nine, AMNLAE held one, Sandinista Youth held one, the CST held three, and the ATC held two. UNAG held two of the guild seats (Booth 1985: 37). Thus, the mass organizations, organs of grassroots democracy directly representing the interests of the popular majority, were given a significant role in policy-making at the national level. Not only were the Sandinista mass organizations strongly represented in the new legislature, but also the awarding of nine seats to the CDS alone indicates the centrality of grassroots local-level direct democracy in the Sandinista conception of governance.

But it is also important to understand that the Council of State shared co-legislative functions with the five-member executive Governing Junta of National Reconstruction (JGRN), three of whose members were Sandinistas. In addition, the Council of State was a relatively weak legislature since the JGRN had exclusive legislative authority over a wide variety of administrative and budgetary matters as well as veto power over legislation submitted by the Council – which had no corresponding veto power of its own over legislation passed by the executive. Nevertheless, the Council passed a substantial volume of key legislation and was also able to influence significantly the content of JGRN bills (Booth 1985: 35).

Eventually, internal opposition from significant components of the Nicaraguan business class as articulated by their political parties, and the pressure of US opposition via the armed counter-revolution (see Weeks 1987) resulted in the abandonment of the representative/participatory Council of State. For the 1984 national elections, a system of straight territorial, political party representation was implemented, but the more democratic European system of proportional representation was favoured over the Anglo-American single-member plurality district. The choice of proportional representation was indicative of the seriousness of the Sandinista commitment to a *genuinely* representative democracy – with single-member districts, opposition parties would have held no seats at all in the new national assembly after the 1984 elections in which the FSLN received 67 per cent of the vote.[11]

TRANSFORMATION OF THE POPULAR/MASS
ORGANIZATIONS

With the shift to a Western-style representative system, the popular and labour organizations lost their direct participation in the legislative process. But what was the extent of their ability to represent the interests of their members before and after this change? To what extent were they able to institutionalize a direct, participatory grassroots democracy? What was the role of the FSLN vis-à-vis both the popular sectors and the governance of the nation? How did the Frente's own internal praxis change over time, and what impact did it have on the ability of the popular/mass organizations to function effectively?

The organizational structure of the mass organizations was simple and uniform. Administratively, they were all organized by geographical area with a national-level headquarters, regional offices, municipal or zonal level branches, and finally, local-level committees. Politically, there was a permanent executive committee, a consultative council to advise it, and a national assembly with real legislative power as the ultimate authority (Serra 1991: 54). There were, accordingly, three levels of leadership with only local level representatives elected by the membership at large. The other levels of leadership were elected by the leadership level immediately below them in a system of indirect election and representation typical of democratic-centralist structures. In many cases, candidates at the higher levels were designated by the directorate of the mass organization for acclamation without any electoral competition at all. In other cases, intermediate level leaders were directly designated by the FSLN itself or were hired to fill their posts as professionals. At the regional and national levels, almost all of the higher directors were named by party authorities (Serra 1991: 56).

Membership in the mass organizations was virtually automatic and in principle open to anyone qualified by virtue of belonging to the relevant social sector. As might be expected, formal levels of membership were therefore quite high, actual participation much lower, and eagerness to seek or accept the responsibilities of leadership, lower still. In fact, the 'natural leaders' of their respective sectors often had overlapping reponsibilites in multiple organizations, and many would, at the same time, be militants of the FSLN. In other cases, such as the CDS, the local leaders were women already overburdened by the 'double day'.[12] Besides confronting the responsibilities of their office, local leaders would often find themselves caught between the needs of their constituents and the specific demands of the organization (Serra 1991: 56).

Democratic centralism has certain advantages such as ensuring the efficiency of administration and control functions, but it also has drawbacks for the development of direct, participatory democracy. In the Sandinista mass organizations, for instance, power tended to become concentrated in the hands of members of the top leadership who were responsible for carrying out the general policy 'orientations' of the FSLN. These orientations or 'lines' would be translated into policies applicable to the membership and jurisdiction of the organization, and would be transmitted or 'sent down' (*bajar la línea*) to the regional level to be adapted to local conditions and sent down further to the local level for execution. Although the democratic-centralist 'transmission belt' is supposed to run both ways – transmitting popular wishes, opinions, and ideas *up* while sending orders and work plans *down* – it tended in practice to be far more efficient in the downward direction. This phenomenon came to be known as 'verticalism'. Zonal- and regional-level leaders of the mass organizations regularly sent reports to the zonal/regional offices of the Frente, but local leaders often found themselves trying to mobilize the *bases* to work on projects in which they had no real sense of ownership or input. More commonly, they simply disregarded irrelevant or unworkable 'plans' while carrying out essentially *ad hoc* activities related to local needs or having their inception with state or other organisms such as nongovernmental organizations (Serra 1991: 57–8; Ruchwarger 1985: 95).

An equally problematic feature of the relationship between the mass organizations and the FSLN was the development of 'interlocking memberships'. The directors and top-level leaders of the mass organizations were for the most part also members (militants) or aspiring members of the FSLN. This dual role created a conflict of interest since the settling of any differences of opinion between the party and the mass organization would be biased in favour of the party. The problem was exacerbated by the change in legislative structure from the Council of State, where the mass organizations had direct representation, to a national assembly in which representation was mediated by political parties, that is, the Frente. Interlocking memberships also worked against openness and pluralism in the organizations by discouraging the recruitment of 'nonpolitical' or at least non-Sandinista members. Party committees within the mass organizations became parallel, and sometimes overriding, structures of authority further undermining autonomy. FSLN cadre, new and old, were also likely to be transferred with little regard for the impact of this shift for the work of the mass organization. In fact, the FSLN drew the bulk of its new members from the ranks of the mass organizations which were perfect 'schools for revolutionaries'. Democratic centralism, coupled with the substantial political power of the Frente itself, tended to resolve this growing contradiction in the party's favour, jeopardizing the autonomy of the mass organizations and the evolution of participatory democracy (Serra 1991: 60; Ruchwarger 1985: 98–9). As Coraggio put it:

> In regard to the government-party relationship, it is a matter of finding mechanisms through which government officials are basically accountable to the people and that the logic of government organization does not become confused with the logic of party organization.
>
> In regard to the relationship between the party and the mass organizations, the central problematic boils down to the question of how to resolve the need ... to guarantee the continuation of the revolutionary process and ... the need to guarantee the autonomy of the mass organizations to make a substantive democracy possible. (Coraggio 1986: 41)

The mass organizations also had complex and contradictory relations with the state. As already mentioned, the mass organizations initially filled a variety of parastatal functions as the old Somocista state collapsed and the new Sandinista state gestated. Just as the FSLN grew and developed as a party and the mass organizations themselves became increasingly bureaucratized, so too did new bureaucratic state structures emerge, gradually supplanting the mass organizations in terms of planning, and delivering services. This was a gradual process, however, and the mass organizations continued to play an important role in articulating the needs of their memberships, and in contributing, at least on a consultative basis, to the policy-making process. Since resources were always scarce, the mass organizations also had an important contribution to make in providing manpower to execute policy and deliver goods and services. They also played a key watchdog role, criticizing government organisms for inefficiency and corruption, while trying to ensure both delivery and fair shares for their constituents. When conflicts erupted between the state and the mass organizations, the FSLN sometimes intervened in favour of the latter. But more often than not, the close relationship between the party and the state reinforced the power of the latter vis-à-vis the mass organizations.[13] In any case, the siphoning off of their best cadre by the Frente and the high level of technical development required in the policy-making process tended to reduce the mass organizations' power and influence (Serra 1991: 59; Ruchwarger 1985: 100–1).

THE COMMUNITY MOVEMENT

From the CDS to the New CDC

In the aftermath of the Sandinista triumph, the Comités de Defensa Sandinista (CDS), successor to the Civil Defence Committees (CDC) of the popular insurrection, became the basic institutions of authority at the neighbourhood level, assuming a variety of administrative, security, stabilization, and development functions. The CDS[14] was already the most diverse of the mass organizations, and it quickly became the largest in terms of membership which was open to anyone over the age of 14 without regard to sex, religion or political affiliation. By 1984, up to 600 000 individuals, organized into 15 000 Neighbourhood Base Committees (CBSs), had been active in CDS projects (Serra 1985: 66).

The CDS was involved in carrying out an array of tasks. To help overcome shortages of basic goods, they promoted production collectives (with AMNLAE) in sewing, ceramics, and handicrafts, and they also organized the planting of community gardens. The CDS assumed responsibility for the distribution of basic consumer goods at official prices through either government stores or licensed local merchants (people's stores). Since this was a rationing system, the CDS was responsible both for taking and maintaining a census of the neighbourhood, and for distributing ration cards. After the Consumer Protection Law of 1984 which restricted the sale of eight basic products to official channels, CDS responsibilities in this area expanded (Serra 1985: 70).

The CDS was also active in literacy and education, contributing 16 630 *brigadistas* to the National Literacy Crusade (out of some 85 000), and organizing Popular Education Collectives for adult education in the *barrios*. In the public health field, the CDS played a vital role in carrying out national vaccination campaigns against polio and other childhood diseases. Other campaigns, coordinated by newly trained health *brigadistas*, targeted malaria, dengue fever, diarrhoea in children, and basic hygiene and sanitation. The CDS mobilized residents to remove rubbish, clean storm sewers, and build latrines (Serra 1985: 71–3).

The CDS was active in wider community development efforts ranging from improvement of squatter settlements to building low-cost housing in *urbanizaciones progresivas*, or sites and services developments. For example, the early urban renewal projects carried out by the Ministry of Housing and Human Settlements (MINVAH), and financed by the World Bank, were reported as owing much of their success to CDS participation. The CDS also mobilized residents for volunteer workdays (*rojos y negros*) to carry out special projects such as building a community centre or a playground (Serra 1985: 73–74).

The most controversial areas of CDS operations were civil defence, militias, and revolutionary vigilance or night-watch patrols. As the counter-revolutionary war heated up after 1981, defence-related activities occupied more and more of the mass organizations' energies. The night watch may not have had much impact on the counter-revolutionary war, but it led to a dramatic reduction in crime while probably preventing sabotage and reducing the potential for other counter-revolutionary actions. The Militias Populares Sandinistas (MPS) mobilized the civilian population for national defence and made an important contribution to the war effort. Since the militias were voluntary, they were much less contentious than registration for the draft under the Patriotic Military Service Law which the CDS was obliged to enforce (Serra 1985: 74–5).

The precipitous decline in participation in the CDS and other mass organizations which began in 1985 was caused in part by the economic adjustment measures implemented because of the impact of the Contra war and the imposition of a commercial and financial embargo by the United States. The distribution of the eight basic commodities was now fully controlled by the state, but even tighter controls could not offset the chronic food shortages caused by Contra destruction, the disruption of food production, and a misguided emphasis on large-scale, capital-intensive projects such as the state milk enterprise at Chiltepe. The CDS was thus responsible for overseeing the fair distribution of increasingly scarce commodities in a time of dire need – a position somewhat inimical to their popularity.[15]

The scarcity of manufactured goods of all kinds, caused by declining terms of trade for Nicaragua's primary exports as well as by declining production, also made it difficult for the government to provide materials for grassroots projects. The investment policies promulgated by the government in 1984 virtually pre-empted public investment in Managua and redirected scarce resources to the countryside in support of the war effort and food production. In addition, the unpopularity of the draft and the individual effects of the growing economic crisis – inflation and the decline in real wages, shortages, unemployment, and the growth of the informal sector – generally lowered the level of motivation and participation. UNAG, which represented the interests of small agricultural producers, was the only popular organization to increase its membership after 1985. UNAG aggressively challenged Sandinista economic policy which, as a result of the need to generate foreign exchange earnings, was tilted in favour of medium-to-large producers of agroexport crops at the expense of small producers of subsistence crops. UNAG demonstrated its autonomy from the FSLN and garnered popular support by responding to the needs of its constituency over and above its allegiance to the party. It successfully lobbied for the changes in agrarian policy demanded by peasant producers, and obtained substantial increases in both the redistribution of land and the granting of individual titles (Williams 1994: 175–6).

But even before the war, the economic crisis, and pressures to carry out unpopular programmes began to stifle motivation and incentive, there had already been marked fluctuations in participation in the CDS. The growing bureaucratization of the movement, its subordination to party imperatives, and abuses by individual coordinators had a negative impact on the level of participation, and resulted in attempts at reform. The first reform, which dealt with the accountability of leaders, took place on the initiative of Comandante Bayardo Arce at the end of 1982. In an open letter to CDS coordinators, Arce stated 'that the CDS leadership and members should express qualities that can be measured by ... their willingness to be the best servants of the people, avoiding and combating opportunism, bureaucracy, favoritism, and bossism'. He described 'arbitrary attitudes and actions that exert influences which are contrary to Sandinista principles', and he listed a number of cases:

> Withholding the sugar distribution card from someone who still does not understand the Revolution ... We know that this method is sometimes used to pressure people into doing CDS tasks, which are supposed to be voluntary.
> Harassment by words and actions of people who profess another ideology – whether religious or political ...
> Falling into an abuse of authority and using a position of responsibility in the organization as a way to enjoy personal and family privileges.
> To allow and lead abuses in carrying out the voluntary night watch, especially in taking repressive measures against those who do not participate in this task. (Quoted in Ruchwarger 1985: 106–7)

The CDS was restructured, and members were gathered in assemblies to elect/re-elect coordinators and leaders at all levels. In February 1984, Comandante Leticia Herrera, national general secretary of the CDS, citing continued abuses, limited the terms of all CDS leaders to one year. Similar nationally mandated sets of elections for CDS coordinators were held in 1985 and again in 1988 (Ruchwarger 1985; Serra 1991: 63). The 1985 reforms were directed at *barrio* CDS elections, and included a more open nomination process, multiple candidacies, and most importantly, secret balloting. Although there was little evidence of actual abuses of power, more than half of the coordinators of *barrio* committees in Matagalpa were re-placed in the more strongly contested 1985 elections. However, Sandinistas were still overwhelmingly victorious in the majority of contests, but then the reforms were not in-tended to make the CDS more independent of the party (Gilbert 1988: 70–1).

By 1988, the deepening economic crisis and the continued overall decline in participation,[16] impelled the deepest reform proposed to date in the CDS. Popular revolutionary hero, Comandante Omar Cabezas, was named the new national CDS coordinator. He initiated an analysis and critique of the CDS, identifying a number of factors to explain the general decline in CDS activity: first, the imposition of a uniform structure and uniform policies on diverse regions and neighbourhoods themselves containing the broad diversity of class and other identities characteristic of Nicaraguan society; second, the top leadership now identified the problem of sectarianism, or the identification of the neighbourhood CDS with the Frente; third, despite the 1985 reforms, individual abuses of power continued, and the institutional pattern of verticalism still pre-vailed; fourth, there was a widespread expectation that along with top-down directives and programmes, there should also be a constant flow of resources from the state (LaRamée and Polakoff 1990: 109–11).

Cabezas' prescription for rectifying the problems of the CDS and revitalizing the mass organization was to turn it into 'a gigantic community movement whereby the community or-ganizes itself to solve its own problems ... with the aid of the government and not the government with the aid of the com-munity' (Cabezas Lacayo 1988a). As Omar Cabezas put it: 'Organize yourselves how you want and for what you want! Those who don't know how (to organize) should get together and figure it out. And if you make mistakes, if you come up against a wall, it doesn't matter. That's how you are going to learn, little by little' (Cabezas Lacayo 1988b). Cabezas' task was to revitalize the organization, making it into a broad, viable democratic movement that represented its participants and worked for them so that they might solve their most im-mediate and pressing community problems. 'Democracy', ac-cording to Cabezas, 'begins at the base', and in order to achieve democracy in the CDS movement, 'we must begin by democratizing the base' (Cabezas Lacayo 1988b). Cabezas emphasized that the Frente would no longer impose a set of demands on the community. Rather, he insisted that people find their own leaders and create their own organizations, without depending on the Frente. The name of the CDS was changed to CDC – Committees of Community Development. Thus, Cabezas began the process of reconceptualizing the purpose of the community organizations and of restructuring them so that they would respond to their constituencies' needs and initiatives.

However, it can also be said that the Frente and the government both shifted the burden of responsibility to the people. In contrast to top-down decision-making, it was up to the people to identify their own leaders, to develop their own initiatives, and to create their own organizations. Essentially, the CDS was drastically decentralized, and the communities were left to organize themselves. This new laissez-faire attitude also presupposed that motivation alone would now substitute for extensive material inputs. Of course, given the scarcity of resources, this position made a virtue of necessity – there was nothing to distribute. The expectation was that a ground swell of repressed popular participation would be fuelled by an economic crisis requiring cooperative solutions.

To be fair, the reform called for new elections and a structural reform reducing the number of zonal committees. Zonal delegates were encouraged to become CDC *promotores* in their own neighbourhoods. Ideally, these 'promoters' or natural leaders, who held the trust and affection of the people, would become the new or renewed organizers. But the assumption that revitalization would take place more or less automatically was overly optimistic. It did not take into account the extent to which the severity of the economic crisis favoured individualistic survival strategies based on mutual suspicion while undermining cooperative solutions based on trust. Cabezas' assumption also failed to account for the effects of nearly ten years of 'sectarianism', 'democratic centralism', and 'abuses of power' on the popular will.[17] In addition, as the then vice coordinator, Enrique Picado, noted, 'there was a contradiction between leaving people to their own means without any direction or guidance, and somehow maintaining control without repressing the initiatives of the community'.[18]

After the Sandinistas' 1990 electoral defeat, the CDC became a nongovernmental organization, and was renamed the Movimiento Comunal (MC) or 'Community Movement'. The challenge facing MC activists and leaders was how to recover from the electoral defeat, and reactivate what had once been a mass movement. In the words of Enrique Picado,

> The electoral defeat hit us all like an earthquake. The Frente didn't prepare us for the possibility of defeat. Imagine ... if I was unprepared, how unprepared were the leaders of the communities, most of whom did not have much education or political awareness. The local leaders were completely demoralized.[19]

However, Máxima Bermudez, current national vice coordinator of the Community Movement, believes that because its transformation began well before the election, the Community Movement, in comparison to the other mass organizations, was 'the least stricken after the election results'.[20]

> As an organization, we succeeded in confronting the election. We didn't need to know who voted for whom, but rather how to undertake the tasks of the community without seeing it connected to a political party. Still, it was difficult. There were entire neighbourhoods that had been entirely immersed in the electoral campaign. That is, there were communities that were completely divided, CDCs that were completely broken up, and other community organizations that completely disappeared from the neighbourhood ... In spite of polarization in our communities, a movement surged to vaccinate the children [in May 1990] ... Our message was, 'Independently of the government, we have to talk about our children and our communities. What we do here will not be good or bad for the government of Doña Violeta; it will be good or bad for our children'. That was our first accomplishment.[21]

The MC's transformation from a mass organization that had been created by, and primarily responsible to the FSLN, into an independent organization embodying a social movement, was very difficult for many reasons. First, the Community Movement had to change its focus in order to gain acceptance from those who either had become disillusioned with the

Frente or had been opposed to it. Enrique Picado explained that during the decade of the 1980s, the CDS had emphasized ideology and abstract ideas.

> There wasn't much correspondence between '*patria libre o morir*' ['a free country or death'], and resolving community problems. We focused on the masses and forgot about the person. Now we have substituted the individual for the masses.[22]

Changing its focus from 'the masses' as the unit of development to the individual and her (or his) community, meant concentrating on local problems. According to Sergio Obando, MC coordinator for the department of Granada, this change has helped the MC to gain people's support and participation:

> It is not reasonable [for the government] to demand that people make sacrifice after sacrifice. And although the economic situation has limited all of us, the MC has proved itself to be an alternative for them to find solutions to their social problems. It has been possible to gain acceptance in this way. The MC is a collective, serving the community. We talk about concrete problems that people have, and not about politics. Before it was reversed.[23]

Second, to gain legitimacy as a truly democratic organization, all leadership positions at all levels would have to be elected ones rather than appointed ones. As noted earlier in this chapter, this represents a significant departure from previous practice.[24] Obtaining maximum participation of community residents in elections so that elected leaders represent community interests is essential to democracy. However, given the current political and economic climate, this has been even more difficult for the MC to achieve than it was a decade ago for the CDS. In addition, elected leaders vary considerably in their capacity or ability to prioritize needs and interests. Therefore, serious effort has gone into *capacitación* – enabling leaders at all levels to successfully diagnose, analyse, and prioritize social problems and needs. According to Máxima Bermudez, building democracy at the base through elections and the *capacitación* of elected leaders is one of the MC's most important tasks:

For us, the municipality is the fundamental elected body of society, and it is on this that we have placed a lot of emphasis. It isn't only whether or not to build a school or to simply decide to build latrines. The community will begin to make more important decisions in the life of the neighbourhood and the municipality.[25]

Third, breaking away from the party and becoming an autonomous organization created a lot of tension and conflict among FSLN members and sympathizers. Máxima Bermudez identified the MC's focus on the community and its independence as the source of that conflict:

> We focus on the problems of the community. We don't belong to any political party, nor to any government. We make our own decisions. We are an organization that corresponds directly to the needs of the community. It seems to us that this is where the power of the organization lies – precisely because we don't respond to anyone's politics ... This change was difficult to implement. Many people in the Frente questioned our style and our concept of community-based struggle. Our autonomy has cost us a great deal ... We are a threat to the political parties, including the Frente, because of our non-partisan, non-sectarian style.[26]

That the Community Movement continues to be associated by many with the Frente has to do with the fact that many of its leaders at all levels – its national coordinators, department coordinators, and community leaders – consider themselves to be 'revolutionaries'. Virtually all of them were either FSLN militants or community activists in the struggle leading up to the Sandinista triumph and during the 11 years of Sandinista rule. That is, the overwhelming majority of MC leaders have a history of personal involvement in various aspects of the economic and social development of their communities. Their work with the MC is clearly an extension of their previous commitment to progressive social change.[27] Many MC leaders maintained their membership in and allegiance to the Frente, although this became more complicated after the 1990 elections when the FSLN divided into two factions – the Sandinista Renovation Movement (MRS), and the Democratic Left (ID). Since the MRS split off from the Frente as a separate party in the spring of 1995, both the MRS and the Frente have been represented among the leadership of the Community Movement.[28] Many leaders were reluctant to discuss their own affiliation, emphasizing that it was a personal decision and had little to do with their actual work in the community. Moreover, adherents to both parties were equally critical of the public statements of affiliation with the MRS by national coordinator Enrique Picado and national vice coordinator Máxima Bermudez. (In an interview with *Barricada Internacional* (1995: 22) Picado asserted he had *not* resigned from the FSLN.)

A testament to their nonpartisanship is the fact that MC leaders and activists not only have been demonized by members of the UNO for being 'Sandinistas', but also have been criticized by the leadership of the Frente for being independent, for supporting a civic method of struggle as opposed to a more bellicose or aggressive one, and hence, for betraying the revolution.[29] In some communities, FSLN leaders have threatened to start their own 'community movement' that would compete with the MC because the MC is 'too independent of the party'.[30] Perhaps the sentiment that MC leaders and activists have betrayed the revolution results from their work with members of all political parties and ideologies, religious groups, international organizations, national government ministries and officials, and nongovernmental organizations.[31] What stands out in sharp contrast to the criticisms MC leaders have received from the Frente is the fact that they have maintained their allegiance to the revolutionary project. In the words of one community leader and activist, 'To be a revolutionary means to be able to change as the context and conditions change. The revolution isn't this thing out there. The revolution is us. We are the revolution. It's not this political party thing – it's working for progress, for the children, for the community'.[32] The political nature of the MC's work is clarified by its national coordinator, 'Our work is not sectarian, but it *is* political. To work to transform reality, that's political. It's a revolutionary project that has its own ideology'.[33]

Essential to the revolutionary project, both ideologically and in practice, was the Sandinistas' commitment to social justice and their 'preferential option for the poor – relieving hunger, malnutrition and misery, and improving housing, health, sanitation and ultimately, the material conditions of life. While in power, the Sandinista government successfully carried out more than 30 popular health campaigns, reduced the infant mortality rate, increased accessibility to medical attention, drastically reduced the illiteracy rate, increased school enrolments and retention rates at all levels, improved housing standards, and established a national social security system.[34] What characterizes MC leaders and activists is their continued commitment to social justice, especially in the areas of health and education. Moreover, defending the rights of children and working for community development and progress have been conceptualized as congruent, noncompeting goals.

The Community Movement and Community Development Projects

Although it is still perceived by many to be an organization of the Frente, the Community Movement is formally an independent and autonomous, nongovernmental organization with a national presence that aims to solve local problems through local initiatives. In the words of one community activist, 'the Movimiento Comunal is not only a structure; it *is* the community'.[35] Community Movement development projects are as diverse as the communities in which they arise. Thus, while for some communities, property issues are the most pressing and urgent problems, in other communities, potable water and electricity are priorities, or literacy and adult education, daycare centres and preschools, or health and sanitation.

The largest and most widespread project coordinated by the MC focuses on children who live in very poor neighbourhoods. The Community Movement operates over 200 *casas comunales del niño* (CCNs), or 'children's community centres' which offer a variety of services including daycare or preschool, first and second grade classes, rehabilitation and occupational training for young teens. In the words of Isabel Morales, the Executive Director of the Children's Community Centres,

> Children are the future of our country; we parents are like a volcano in ashes that no longer produces anything for the homeland. Children are the seedbeds that we bear so that

they may produce something better than we did. (Quoted in Urcuyo 1994: 16)

The daycare centres and preschools have their origins in the *comedores infantiles comunales* (CICs) or infant centres of the previous decade which had been established in order to eliminate hunger and malnutrition, and respond to the high mortality rates among infants and children. These centres had received support from the Ministry of Social Welfare (INSSBI), the Ministry of Health (MINSA), the Ministry of Education (MED), and numerous nongovernmental international organizations and solidarity committees (many of which had provided funding for the construction of permanent centres). Because hunger and malnutrition were viewed as community problems with a community solution, organizing parents to participate in the building of the centres and in their maintenance and operation, was critical to their functioning.

In the late 1980s, Frente and community leaders who were involved in the development of the CICs determined that the centres had a number of problems: instability and inconsistency in the delivery of food to the centres, difficulties in getting parents to provide supplementary food, insufficient follow-up on the nutritional status of the children participating in the programme, and a high rate of staff turnover (Urcuyo 1994). Since 1990, these problems have been exacerbated as a result of cuts in spending on education and welfare and the privatization of the health care system. The children's community centres have had to depend primarily on assistance from external sources – the Evangelical Committee for Development Assistance (CEPAD), the World Food Programme (PMA), and international solidarity committees and organizations (although these too, have declined significantly in their support of projects in Nicaragua since the elections). In addition, because the Chamorro government's neoliberal policies have disproportionately burdened, and most severely affected poor families – which constitute more than 70 per cent of the population (Evans 1993: 10) – many centres have experienced a decline in parents' ability to contribute their time and support. Thus, community participation which was conceptualized as the foundation of the children's centres (and essential to the success of all social-sector programmes), has become increasingly difficult to realize. The majority of daycare centres continue to rely on a rotating schedule of women from the community to cook the children's lunch. The women are expected to provide wood for cooking and to supplement the meal with additional food. Many centres have problems with parents being unable (and in some cases, unwilling) to keep their commitment to the school and to the children. Given their economic circumstances – the extraordinarily high unemployment rates in all of these communities, and the fact that many women are single heads of household with children of their own – the burden of providing wood and supplementing the meal for a large number of children, is one that many mothers cannot bear.[36] Illness and disease, which are common among families that are impoverished and undernourished, were also reasons for parents being unable to cook the meal of the day when it was their turn, or teachers being unable to teach their classes.[37] In addition, parents may feel obligated to pay something to the volunteer teachers of the centres, but more often than not, they find themselves without the resources to do so. For example, in one centre – an open-air structure with a bamboo roof that doubled as a church on Sundays – in a community on the outskirts of León, parents were reluctant to participate when they were asked to make a small contribution to the teacher who had been working with their children during the previous six months without receiving any form of recompense.[38] Also, due to the rising costs in services such as water and electricity, many of the centres that have these 'luxuries', can no longer afford to pay for them. In Granada, for example, services to one centre were cut off because they were one month behind on payment of their utility bills.[39] Without any other source of funding, the costs of maintaining the centres must be transferred to parents and community members, who generally are not in a position to provide financial support.

A few centres have solved these problems by becoming virtually self-sufficient. In the municipality of Matagalpa, for example, there are five daycare centres, each of which is affiliated with a *micro-empresa* or 'small business' collective that earns just enough to ensure that the centre always has electricity; well-rounded meals are provided on a daily basis for 80 to 120 children; and each member of the collective – the workers in the business, the teachers, the cook and the administrator of the school – is paid approximately 200 córdobas per month (or just less than $30 in US currency).[40] The centres that have achieved self-sufficiency not only provide employment for several individuals, they also avoid many of the difficulties that plague other, nonself-sufficient centres.[41]

Although there are costs (either actual or 'in-kind') associated with sending one's children to the Community Movement's daycare centres and preschools, they are minimal in comparison to the costs of entering first grade in the government's 'public' schools. Beginning in 1990, students have had to pay a monthly fee, purchase school uniforms (and shoes), buy their own books and notebooks, and supply their own pencils and crayons. Because of the severity of the economic crisis, many families simply cannot afford to send their children to school. There are, therefore, many older children and youth who are hungry and in need of attention, and, although officially the preschools only accept children from the age of three months old to five years old, the majority of centres find it difficult to turn away 'older' children. The Community Movement coordinates several different kinds of centres which attend to over 27 000 older children or youth nationwide, but the need is obviously much greater.[42] In Subtiava, for example, there is a centre for *niños del basurero* or 'children of the garbage dump', which offers lunch, occupational training, and a sports and recreation programme for teenagers who literally had been found searching for food in garbage dumps. In León (and Managua), there are rehabilitation centres for young drug abusers, many of whom had been abandoned by their parents before coming to these centres; and centres for young girls who have been identified as at risk of becoming teenage mothers. These centres provide a positive environment, are staffed by understanding and caring individuals, and offer real skills in an attempt to prevent children from going back to living out on the street.[43]

A few communities are able to support an integrated approach to youth development. One neighbourhood on the outskirts of Estelí, for example, offers evening classes for children and teenagers which include workshops in dressmaking and tailoring, athletic activities like judo, and consciousness-raising groups in which young people talk about their relationships with and responsibilities to each other, parents, and their community. The centre also houses a library and reading room where children work on school projects and concentrate on their studies. Centres such as this one encourage young people to stay in school and continue their education, provide them with marketable skills, and help them to develop a consciousness of themselves as social actors with both rights and responsibilities. The success of this centre in involving a large number of children from the community appeared to be based primarily on the energy, charisma and will of its main benefactors – a family from Barcelona, Spain that has dedicated several years of work to this project, and financial assistance from a solidarity committee in Barcelona.[44]

In 1992, the Community Movement initiated the popular adult education project, a scaled-down version of the popular education centres of the 1980s and the Sandinistas' literacy programme – which had its origins in the pedagogy of Brazilian educator and philosopher, Paolo Freire. Literacy skills are taught by focusing on the experiences of community members and the everyday problems they confront such as health and disease, sanitation, access to land and agricultural production. The *maestros populares* or popular educators are young people in their teens who essentially volunteer to lead small group discussions and teach reading and writing to adults in their community. For example, in Santa Cruz, in the department of Estelí, there are seven *maestros populares* who are responsible for 42 adults. The teens were trained by the MC, but the initiative to organize the project was their own. Two of the teenagers are physically handicapped and more than half of their students are handicapped adults. In the words of one teenager, 'Literacy is not only about learning to read and write; it is also about broadening a person's life. I don't know very much, but one has to help with the little that one knows'.[45] Many adults in the literacy classes have taken an interest in solving the community problems they discuss such as health care, sanitation and potable water which tend to be major concerns in communities throughout Nicaragua.

Just as the popular education project had its roots in the education programmes of the previous decade, so too the

MC's health and sanitation projects have been based on the Sandinista social programmes that preceded them. The MC conceptualizes health as something more than access to medical care and services. According to Máxima Bermudez, 'Health means having a dignified life which includes having decent housing, potable water, better hygienic facilities, electricity. Health is environment; it's education.[46] The Community Movement's goal is to give communities the education and skills they need in order to control their own health and defend their right to the health care services it believes the government is obligated to provide. The focus is on preventative medicine. MC health promoters emphasize community-level health care by organizing committees for potable water, latrine construction, and vaccination campaigns. The MC also organizes and trains popular health *brigadistas*, or volunteer health workers, to educate the residents in their community to prevent disease, and provide basic health services, vaccinations and medications. Training *brigadistas* has been a daunting and impressive undertaking. For example, in the five municipal districts of the department of Estelí, well over 600 *brigadistas* have attended workshops in El Crucero sponsored by international NGOs and UNICEF, in order to qualify. Nationwide, the MC has trained more than 20 000 *brigadistas*.[47]

The Community Movement has experienced a number of difficulties implementing their sanitation projects, specifically in the construction of latrines. While they have been reasonably successful in obtaining funding for materials, by the time they receive the funds, costs increase. As a result, the number of latrines projected for construction has had to be reduced and several families that were promised latrines were not able to get them. The distribution of materials for construction has also been problematic. In some cases, once delivered to the community, the materials have mysteriously disappeared. Instead of being used to build latrines, materials were used for other purposes, primarily as a source of cash for more immediate needs like food. Furthermore, in some communities (Estelí, for example), latrine construction has been carried out by a committee of individuals who have become specialists in a particular aspect of the construction, while in other communities (like Matagalpa) each family has been responsible for building its own latrine. A common problem in the latter case has been the incorrect measurement of dimensions and the subsequent waste of materials.[48] The preference for individual solutions in Matagalpa was apparent in other ways. In the *barrio* 'Francisco Moreno' – declared a 'danger zone' for having the highest number of cases of diarrhoea and associated illnesses – no one was willing to share a latrine even though the demand was greater than the supply of materials, and many families lived on too small a plot of land to house a latrine at a safe enough distance from their own house and their neighbours' houses. The community avoided the problem of deciding which families would be the beneficiaries by employing a lottery system and thus leaving the decision to fate or luck. This decision can be interpreted in a number of ways: it might exemplify the community's fear of the sectarianism and favouritism of the CDS of the past; it might also exemplify their resistance to being in control or taking responsibility for their decisions, or to act as a community.

The children's community centres and the health projects both highlight the extent to which the MC has become decentralized and what the disadvantages of decentralization are. There appears to be very little communication between communities regarding their successes and failures in implementing projects. People are left to learn the hard way, sometimes by repeatedly making mistakes before figuring out what kinds of strategies – for raising money, getting supplies, and organizing community cooperation and participation – work best in their community. The children's community centres and the community health centres or clinics, for example, vary considerably in their physical durability, structural stability, the ways in which they are organized and run, the degree to which they have been able to establish themselves as institutions of the community, and the extent to which community members participate in the projects. Organizing community participation remains one of the most significant challenges the MC, or any organization, for that matter, faces in Nicaragua. One community leader and longtime activist explained why this has become so difficult:

> People have changed a lot since the Eighties. Now people don't have as much motivation to participate. They'll say, 'What for? What's the point?' And the economic situation is

so horrifying that one doesn't see a way out of it. They become disillusioned and lose all hope.[49]

For reasons mentioned earlier, it is obvious that the economic crisis has had a significant impact on participation. It is also apparent that many Nicaraguans have been demoralized by seeing their previous gains steadily eroded. Indeed, a sense of hopelessness pervades many communities.

In addition to these obstacles, the Community Movement must deal with political reality and overcome the polarization that has divided many communities throughout the country. Managua, in particular, is a deeply divided city. In 1990, after he became mayor, Arnoldo Alemán created a citywide organization called the Juntas Comunitarias de Hora y Progreso or Community Juntas of Time and Progress (JCOHP). According to the District 3 delegate to the mayor's office, communal committees of the JCOHP exist in all of the *barrios* of Managua. He compared the JCOHP to the CDS, and commented on the MC's relationship to the FSLN:

> The JCOHP is similar to the CDS, but it is under the authority of the mayor. The JCOHP also differs from Omar Cabezas' organization because he had the idea of using the organization for political ends. In contrast, we don't get into politics. We work for the people. The Movimiento Comunal is identified with the Frente. They just want to show that they are better than we are. But they didn't do anything in ten years.[50]

According to Máxima Bermudez, the JCOHP 'has created conflicts in the community. We have proposed to the JCOHP that we not fight but rather that we join resources for the benefit of the community. In a few cases, if the JCOHP leader was sensible and not highly partisan, we have succeeded'.[51] Enrique Picado criticized the JCOHP and the mayor for trying to convert community activists into JCOHP supporters, and for their antidemocratic tendencies:

> The municipal districts are returning to a Somocista structure. The mayor's representatives were always the ears of the authorities of Somoza's National Guard. They have a mentality of revenge. They certainly don't go around thinking about democracy.[52]

In addition to the JCOHP, there are other community development organizations affiliated with the municipal, departmental, or national government. For example, GUAPISA, or the 'Group for Social Assistance', is a national governmental organization under the direction of Presidential Minister, Antonio Lacayo. All of these organizations are vying for community support and allegiance, and the competition has become especially intense, as the 1996 elections draw near. Máxima Bermudez pointed out that economic conditions are so bad and people are so impoverished that 'the community must take advantage of all of the resources it can'.[53] However, the support that many of these government-sponsored programmes provide is contingent upon the community not affiliating itself with any other organization, and especially not with the MC.

Political polarization has been most evident in the struggle over property. Many property owners who fled Nicaragua at the time of the Sandinista triumph, have returned to reclaim their former lands, houses, and factories. In September 1994, the government created the Office of Territorial Organization (OOT) to settle property disputes and review all of the land, houses and property titles that had been granted by the Sandinistas (especially in Laws 85, 86, 88). According to Máxima Bermudez, the review process,

> ... is a bureaucratic nightmare that impedes rather than solves the problem of property ownership. The OOT has been used for political ends to deny the right to property to thousands and thousands of citizens whom we have been trying to protect. Property is a problem with a social character. Therefore, we have had to support the rights to property.[54]

The Community Movement has been involved in legal proceedings on behalf of individual families and community organizations that have occupied these contested properties since the revolution, regardless of their current political affiliations. In addition, the MC has assisted in organizing brigades against evictions and has carried out other actions such as lobbying political parties, the Church, the government, and members of the National Assembly, in an attempt to influence legislation regarding property rights.[55] In Diriamba, Carazo, for example, representatives of the MC both at the local level in Diriamba, and at the national headquarters in Managua, have assisted families living in *cuarterías*, which are extremely impoverished and crowded 'public housing' areas,[56] in their fight to prevent eviction, defend their homes and legally obtain public housing status. There are 37 *cuarterías* with a total of 354 units ('houses') and 1700 residents in Diriamba. Many *cuartería* residents have lived there for more than 45 years. Before the Sandinista victory, *cuartería* residents paid a monthly fee to landlords who tended to be wealthy businessmen, lawyers and other professionals. When the Sandinistas came to power, *cuarterías* were declared to be in the public interest and domain, and residents were no longer required to pay monthly rental fees. However, the Sandinistas did not give *cuartería* residents legal title to the lands or houses. Since 1990, the former landlords of the *cuarterías* have returned either to extract their monthly fees, or to evict their former tenants and reclaim the properties. The Community Movement, therefore, has been playing a central role in defending those who live in the most marginal circumstances.[57]

'Tierra Prometida' ('Promised Land'), a squatter settlement in Managua, is another example of the Community Movement's support of the poor in conflicts over property. Established in 1991 by seizing 50 manzanas of previously abandoned land, and currently housing 864 families, 'Tierra Prometida' is representative of the divisive political battles over property which have erupted in many communities since the 1990 elections. A commission elected by the community worked with leaders from the MC's national headquarters in an attempt to obtain legal title to the land. The commission succeeded in getting the mayor, Arnoldo Alemán, to grant 'public land' status to the settlement. Six months later, however, the mayor revoked the decree. Apparently, the former 'owner' materialized and demanded recompense for the value of the land. A new commission was formed by electing two community representatives from the Movimiento Comunal and two community representatives from the mayor's parallel organization, the JCOHP. The new commission negotiated an agreement specifying a down payment and monthly mortgage rate based on the square footage of space each family occupied.[58] The owner signed the agreement but the mayor refused to approve it. Two additional 'owners' appeared. Thus, three individuals were claiming to own the land occupied by 'Tierra Prometida', but none had written documentation that delineated the boundaries of their property.[59] The two representatives from the JCOHP withdrew from participating further, while the MC representatives have continued their attempts to negotiate a settlement for the whole community.

According to Máxima Bermudez, for many poor Nicaraguans, the threat of losing the plot of land on which they built their houses, has been a common problem and has served to forge connections between individuals of different political ideologies, rather than contribute to further polarization. In other words, the struggle over property has served as a catalyst for people to organize in order to solve other common problems, like poor sanitation, lack of potable water, disease, and illiteracy.[60] While this may well have been true elsewhere, it does not appear to have been the case in 'Tierra Prometida'. Instead, 'Tierra Prometida' demonstrates the extent to which some local officials will go to create obstacles that will effectively block the fulfilment of even the most basic needs, like housing. In contrast, the residents of the *cuarterías* in Diriamba – as well as in other municipalities like Masaya, for example – confront less resistance from local officials, and therefore can reasonably hope for improvement in their circumstances.[61]

The power of local officials to negatively influence the quality of life of the majority is no more evident than in the municipality of Matagalpa where the most critical and urgent problem has been the shortage of water. Matagalpa's water system is an antiquated one with the capacity to service a population of 20–25 000. Migration – a result of the Contra war, unemployment in the rural areas and the economic crisis – and natural growth have increased the municipal population to over 100 000. There are 45 neighbourhoods in Matagalpa, ten of which do not get any water, a few, like 'Reparto Sandino' receive water once every two weeks, 12 do not have potable water, and the majority get water for only one half-hour per day.[62] Deforestation and erosion of the mountainsides have contaminated the two river basins which serve as sources so that even those neighbourhoods receiving water on a 'regular' basis do not receive clean water. Shortly before the

1990 elections, the municipal government and CDC leaders had successfully negotiated a $20 million water project with the German government. After the Sandinistas lost the elections, a new mayor took office who blocked the project. The MC negotiated a new water project with a consortium of 'sister city' organizations, but the mayor resisted. Apparently he had decided that since the proposed water mains would not have passed through his *finca*, and the project would not have been completed during his term in office, he didn't want to have anything to do with it. The MC presented the mayor with a proposal to build a water tank in the poorest and most crowded neighbourhood, 'Francisco Moreno', which is home to over 7000 residents. The mayor refused the proposal; instead he built a water tank in a more well-to-do neighbourhood with 100 residents.

Deterioration of the quality of life for the majority, which began with the Contra war and the US's economic embargo of Nicaragua in the 1980s, has accelerated rapidly during Chamorro's term in office. The little that the MC has been able to salvage or has struggled to protect is minute in comparison to what has been lost. The UNO government's structural adjustment programme and its neoliberal policies have privileged the wealthy and assaulted the poor. Many others who had been managing to survive, have now fallen into abject poverty. Still, the MC goes on. In the words of one MC leader and activist, 'We can't just stand by and watch everyone die of hunger. We have to do *something*'.[63] The question is, can the Community Movement, as it is currently structured, really make a difference in an environment that is hostile to social justice? Can it reach enough people, can it provide people with the desire to take control of their lives again; can it organize enough people to defend their own rights; can it convince them that they can make a difference, that it is worth fighting back, worth the sacrifices necessary to attain a truly equitable and democratic society?

AMNLAE AND THE WOMEN'S MOVEMENT

Women's activism in Nicaragua, as in many other Latin American countries, was sparked by the new theology of liberation in the 1960s. As women became involved in the Christian base communities, they began to question their objective conditions of life and the structure of social and economic relations that produced those conditions. In the struggle before the Sandinista triumph in 1979, women were mobilized as combatants and military officers,[64] messengers, educators, 'Mothers of Heroes and Martyrs', in protests and hunger strikes, as participants in semiclandestine and clandestine activities, and in the Civil Defence Committees. After 1979, women were encouraged to participate in the paid labour force in greater numbers than ever before,[65] in the mass organizations, the health campaigns, the popular education projects,[66] the volunteer militia, and in the distribution of food subsidies. Their mobilization in the defence and consolidation of the revolution provided them with new responsibilities, new identities, and a new consciousness regarding their status in society. The decade of Sandinista rule (1979–90) created opportunities for challenging conservative and reactionary attitudes towards women in society and for promoting women's rights. The revolution provided an ideological orientation of liberation that 'made it possible for women to break with the past and mobilize to demand equality' (Yanz 1981: ii).

The Frente's relationship to the women's movement was typical of its relations with the other mass organizations, which, as we have seen, primarily served as mechanisms through which people were mobilized to implement party policy with relatively little autonomy to determine their own agenda. Despite the Sandinistas' formal commitment to the emancipation of women, demonstrated as early as 1969 in the 'Historic Programme of the FSLN', the outcomes were mixed in terms of the ability and willingness of the party's top leadership to respond to women's needs and interests and develop policy in a timely fashion to improve the status of women in legal, economic, political, and social spheres. Thus, it was possible for poet Rosario Murillo (President Ortega's *compañera*) in 1985 to declare,

> I believe that in a Revolution, a specific women's organization can't exist as it would be a way of perpetuating inequality. We don't talk about creating specific organizations for men and of men, in spite of their unequal situation vis-à-vis

the exploited or oppressed in a class society. (Quoted in Collinson 1990: 143)

The women's movement, embodied in a mass organization, suffered on two counts. First, it laboured under the expectation that a single organization could adequately represent all women and address the diversity in women's material conditions of life, their social class, ethnicity, and aspirations. In other words, treating 'women' as an undifferentiated or homogeneous 'category' was problematic since women have distinct and conflicting interests, experiences, needs, identities, and allegiances (Molyneux 1986). Indeed, 'a feminism organized around a unitary 'woman' in effect privileged certain voices and marginalized others' (Westwood and Radcliffe 1993: 23). In particular, AMNLAE has been criticized as having had primarily a middle-class orientation (Deighton et al. 1983; Collinson 1990), and thereby being unable to attend to the needs of rural women, the urban poor, and indigenous women. Second, the women's movement, as embodied in AMNLAE, was 'organically structured by and responsible to the party'.[67] The Frente determined its leadership, established its policies and methods of operation, and set its agenda. In essence, AMNLAE was not unlike its previous incarnations, AMPRONAC, APMN, and OMDN.[68] It was an instrument of the party and dependent on the top-level male party leadership. Feminist and labour party adviser to the National Workers' Front (FNT), Ruth Herrera explained,

> The Frente always had the AMNLAE leadership more committed to its membership in the party than to its leadership role for women ... The tasks carried out by AMNLAE placed a higher priority on the party than on women ... The FSLN listened to us, but they never took our demands seriously.
> (Quoted in *Barricada Internacional* 1992: 22–31)

Indeed, 'this lack of autonomy in a succession of women's organizations stifled or submerged the possibilities for developing a truly feminist movement' (Randall 1994: 17).

AMNLAE's early goals included maintaining 'the mobilization of women around the defense and consolidation of the revolution' (Carrión quoted in Deighton et al. 1983), organizing women as women, and encouraging women's participation

180   *The Undermining of the Sandinista Revolution*

in other mass organizations (Collinson 1990: 141). AMNLAE worked successfully with the CDS in organizing the literacy crusade of 1980 which trained 100 000 popular educators to teach literacy skills, and the vaccination campaign which, by 1982, had trained 78 000 health *brigadistas* who reached 85 per cent of the population (Deighton et al. 1983).

On the legislative front, AMNLAE demanded legal equality for women, legislation to equalize the burden of housework and childcare, the creation of employment opportunities and improved conditions of work for women, equal pay for equal work, and the establishment of daycare centres for working mothers. Between 1981 and 1982, AMNLAE proposed new laws on adoption, family relations, and 'nurturing' to the Council of State (Ruchwarger 1987: 189–92). These bills generated a great deal of controversy nationwide as well as in the Council. After heated debate, and several rounds of revisions, they were passed by the Council and presented to the JGRN which subsequently failed to ratify them (Molyneux 1985: 153–5). The proposal to include women on an equal footing in the law on national military service (conscription) did not pass the Council of State, although it was supported by large numbers of women (Molyneux 1986: 302).

AMNLAE's membership increased rapidly in the early years of the revolution with over 700 committees and 30 000 participants by 1983 (Deighton et al.: 43), and as many as 85 000 by the end of 1984.[69] However, as the Contra war intensified and it became clear that AMNLAE would push back its own agenda in support of the Frente's, membership and participation declined precipitously. In other words, 'Women's issues and the needs of the revolution were too often placed in opposition to one another' (Randall 1994: 28). AMNLAE began to lose touch with its base and did not really have an opportunity to develop its own analysis of gender (Collinson 1990: 142).

In 1986, women's activism was re-energized nationwide by grassroots town meetings or 'cabildos' organized by AMNLAE to discuss provisions for women's rights in the new constitution. Abortion, reproductive rights, family planning and access to birth control, domestic violence and rape, divorce laws, women's economic dependence on men, and the unshared burden of housework and childcare were the primary concerns elaborated on in these discussions (Collinson 1990). The high level of participation in the 'cabildos' demonstrated that 'women's issues' were not a fabrication of middle-class feminists but were also of concern to peasant women and working-class women (Collinson 1990). While many of these concerns were not adequately addressed in the final version of the Constitution, the legal rights of women did improve significantly. Among its other provisions, the Constitution established equality before the law, equal pay for equal work, and equality of rights and responsibilities between men and women (Chuchryk 1991: 155).

By 1986, AMNLAE was debating the relationship between its role as a mass organization and its potential to lead a wider social movement of women. This debate was settled by the FSLN's 1987 Proclamation on Women, which not only reinforced AMNLAE's subordinate and dependent position vis-à-vis the party, it also demonstrated the Frente's continued conservatism regarding women's status in society (Chuchryk 1991; Collinson 1990). For example, the proclamation stated, 'The struggle to wipe out discrimination against women cannot be separated from the struggle to defend the revolution' (quoted in Collinson 1990: 137) and 'We will struggle so that women can fulfill their maternal function and family responsibilities under ever-improving conditions and in a way that these responsibilities do not become insurmountable obstacles to their own personal growth and development' (quoted in Chuchryk 1991: 155). Indeed, 'Possibly no other party has issued such a mainstream policy document on women's oppression while in government' (Collinson 1990: 145).

Although criticized for reinforcing women's traditional roles, the proclamation also guaranteed every individual 'the right to physical, psychological and moral integrity', made 'cruel and degrading behavior punishable by law', and declared that 'machismo and other forms of discrimination against women inhibit(ed) the development of the whole society' (Collinson 1990: 145). In addition, the proclamation provided the foundation for AMNLAE's reorganization and its new emphasis on more locally derived demands and needs. More important, the laws that were passed soon after the proclamation, officially changed the definition of the family, granted full equality to women, authorized police to intervene in situations of domestic violence, allowed women to file for divorce for the first time, and imposed regulations on industry for the provision of childcare services. Clearly, these laws represented great strides for women's rights. In addition, it is clear that women had benefited greatly from Sandinista social welfare policies, especially the provision of food subsidies (until 1988), and free health care and education. But they also endured an increased workload: they had joined the paid workforce in greater numbers than ever before, they had been mobilized to participate in the other mass organizations – their neighbourhood associations (CDS), and labour unions, for example – and they were still the primary caretakers of their homes and children, experiencing little change in their relationships with men generally.

Thus, while many of AMNLAE's articulated demands and goals were eventually met, women's subordination continued in other ways (Molyneux 1986). This can be attributed to the fact that AMNLAE always had an ambiguous and contradictory role vis-à-vis the revolutionary state. Even though the state and the party both had a formal commitment to women's emancipation and participatory democracy, AMNLAE was still an organization created by and for the *party* and not by and for *women*. National Assembly member, Dr. Mirna Cunningham, explained:

> Those of us who have been working all these years in the popular sectors, we're convinced that all the models up to now have lacked this vision: a genuine understanding of women and race. We haven't been able to develop authentic movements that retain sufficient autonomy while at the same time articulating the larger, overall struggle ... We've known how to talk the talk; we've got the discourse down pat. What we haven't been able to do is raise people's consciousness in a more profound and far-reaching way. (Quoted in Randall 1994: 76–7)

Although many of the women in the Frente itself had lobbied the male-dominated leadership for women's rights for many years, they had limited success.[70] Since women were not represented among the party's main leaders,[71] they had to depend on an all-male leadership that was generally unconcerned about advancing women's interests. Both as a mass organization and as representative of a movement, AMNLAE 'was clearly unable to fulfill its promise' (Randall 1994: 28). AMNLAE could not free itself from the structure that had created it; equality, emancipation, and the interests of all women were much more difficult to realize.

After 1988, as a result of the increasing severity of the economic crisis, hyperinflation and the implementation of structural adjustment, the '*compactación*' of the state and state services, and the discontinuation of food subsidies, participation in all of the mass organizations, including AMNLAE, declined even further and the quality of women's lives, in particular, deteriorated substantially. Structural adjustment placed the heaviest burden on women because of their responsibilities as primary caretakers of family well-being (Moser 1993). Furthermore, the neoliberal policies promulgated and implemented by the Chamorro government since 1990 have had an even more devastating impact on women's material conditions of life and on economic life generally. With official unemployment and underemployment at over 70 per cent (*Envío* 1995: 5),[72] and the virtual privatization of health care services and education, the standard of living has deteriorated substantially. As a result of these changes, women, especially, have been subjected to increased psychosocial violence – that is, the violence of hunger and malnourishment, of being unable to provide even the minimum level of subsistence for their families, the violence of having to prostitute themselves in order to survive – as well as an increase in domestic violence:

> Sometimes the children believe that I don't give them any (food) because I don't want to. They can't begin to understand ... I feel so bad; it is a suffering that completely devastates me. I want to (give to my children), but I can't. In the Sandinista system, women made great strides; women had the support of the government, (for example), our children went to school, they were given notebooks, pencils ... that benefited women. Now we are completely marginalized, you have to pay for school, everything is different. (Quoted in Fernández Poncela 1993)

What has become of AMNLAE and the women's movement in Nicaragua since 1990, and how can we assess the impact of the revolution on women's lives? The Sandinistas' defeat at the polls was a tremendous blow to AMNLAE. Community leader and activist Rosa Ceballo explained, 'Of all the mass organizations, AMNLAE was the most dependent upon the party, so that when the FSLN lost the elections in 1990, AMNLAE was devastated the most'.[73] In response to past criticisms, and in line with the plan for its reorganization as outlined in the Sandinistas' Proclamation on Women, AMNLAE underwent a major restructuring. Dora Zeledón, AMNLAE's national coordinator, emphasized AMNLAE's independence from the party:

> AMNLAE is an autonomous movement that defines its own policies and actions, without being subordinated to any political party or government body. Without losing sight that it is a revolutionary project, its character is broad-based and has wide appeal. (Zeledón 1993)

However, AMNLAE is still perceived to be primarily responsible to the Frente. According to Máxima Bermudez, vice coordinator of the Community Movement, 'AMNLAE is not yet an autonomous organization ... It was the organization hardest hit by the elections, and it is diminishing in its strength and influence. It can't offer women what we need'.[74] Rosa Ceballo noted that, 'AMNLAE still has close ties to the party. It has stayed above everyone. Women can accomplish more and are better represented by the Community Movement which doesn't distinguish between women – whether we are feminists or non-feminists'.[75] The leader of the women's section of UNAG and member of the National Assembly, Benigna Mendiola criticized AMNLAE's tendency to centralize, and its insensitivity to peasant women's realities:

> I've always thought that the best thing instead of just talking, is for women to fight for their rights wherever they are: in the Sandinista Workers' Federation (CST), the Farm Workers Association (ATC) or the Luisa Amanda Espinosa Women's Movement (AMNLAE) ... There's no need to centralize the movement. Each woman's way of thinking must be respected, but we must meet when there are problems which impede our collective development ... I respect the work of the women organizing this meeting. On the other

hand, we haven't always had their support. It's not the same to be in the reality of the countryside as it is to contemplate philosophical questions ... In the past we've had problems with certain AMNLAE activists. They want to transform the mentality of the peasant overnight. (Quoted in *Barricada Internacional* 1992) [76]

It is interesting to note that Rosa Ceballo and Benigna Mendiola articulated a similar position – that women's interests would be better served and women would be better represented by local organizations. Decentralization, together with an emphasis on local solutions to local problems, has, in fact, ensued. [77]

Thus, although AMNLAE's numbers have continued to decline, [78] the women's movement in Nicaragua cannot and should not be reduced to AMNLAE. Since the late 1980s, and especially after 1990, the 'women's movement' has resurged as an obvious challenge to 'the FSLN's reluctance to move feminist issues off the back burner' (Stahler-Sholk 1995: 238). [79] It has manifested itself in the proliferation of women's organizations from small local organizations with very specific goals, to larger organizations with a broader presence which have surfaced throughout the country. Though somewhat fragmented and locally specific, and generally lacking national coordination, these nongovernmental women's organizations are independent of party politics and closely in tune with women's specific experiences and needs.

The activities of these organizations include consciousness-raising workshops and theatre groups that deal with issues like domestic violence, gender relations, and sexually transmitted diseases, special radio programmes for youth and adolescents, agricultural and craft production collectives, retraining institutes, reproductive rights activism, family planning and health services. For example: Fundación 'Puntos de Encuentro' ('Meeting Points' Foundation) in Managua deals primarily with violence against women through workshops and radio programmes; Servicios Integrales para la Mujer (Integrated Services for Women), and El Centro de Adolescentes y Jóvenes (The Centre for Adolescents and Youth) in Managua together provide information, workshops and courses in sex education, teenage pregnancy, family planning, sexually transmitted diseases, counselling services for victims of sexual abuse and domestic violence, and reproductive health care services; Centro de Mujeres Desempleadas (Unemployed Women's Centre) which boasts a membership of over 700 women and reaches women throughout the department of Estelí, provides training courses for women in traditional trades (sewing, beautician and hair styling skills) and nontraditional trades (taxicab driving, painting) and has an expanding soya bean production project;[80] Instituto 'Mujer y Comunidad' ('Woman and Community' Institute) in Estelí works with the youth of the community by holding workshops and radio programmes on gender and relationships, provides credit for small businesses, and is involved in agricultural and animal husbandry projects. While the Institute has served primarily rural women, it has recently elaborated credit programmes for urban women. All of its projects focus on gender issues.[81] In addition to these organizations, there are scores of other organizations – like the women's centre in Matagalpa, a women's collective which includes among its activities a popular theatre group that performs skits in the towns and villages surrounding Matagalpa on gender related issues,[82] and an all-women's agricultural production cooperative in Somoto.

Perhaps the most significant impact of the revolution on women concerns their mobilization and participation, and the consequent transformation of their consciousness from that of passive victims or objects to that of social subjects capable of effecting social change. As throughout the period of Sandinista rule when women were most active at the grassroots level and in the lower levels of government, the legacy of the revolution is the continued mobilization, participation and 'conscientization' of Nicaraguan women.

The impact of the revolution on women has been very positive. It has awakened our consciousness so that we are more sensitized to the problems in the community. It has taught us to collaborate with each other. It has given us an awareness of ourselves as active subjects in the process of social change. The revolution depended on women's participation in public life. It was a radical change from before and provided a foundation for further action. Once your consciousness is raised you can't go backwards; once your eyes are opened, you can't close them up again. Children are different too. Kids now have their own political analysis and make their own decisions. They feel themselves to be active subjects who have the capacity to decide what to do. They know they have to fight to defend their rights.[83]

In other words, the revolution transformed a 'culture of silence' – one that develops when marginalized individuals are prevented from self-determination and reflection – into a culture of awareness (Freire 1970). In this respect, women have been the main beneficiaries of the revolutionary process.

The Nicaraguan case teaches us a number of lessons. We have learned that for any challenge to male dominance to be truly successful, it must be connected to substantive changes in society – that is, to widespread structural changes in the ways in which the economy, political life and social life are organized, but that such widespread structural changes in society do not by themselves guarantee liberation for women. They may, however, allow the struggle for emancipation to take place. We further learn that sexual politics can't be separated from the politics of class or race. The experiences of Nicaraguan women also highlight the importance of analysing sexual politics in the broader context of national and international politics. The process of women's politicization in Nicaragua challenges mainstream notions of what constitutes political behaviour and political activity. That is, conventional politics do not account for the breadth of women's participation in Nicaragua. Indeed, many of the social movements throughout Latin America in which women are claiming their rights as citizens, human beings, and mothers, demand a redefinition of 'politics' (Fisher 1993). An alternative understanding of women's participation lies in the fabric of everyday life, where women's resistance cannot necessarily be defined as 'feminist', 'socialist', 'radical', or 'liberal', but rather, as something informed by a 'logic of survival' (Aptheker 1989: 170). Armed only with their new identities as social subjects which were forged during the revolution, perhaps women will find the seeds of progressive social change in their daily activities, responsibilities, and relationships.

FROM MASS ORGANIZATIONS TO NGOS: WHITHER THE REVOLUTION?

With the benefit of hindsight, it might seem as though the transformations undergone by the Sandinista mass organizations since the 1990 elections (not to mention their earlier problems in the 1980s) both parallel and reflect a continentwide historical process. Although a strong case for Nicaraguan exceptionalism might be made – after all, a revolution *did* occur – the international constraints under which the Sandinistas operated, the broad-based nature of the movement which brought them to power, and finally, their contradictory relationship with their own social/political base, all seem to correspond with general changes in the potential for national sovereignty, in the relationship between the state and civil society, and in the very nature of social movements throughout the Americas.

The potential for national sovereignty in what used to be called 'Third World' nations has everywhere undergone a precipitous decline. In Latin America, that decline began with the failure of the populist import-substitution industrialization (ISI) model for national development. The consequent spread of military dictatorships with their disastrous social and economic policies led inexorably to the debt crisis, structural adjustment programmes, the neoliberal/free-market development model, and the dismantling of the 'welfare state'.[84] Only after these world-historical processes had virtually guaranteed a new phase of capital expansion without hindrance from the threat of revolutionary movements, was there a slow, partial return to a purely formal democratic rule, hamstrung by structural adjustment programmes. Yet, for all the effort put into repression and demobilization in the 1960s, and 1970s, giving rise to widespread economic marginalization, the 1980s, Latin America's 'lost decade', was also the decade of a widespread popular mobilization taking the form of so-called 'new social movements' (Escobar and Alvarez 1992: 1–2).

While Central America followed, in large measure, the wider Latin American pattern, certain historical preconditions resulted in an isthmusian detour. These peculiarities included virtually total political domination by the United States, extremely low levels of development based on dependent agroexport economies, and arising out of both these factors, a history of violent, repressive oligarchic rule. Unlike Argentinians or Brazilians, Nicaraguans could not even aspire to a return to authoritarian populism; they had yet to experience the slightest breath of national sovereignty or formal democratic institutions. They mobilized for armed revolution, because that was the only path open to them out of their historical cul-de-sac.[85] Overthrowing the Somoza dictatorship provided Nicaraguans with the opportunity to replicate what had elsewhere been an earlier phase of national development, but they were forced to carry out the experiment in a small, dependent economy, and against the implacable hostility of the United States acting on behalf of transnational capital.

The Sandinista mass organizations – though born of revolutionary mobilization by the FSLN, and triumphant in their struggle against the dictatorship – entered into a relationship with a party and a state in power, in some ways similar to that previously experienced by social movements elsewhere during the populist era. The difference, of course, is that the role played by the populists was now played by a popular revolutionary regime which, unlike the populists, sought to create a genuinely participatory democracy and had the will to effect a meaningful redistribution of wealth and power. But military aggression, economic embargo, and the 'triumph of capitalism' over 'really existing socialism' fatally undermined the experiment. The free and open electoral franchise, perhaps the Frente's most enduring legacy, led ironically to the imposition of a neoliberal state virtually identical to those wielding power everywhere in the Americas. Nicaragua had caught up with history. And like their counterparts across the region, the Nicaraguan people and their popular organizations entered the 'new world order' and seemed to have joined the wider universe of 'new social movements'.

The concept of 'new social movements' (NSMs) intends to embody a new approach to the analysis and understanding of what is held to be a significant change in the nature and scope of collective action. More specifically, the proponents of the NSM idea intend to address what they see as a proliferation in the forms of collective action, and the identities expressed via those new forms. Thus, NSMs allegedly represent a shift away from traditional actors – class-based organizations such as labour movements and leftist political parties oriented towards major revolutionary changes and the alteration of the balance of power in the state – to new types of actors such as community movements, women's groups, civil rights groups, indigenous organizations and environmental movements, oriented towards smaller-scale, more directly democratic and participatory forms of struggle, often denying the legitimacy of political parties, and generally eschewing direct confrontation with the state (Escobar and Alvarez 1992). The concept of 'civil society' has been extensively deployed by both NSM participants and the social scientists who observe them, to situate these new phenomena politically. As Vilas points out:

> The term 'civil society' is broad. Today it includes everything from daily life and interpersonal relations in the home, to questions of territory, purchasing power, ethnicity, gender and generation. Liberal-capitalist tradition distinguishes between the public and private spheres; the term civil society points to the articulation between them. It implies a questioning of such 'borders', and indicates the role of the 'private sphere' in the gestation of conditions for collective 'public' action, and in the reproduction of the political and social order. Thus the concept of civil society refers to a sphere of collective action distinct from both the market and 'political society' – parties, legislatures, courts, state agencies. Civil society is not independent of politics, but clearly, when people identify themselves as 'civil society', they are seeking to carve out a relatively autonomous sphere for organization and action. (Vilas 1993: 38)

The CDS had apparently already begun something like a metamorphosis into a 'new social movement' under Omar Cabezas' leadership between 1988 and 1990 when it became the Committees for Community Development (CDC) with the watchword of self-organization. After the FSLN's electoral defeat, it underwent another name change – to 'Community Movement' (MC) – and became an autonomous nongovernmental organization (NGO) without formal party affiliation, and ostensibly decentralized to the community level. AMNLAE also declared itself autonomous from the Frente, but the women's movement had already spun out of its orbit and was rapidly generating a broadly decentralized network of specialized organizations attending to women's needs. The rejection of AMNLAE by a new generation of activists was symbolic of the repudiation of both authoritarian and hierarchical practices and the subordination of women's interests. Thus, the Nicaraguan women's movement exemplifies the new conception of social movements as the building of 'collective identities' – a deliberate balancing of the struggle for power and emancipation with the cultural struggle for identity (Escobar and Alvarez 1992: 4). Interestingly, Calderón *et al.* argued that the NSM phenomenon is exemplified, among other cases, in the trajectory of the national liberation movements in Central America 'where issues of social transformation and national autonomy are increasingly problematized in relation to the democratization of politics and society' (Calderón et al. 1992: 22).

Like social movements across the Americas, Nicaragua's (formerly) Sandinista popular/mass organizations were seemingly adjusting to a reality characterized by the multiplication of social demands on an increasingly unresponsive state along with the growing obsolescence of political parties (a crisis of representation) expressed in their inability to effectively aggregate demands and meet their constituents' needs. This reality generated everywhere a quest for greater autonomy on the part of the popular/social movements, however limited and illusory this autonomy might prove to be. In fact, the key demands of NSMs for autonomy and participation emerged precisely because of the shortcomings of previous models. Whatever the causes of its failures, the revolutionary model in Nicaragua ultimately proved bitterly disappointing in its outcomes for the popular majorities, and this disillusionment was so great that, by the time of the 1990 elections, the population had been virtually demobilized. But, the 'terrible tension' which has everywhere arisen between society and the state, rather than engendering paralysis, has been said to impel a growing 'hope and expectation, increasingly generalized, of installing or reestablishing democracy' (Calderón *et al.* 1992: 24–5) – and it might be added, a true democracy transcending the ersatz populist variety.

The populist state, typically a corporatist regime, relied on the cooptation of popular social forces through a variety of clientelist and patronage mechanisms to maintain its power.

The impossibility of continuing these practices in the era of neoliberalism with its permanent fiscal crisis and loss of national sovereignty, has precipitated a search for 'a new institutional scheme ... in which conflicts and demands are recognized and processed' (Calderón et al. 1992: 24–5). Indeed, it could be argued that the Sandinista regime manifested many of the characteristics of Latin American populism, particularly as demonstrated by the Frente's tight control of the urban labour movement.[86] The initial autocritique of the CDS culminated in Cabezas' admission that the FSLN's relationship with the popular movement, while driven by revolutionary democratic theory, was characterized more by an authoritarian and clientelist (populist) practice. Consequently, the concern with autonomy, small-scale decentralization, and democratic procedures evinced by the Nicaraguan grassroots organizations since the elections of 1990, seems to correspond with the new direction taken by social movements across the continent. And, it might also be said that the persistence of popular participation in Nicaragua since the elections corresponds with the general 'hope and expectation ... of installing ... democracy'.

But if the goal is to attain democracy in both political *and* economic realms, how far, for all their hopefulness, can decentralized 'movements' – made up of fragmented, locally based, autonomous organizations – realistically expect to go? In other words, are 'identity politics' sufficient for the kind of societal transformation that would be necessary in order to guarantee basic civil rights – safety and security, a voice in government, freedom from discrimination, and access to health care, education, food, decent housing, and dignified work – to all members of society? What are the limitations of exclusively locally based solutions to problems that are widespread and structural?

Calderón et al. conclude that identity-centred actions are insufficient to 'oppose present national and global power relations'. They base their conclusion on an analysis of the international economy and recent transformations in relations between capital and technology including,

the cultural homogenization of the market, due to the increased pervasiveness of the mass media; loss of development visions and the destruction of the welfare state; and, of course, the external debt and the central role of finance capital in the economy. These transformations are perhaps most clearly reflected in the increasingly crucial role played by information technologies in organizing relations of domination and of daily life; in other words, they are manifested in the growing concentration and centralization of decisions in the hands of phantasmagorical elite. (Calderón *et al.* 1992: 27)

While the foreign elites who control economic decisions and the dissemination of funds, technology, and information (or disinformation) are invisible, the local elites in Nicaragua seem real enough. Physical evidence of their existence is omnipresent in Managua, for example, in its elaborate cathedral, rotundas (traffic roundabouts) and expensive fountains, its shopping centres with a cornucopia of gourmet foods, its latest models of automobiles, and its construction of luxury homes and hotels throughout the city and its outskirts. Meanwhile the overwhelming majority of people are unable to satisfy even their most basic needs. It would appear then, that class inequality is still an essential aspect of Nicaraguan society. Vilas explains the continued relevance of class analysis even in the context of a paradigm shift:

A deterministic emphasis on class is unsatisfactory because it leaves out other dimensions which are as relevant – or more so – in particular situations. But to replace class reductionism with class rejectionism is no improvement at all; on the contrary, it impoverishes our analysis. Class is also central to an understanding of civil society (which is) distinct from political society, but is not alien to politics. (Vilas 1993: 40)

The importance of class is demonstrated by the fact that throughout Latin America, the sector of civil society that has been mobilized to change society – mobilized against human rights abuses, against government policies and the high cost of living, and in defence of citizenship – consists of the poor and the powerless, with some participation of the middle classes but with 'little, if any, involvement of people from the wealthy classes' (Vilas 1993: 41).

Although many of the popular organizations in Nicaragua are formally independent of political parties, their agenda is not apolitical, and they do not operate in a political or economic vacuum. Indeed, the environment in which they exist is fervently inimical to popular organizing and obsessively protective of elite interests. It is also an environment characterized by the erosion of class as an identity, in large part due to the neoliberal economic agenda of the 'new world order'. The most salient components of that agenda are:

> the de-salarization of the work force, the growing fragmentation of labor markets, the growth of the informal sector, the crisis in the precarious systems of social security, the weakening of the leadership capacity of unions as well as their ability to achieve demands, and the shrinking number of votes garnered by leftist political parties. (Vilas 1993: 41)

Thus, even though class *identity* has diminished, class is still *structurally* one of the most significant divisions and sources of conflict in Nicaraguan society. While the obstacles to achieving popular democracy during the decade of the 1980s were the counter-revolutionary war and the economic embargo which exacerbated the Frente's sectarianism, abuses of authority, and verticalism, the principal obstacle in the 1990s has become the state itself and its promotion of neoliberal economics. As MC national coordinator Enrique Picado questioned, 'How can we deepen or even sustain an organization with this great obstacle?'[87] Could it not in fact be argued that decentralizing the 'movement', while solving some of the problems and correcting some of the mistakes previously made by the Sandinistas, has diluted the potential power and influence of the masses, and thereby weakened their ability to effect social change under the current system of government?

Under the circumstances, however, it is difficult to imagine that any other approach would work. In the case of the MC, the leadership confronted a dual crisis of demobilization and resource scarcity. It made sense to capitalize on years of experience in community development coupled with an established credibility with international funders and overseas NGOs. MC leaders repeatedly affirmed that, in their view, the low level of participation was temporary and conjunctural, and that they were up to the task of rebuilding the movement from below on the basis of a nonparty, nonsectarian logic. In a sense, they have measured their success more in terms of the numbers of key cadre and new leaders actively involved in the continuing struggle, than in the level of mass participation, *per se.* They were certainly proving that communities could be mobilized around specific issues affecting the interests of the majority of residents, even if under the difficult economic circumstances confronting the majority, high levels of participation were difficult to sustain.

The 'new' women's movement, as represented by a multitude of smaller, independent organizations, on the other hand, evinced a steady increase in interest and participation. There are at least two explanations for this difference. The first explanation views the evolution of the women's organizations as a response to frustration with the Frente for its intransigence regarding women's 'traditional' role in society, and a decade of virtually unfulfilled promises. Once the Frente no longer dominated the national political agenda, women's organizations proliferated because they were able to unleash their own agenda and attend to their own needs. Thus, it is possible that the women's organizations are perceived as truly independent of political parties, in contrast to the MC which is still perceived to be an organization of the Frente.

Another explanation is that the revolution created the possibility for people to become conscious of their social identities, including their rights as citizens and their responsibilities as social actors engaged in the process of making their own history. The revolutionary project raised women's consciousness as women as well as their social consciousness as the active subjects rather than the passive objects of policy. It is in this explanation that we observe a convergence between activists in the Community Movement and in the women's movement, because the revolution also provided people with the knowledge that social and economic life can be organized differently and that they themselves are capable of bringing about social change.

It is indeed remarkable that the popular organizations have proved to be as resilient, and the commitment to social justice as ineradicable, as they have been. Perhaps there is a grain of truth in the proposition of Nicaraguan exceptionalism, and the revolution really made a difference after all. Certainly

196   *The Undermining of the Sandinista Revolution*

there is no nongovernmental organization quite like the Movimiento Comunal elsewhere in Latin America in terms of its scope and vision for community development. In his analysis of the 'regime transformation' literature, Williams (1994) argues that Nicaragua might be seen as a unique case in having created a more inclusive model of democracy by incorporating both representative and participatory components. Although constraints, both inherited and acquired, thwarted the full development of grassroots democracy, the legacy of ten years of popular mobilization made the consolidation of a limited elite-dominated democracy problematic.[88] It has also made it impossible for the FSLN, as a self-styled, reborn 'orthodox' left party to reassert its dominion over the popular organizations which it created and once effectively controlled. Confronted by the neoliberal state and the inexorable rollback of the modest gains in social justice and development experienced during the 1980s,

> ... the same strata that were once mobilized for insurrection began to reorganize to demand what they had come to see as their rights. Evidently, whether the FSLN remains at the forefront of those struggles or not, the Sandinista revolution made social subjects out of those who were once the mere objects of policy. (Stahler-Sholk 1995: 250)

The leaders and activists in the popular organizations are, however, unmistakably at the forefront of those struggles. They are the true 'Sandinistas' – the living legacy of the revolution, regardless of their current party affiliation. What is most striking to the observer, is their relentless dedication to their communities and commitment to the revolutionary project, as well as their unwavering hope for a better future, in spite of – or perhaps because of – their experiences, and the obstacles they have encountered.

REFERENCES

Aptheker, Bettina. 1989. *Tapestries of Life: Women's Work, Women's Consciousness and the Meaning of Daily Experience.* Amherst: University of Massachusetts Press.

Barricada Internacional. 1992. 'Seeking Unity in Diversity'. March: 22–31.
——. 1994. June.
——. 1995. 'The Community Movement's Autonomy: Our Most Precious Possession'. October.
Benería, Lourdes. 1982. 'Accounting for Women's Work'. In Lourdes Benería (ed.), *Women and Development: The Sexual Division of Labor in Rural Societies.* New York: Praeger.
Booth, John A. 1985. 'The National Governmental System'. In Thomas W. Walker (ed.), *Nicaragua: the First Five Years.* New York: Praeger.
Cabezas Lacayo, Omar. 1988a. 'Anuncios en Asamblea Realizada el 2 de Julio en la Ocasión del Décimo Aniversario de los CDS'. Mimeograph.
——. 1988b. 'Entrevista a Omar Cabezas,' by Mariuca Lomba. *Pensamiento Proprio,* 52, July–August.
Calderón, Fernando, Alejandro Piscitelli and José Luis Reyna. 1992. 'Social Movements: Actors, Theories, Expectations'. In Arturo Escobar and Sonia E. Alvarez (eds), *The Making of Social Movements in Latin America: Identity, Strategy and Democracy.* Boulder, CO: Westview Press.
Chuchryk, Patricia. 1991. 'Women in the Revolution'. In Thomas W. Walker (ed.), *Revolution and Counterrevolution in Nicaragua.* Boulder, CO: Westview Press.
Collinson, Helen. 1990. *Women and Revolution in Nicaragua.* London: Zed Books.
Coraggio, José Luis. 1985. *Nicaragua: Revolution and Democracy.* Boston: Allen and Unwin.
Deighton, Jane et al. 1983. *Sweet Ramparts: Women in Revolutionary Nicaragua.* London: Spider Web Offset/War on Want, Nicaragua Solidarity Campaign.
Dore, Elizabeth and John Weeks. 1992 a. 'Up From Feudalism'. *NACLA Report on the Americas* 26 (3), December.
——. 1992b. 'Introduction: Theory and Protest in Latin America Today'. In Arturo Escobar and Sonia E. Alvarez (eds), *The Making of Social Movements in Latin America: Identity, Strategy and Democracy.* Boulder, CO: Westview Press.
Evans, Trevor. 1993. 'Nicaragua: An Introduction to the Economic and Social Situation'. Managua: CRIES Working Paper, October.
Fagen, Richard, Carmen Diana Deere and José Luis Coraggio (eds). 1986. *Transition and Development.* New York: Monthly Review Press.
Fernández Poncela and Anna Fernandez. 1993. 'Los Desajustes del Ajuste: Las Mujeres en Nicaragua'. Unpublished paper.
Fisher, Jo. 1993. *Out of the Shadows: Women, Resistance and Politics in South America.* London: Latin America Bureau.
Freire, Paolo. 1970. *Pedagogy of the Oppressed.* New York: Continuum Press.
Gilbert, Dennis. 1988. *Sandinistas.* Oxford: Basil Blackwell.
Harris, Richard and Carlos Vilas (eds). 1985. *Nicaragua: A Revolution Under Siege.* London: Zed Books.
IHCA (Central American Historical Institute). 1995. *Envío,* 14, 7 April.
Jelin, Elizabeth. 1990. *Women and Social Change in Latin America.* London: Zed Books.
LaRamée, Pierre. 1995. 'Differences of Opinion: Interviews with Sandinistas'. *NACLA Report on the Americas,* March/April.

198   *The Undermining of the Sandinista Revolution*

LaRamée, Pierre and Erica Polakoff. 1990. 'Transformation of the CDS and Breakdown of Grassroots Democracy in Revolutionary Nicaragua'. *New Political Science*, 18/19, Fall/Winter.

Lowy, Michael. 1986. 'Mass Organizations, Party, and State: Democracy in the Transition to Socialism'. In Richard Fagen et al., *Transition and Development*. New York: Monthly Review Press.

Marchetti, Peter E. 1986. 'War, Popular Participation and Transition to Socialism: The Case of Nicaragua'. In Richard Fagen et al. *Transition and Development*. New York: Monthly Review Press.

Molyneux, Maxine. 1985. 'Women'. In Thomas W. Walker (ed.), *Nicaragua: the First Five Years*. New York: Praeger.

———. 1986. 'Mobilisation without Emancipation: Women's Interests, State and Revolution'. In Richard Fagen et al., *Transition and Development*. New York: Monthly Review Press.

Moser, Carolyn. 1993. 'Adjustment from Below: Low-income Women, Time and the Triple Role in Guayaquil, Ecuador'. In Sarah Radcliffe and Sallie Westwood (eds), *ViVa: Women and Popular Protest in Latin America*. London: Routledge.

NACLA Report on the Americas. 1995. 'Introduction to Hope: The Left in Local Politics'. 29 (1), July/August.

Nuñez Soto, Orlando. 1986. 'Ideology and Revolutionary Politics in Transitional Societies'. In Richard Fagen et al., *Transition and Development*. New York: Monthly Review Press.

Quandt, Midge. 1994. 'Sandinismo: A Tenuous Unity'. *Against the Current*, November/December.

Radcliffe, Sarah and Sallie Westwood (eds). 1993. *ViVa: Women and Popular Protest in Latin America*. London: Routledge.

Randall, Margaret and Lynda Yanz. 1981. *Sandino's Daughters: Testimonies of Nicaraguan Women in Struggle*. Vancouver: New Star Books.

Randall, Margaret. 1994. *Sandino's Daughters Revisited*. New Brunswick: Rutgers University Press.

Ruchwarger, Gary. 1985. 'The Sandinista Mass Organizations and the Revolutionary Process'. In Richard Harris and Carlos Vilas (eds), *Nicaragua: A Revolution Under Siege*. London: Zed Books.

———. 1987. *People in Power: Forging a Grass-roots Democracy in Nicaragua*. Massachusetts: Bergin and Garvey.

Serra, Luís Héctor. 1985. 'The Grass-roots Organizations'. In Thomas W. Walker (ed.), *Nicaragua: the First Five Years*. New York: Praeger.

———. 1991. 'The Grass-roots Organizations'. In Thomas W. Walker (ed.), *Revolution and Counterrevolution in Nicaragua*. Boulder, CO: Westview Press.

Spalding, Rose, J. (ed.). 1987. *The Political Economy of Revolutionary Nicaragua*. Boston: Allen and Unwin.

Stahler-Sholk, Richard. 1995. 'Sandinista Economic and Social Policy: The Mixed Blessings of Hindsight'. *Latin American Research Review*. 30 (2).

Urcuyo, Braulio. 1994. *Casas Comunales del Niño*. Managua: Valdez y Valdez.

Vanden, Harry and Gary Prevost. 1993. *Democracy and Socialism in Sandinista Nicaragua*. Boulder, CO: Lynne Reiner.

Vanderlaan, Mary. 1993. 'Nicaragua in the New World Dis(Order): Free Trade, Liberalism, Security, and the Crisis of Development'. *New Political Science*, 26, fall, 65–88.

Vilas, Carlos. 1986a. *The Sandinista Revolution, National Liberation and Social Transformation in Central America*. New York: Monthly Review Press.

——. 1986b. 'The Mass Organizations in Nicaragua: The Current Problematic and Perspectives for the Future'. *Monthly Review*, November.

——. 1993. 'The Hour of Civil Society'. *NACLA Report on the Americas*. 27 (2), September.

Walker, Thomas W. (ed.). 1985. *Nicaragua: the First Five Years*. New York: Praeger.

——. 1991. *Revolution and Counterrevolution in Nicaragua*. Boulder, CO: Westview Press.

Weeks, John. 1987. 'The Mixed Economy in Nicaragua: the Economic Battlefield'. In Rose J. Spalding (ed.), *The Political Economy of Revolutionary Nicaragua*. Boston: Allen and Unwin.

Westwood, Sallie and Sarah Radcliffe. 1993. 'Gender, Racism and the Politics of Identity'. In Sarah Radcliffe and Sallie Westwood (eds), *ViVa: Women and Popular Protest in Latin America*. London: Routledge.

Williams, Harvey. 1991. 'The Social Programs'. In Thomas W. Walker (ed), *Revolution and Counterrevolution in Nicaragua*. Boulder, CO: Westview Press.

Williams, Philip. 1994. 'Dual Transitions from Authoritarian Rule: Popular and Electoral Democracy in Nicaragua'. *Comparative Politics*, January: 169–85.

Yanz, Lynda. 1981. 'Preface'. In Margaret Randall and Lynda Yanz, *Sandino's Daughters: Testimonies of Nicaraguan Women in Struggle*. Vancover: New Star Books.

Zeledón, Dora. 1993. 'Mujer y poder'. *Barricada*, 2 October. 1993.

NOTES

1. The authors' names appear in alphabetical order. Both the research for and writing of this chapter were collaborative efforts.

2. Pearse and Steifel (cited in Marchetti 1986: 305) define popular participation as, '... the organized efforts to increase the control over resources and regulating institutions by groups and movements of workers and peasants previously excluded from such control'. More simply put, popular democracy means, '... all those forms through which the working class and popular sectors participate in the socialist project' (Nuñez Soto 1986: 246).

3. See the excellent discussion of these issues in Vanden and Prevost (1993: Chapter 1).

4. This discussion is partially adapted from LaRamée and Polakoff (1990).

5. This new order involves a fundamental shift in the relationship between the economic and political spheres. As Nuñez Soto (1986: 233) argued, '[a]fter a revolution has occurred, the operation of the superstructure, consciousness and action on the economic base and on society gains more relevance than before. Because of the importance of ideology in the revolutionary process, the implementation of economic measures during the transition (to socialism) should not be discussed apart from political tasks and measures. Once the revolution has taken power, political practice becomes political and political-economic practice'.

6. As Vilas (1986a: 148) noted, '[o]ut of necessity, the people organized in these structures directly managed a whole array of tasks and activities that were beyond their experience in a true version of popular democracy'.

7. Vilas (1986a: 13) argued that 'revolutions in dependent capitalist societies raise four basic and interrelated questions'. These are class (the nature of the popular subject), national sovereignty, development, and democracy. Three of the four questions – class, development, and democracy – are virtually synonymous with the question of participation and the role of the popular organizations.

8. See Gilbert (1988: 59–62) for a useful and concise account of this symbiotic relationship between party and state as it evolved in the Nicaraguan revolution.

9. For an in-depth presentation of this historical background and analysis see Vanden and Prevost (1993: Chapter 2).

10. As Weeks (1987: 45) put it, 'Even before Somoza fell, the FSLN defined a primary goal of the post-triumph society to be national unity ... explicitly includ[ing] members of the propertied classes if they proved to be "patriotic". The mixed economy was a vehicle by which this unity would be forged, involving the peaceful coexistence of a large private sector, small-scale producers ... and a sector of socialized property'.

11. It might also be said that proportional representation made it possible for the Sandinistas to hand over power after their electoral defeat in 1990 – proportional representation allotted them 42 per cent of the seats where single-member districts would have meant their complete political annihilation and most likely the destruction of the embryonic democracy they had created.

12. Benería (1982: 134–5) pointed out that when measuring women's work, it is important to take into account unpaid labour performed in the domestic or 'private' sphere – the labour involved in daily household maintenance, subsistence production, and 'informal sector' activities (such as selling or trading goods produced in the home' – in addition to paid labour performed in the capitalist or 'public' sphere. The 'double day' refers to the fact that women virtually everywhere are primarily responsible for household work even when they have a workload equivalent to men's, outside of the domestic sphere. Beginning in the early 1970s, as greater numbers of women entered the paid labour force worldwide, the double day became an increasingly common phenomenon.

13. For a more detailed discussion of these problems see LaRamée and Polakoff (1990). For instance, the Frente, through the CDS, would put pressure on INA and INEE, the water and electric utilities, to reach agreements with squatter settlements permitting the use of illegally tapped services, and arranging for escrow payments. Meanwhile, the Ministry of Housing and Human Settlements (MINVAH) continued to threaten (and sometimes tried) to evict squatters, while generally refusing to negotiate with community representatives seeking legalization. By all accounts, this policy was supported by the FSLN until just prior to the 1990 elections when the party distributed bogus 'certificates of occupation' to squatters in a bid to win their support.

14. The most basic level in the CDS structure was the 'block committee', referred to as a CDS, which represented the residents of a block or street. At the neighbourhood level, the CDS was sometimes referred to as a Comité de Barrio Sandinista (CBS), and functioned as a committee consisting of the block-level coordinators. At the municipal/zonal, regional, and national levels, the term CDS was used.

15. According to our observations in one squatter settlement in 1988, no distribution mechanism, however fair, was considered acceptable to the majority of residents. For example, it seemed preferable to many that if all members of the community could not receive a particular good, then no one should have any.

16. There were significant exceptions to the decline in participation. LaRamée and Polakoff (1990) found high levels of involvement in the newest (post-1984) squatter settlements in Managua; Ruchwarger (1987) describes a vibrant grassroots process in Georgino Andrade, a post-1979 squatter settlement.

17. For a more detailed discussion of these problems see LaRamée and Polakoff (1990).

18. Authors' interview with Enrique Picado, MC national vice coordinator, Managua, January 1991. After the 1990 elections, Enrique Picado continued in his position as vice coordinator (with Miguel D'Escoto replacing Omar Cabezas as national coordinator). Later, Picado was elected national coordinator and Máxima Bermudez was elected national vice coordinator.

19. Authors' interview with Enrique Picado, MC national coordinator, Managua, June 1991.

20. Author's interview with Máxima Bermudez, MC national vice coordinator, Managua, December 1994.

21. Author's interview with Máxima Bermudez, MC national vice coordinator, Managua, December 1994.

22. Authors' interview with Enrique Picado, MC national coordinator, Managua, January 1991.

23. Authors' interview with Sergio Obando, MC department coordinator for Granada, June 1995.

24. As previously mentioned, typically only local level representatives were elected by the membership at large. The leaders in the highest posi-

tions (that is, those at the regional and national level) were generally designated by the FSLN.

25. Author's interview with Máxima Bermudez, MC national vice coordinator, Managua, December 1994.

26. Authors' interview with Máxima Bermudez, MC national vice coordinator, Managua, June 1995.

27. Authors' interviews with MC department and municipal coordinators in Managua, Masaya, Granada, Diriamba, León, Matagalpa, and Estelí, June 1995.

28. For further discussion of the differences leading up to the split, see LaRamée (1995:) interviews with Dora María Téllez (MRS) and Victor Hugo Tinoco (ID).

29. Author's interview with Máxima Bermudez, MC national vice coordinator, Managua, June 1995. In fact, the Frente launched a campaign against the MC in *Barricada*, with headlines like, 'Dangerous passivity of leaders: they don't act nor permit you to act in the Community Movement'. The circumstances preceding these criticisms concerned the MC national executive committee's suspension of the organization's participation in the march leading to the 'cabildo' of 24 March 1995.

30. Authors' interview with Janet Castillo, MC municipal coordinator for Matagalpa, June 1995. In other cases, MC leaders find themselves unwelcome in either FSLN or MRS circles. The Frente's threat could also be interpreted as the party leadership's response to Picado's and Bermudez' public announcement of their affiliation with the MRS.

31. Indeed, according to Máxima Bermudez, in Somoto, Matagalpa and León, for example, members of the ex-Resistance work cooperatively with the MC on community projects.

32. Authors' interview with María Auxiliadora Romero Cruz, MC coordinator of the *centros infantiles* (daycare centres) in Matagalpa, June 1995.

33. Authors' interview with Enrique Picado, MC national coordinator, Managua, January 1991.

34. For an analysis of the FSLN's achievements in the areas of health, education, housing, and social welfare, and of the erosion of the social programmes they established while in power, see Williams (1991: 187–212).

35. Authors' interview with Noel Palacio, MC adult education coordinator for the popular education project in Estelí, June 1995.

36. We heard frequent complaints from mothers about how much extra fuel was required to cook the black beans which were distributed to the centres, compared to the red beans which are customarily eaten in Nicaragua. Parents and teachers also mentioned that the children complained about the black beans being 'burnt'. Apparently they still managed to eat them.

37. We visited several different children's centres in each of the departments of León, Granada, Masaya, Carazo and Matagalpa, and had the opportunity to meet both with teachers and parents at each centre. We also interviewed the MC coordinators and/or vice coordinators of

the departments and municipalities, and the coordinators of the CCN in each area we visited.

38. Site visit with Juanita Silva, MC preschool coordinator in Subtiava, June 1995.

39. Authors' interviews with Sergio Obando, MC department coordinator for Granada, and Guillermo Garcia, director of Coros de Angelos (Choir of Angels), and site visits in Granada, June 1995.

40. The *micro-empresas* in Matagalpa consisted of four *molinos* or flour mills where primarily corn is ground into *masa* for *tortillas*, and one retail meat stand. Authors' interview and site visits with María Auxiliadora Romero Cruz, MC coordinator for the *centros infantiles* (daycare centres) in Matagalpa, June 1995.

41. There are risks associated with starting a small neighbourhood business. To maximize success, the new business should avoid competing with similar businesses for the same customers and not duplicate services already present in the community. The service provided should be within the economic means of the people in the neighbourhood. In addition, the initial investment in materials, tools, and so on, is often beyond the reach of the majority of Nicaraguans and therefore requires a source of capital. Many nongovernmental organizations support projects that aim to be self-sufficient by donating start-up costs as was the case in Matagalpa.

42. Author's interview with Máxima Bermudez, MC national vice coordinator, Managua, December 1994.

43. Authors' interviews with Francisco Silva, MC department coordinator for León, and Juanita Silva, regional coordinator for the children's centres in Subtiava, and site visits in Subtiava and León, June 1995.

44. Authors' interviews and site visits with Lourdes Ponce Noria and family, Estelí, June 1995.

45. Authors' interviews with the *maestros populares* in Santa Cruz, Estelí, June 1995.

46. Author's interview with Máxima Bermudez, MC national vice coordinator, Managua, December 1994.

47. Authors' interviews with the five MC district coordinators for the department of Estelí, June 1995.

48. Authors' interview and site visits with Janet Castillo, MC municipal coordinator for Matagalpa, June 1995.

49. Authors' interview with María Auxiliadora Romero Cruz, MC coordinator for the *centros infantiles* (daycare centres) in Matagalpa, June 1995.

50. Authors' interview with District 3 delegate to the mayor's office, Managua, January 1991.

51. Author's interview with Máxima Bermudez, MC national vice coordinator, Managua, December 1994.

52. Authors' interview with Enrique Picado, MC national coordinator, Managua, January 1991.

53. Author's interview with Máxima Bermudez, MC national vice coordinator, Managua, December 1994.

54. Ibid.

55. Ibid.
56. *Cuarterías* are small, marginal plots of land or buildings divided and subdivided into even smaller rooms or shacks to accommodate anywhere from two to eleven families that share a 'patio' with a common cooking area and a communal latrine. *Cuarterías* are common in many urban areas in Nicaragua.
57. Authors' interview and site visits with Aurelila Cruz, MC department vice coordinator for Carazo, and with members of Diriamba's Committee of the *Cuarterías*, Diriamba, June 1995.
58. Authors' interview with Miguel Espinosa, community activist and MC neighbourhood coordinator in 'Tierra Prometida', Managua, June 1995.
59. Ibid. The authors also had the opportunity to read the original agreement that had been signed by the first 'owner' and the community representatives.
60. Author's interview with Máxima Bermudez, MC national vice coordinator, Managua, December 1994.
61. Author's interview with Manuel Cano, MC department coordinator for Masaya, June 1995.
62. Authors' interview with Janet Castillo, MC municipal coordinator for Matagalpa, June 1995.
63. Ibid.
64. Randall (1981: iv) reported that women were 30 per cent of the combatants in the Sandinista army in 1979, but only 6 per cent of the total number of officers with 9 per cent in the highest rank of guerrilla commanders. One year later the percentage of female combatants dropped to 8–10 per cent; by 1989, women constituted only 6 per cent of the permanent army (Chuchryk 1991: 158).
65. For a discussion of women's labour force participation, see Chuchryk (1991: 148). She noted that in 1977, women constituted 28 per cent of the economically active population (EAP); by 1989, they were 48 per cent of the EAP and were overwhelmingly represented among informal sector workers.
66. Women made up 60 per cent of the newly trained literacy teachers, 95 per cent of the popular educators, 75 per cent of the health brigadistas, and 75 per cent of the local CDS leaders (Deighton et al. 1983).
67. Doris María Tijerino Haslám, member of the National Assembly and formerly Chief of Police and AMNLAE coordinator under the Sandinistas, Presentation at New York University, 30 March 1995. There is, however, some disagreement concerning the way in which the movement was tied to the party. Chuchryk (1991: 157), for example, claimed that 'the links between the movement and the party were not organic, and the direction of the flow of influence was not always clear'. At the same time, she emphasized the party's ambiguous, and primarily conservative, thinking about women's roles in society.
68. The Organization of Democratic Women of Nicaragua (ODMN) was founded in 1966 by the Socialist Party; the Patriotic Alliance of

Nicaraguan Women (APMN) was founded in 1969 (Randall 1994). The Association of Nicaraguan Women Confronting the National Problem (AMPRONAC) was founded in 1977. Its membership rose from 60 in 1977 to 8000 by July 1979 (Deighton *et al.* 1983: 39). AMPRONAC's activities included organizing demonstrations, occupying churches, circulating petitions, carrying messages from political prisoners to their families, and pressuring the Somoza government to reveal the whereabouts of those who had been 'disappeared' (Deighton et al. 1983: 40). AMPRONAC demanded an end to the repression, stabilization in the cost of living, and repeal of all laws that discriminated against women. In 1979, when the Sandinistas assumed control of the government, AMPRONAC changed its name to the Association of Nicaraguan Women Luisa Amanda Espinosa (AMNLAE) in memory of the first female soldier to die in combat.

69. There is some discrepancy between reports of membership numbers. While Molyneux (1986) reports 85 000 members and chapters in ten (out of 16) departments, Williams (1994: 169–85) reports a membership of 60 000 in the same year.

70. See, for example, interviews with Michele Najlis and Milú Vargas in Randall (1994).

71. Women made up 33 per cent of the FSLN membership at the time of the triumph in 1979 (Vanden and Prevost 1993). This fell to 22 per cent in 1984 (Molyneux 1986). At the same time, although women held 37 per cent of the leadership positions in the party (Vanden and Prevost 1993), there were no women in the top leadership positions of the national directorate. Just before the 1990 elections, women filled 40 per cent of the seats in the National Assembly, two of the ministries were headed by women, the Chief of Police was a woman, but still none of the nine members of the Sandinista directorate were women (Collinson 1990). The Frente has since responded to criticisms regarding the exclusion of women in the directorate. At the FSLN special congress held in May 1994, it was decided that 30 per cent of the elected leadership at all levels would be reserved for women and that the directorate would expand to 15 (Quandt 1994: 15–19). Thus, five women were elected to the national directorate including Mónica Baltodano, Benigna Mendiola, Dorothea Wilson, Mirna Cunningham, and Dora María Téllez (*Barricada Internacional* 1994). Mirna Cunningham and Dora María Téllez withdrew from the national directorate when the party split into two factions – the Democratic Left led by Daniel Ortega, and the Renovation Movement led by Sergio Ramírez and Dora María Téllez.

72. Also cited in presentation by Victor Hugo Tinoco, member of the National Directorate of the FSLN, in New York City, April 1995.

73. Authors' interview with Rosa Ceballo, district coordinator of the Community Movement for Condega, Estelí, June 1995.

74. Authors' interview with Máxima Bermudez, MC national vice coordinator, Managua, June 1995.

75. Authors' interview with Rosa Ceballo, district coordinator of the Community Movement for Condega, Estelí, June 1995.

76. The meeting referred to here is the Women's Conference held in January 1992. Over 800 women representing a diverse array of organizations and groups participated in the conference.
77. For a good discussion of the advantages and disadvantages to the decentralization of left politics, see *NACLA Report on the Americas* (1995).
78. As noted by Prevost (in his introduction to this volume) AMNLAE membership has declined, but it still maintains its programmes and centres throughout the country.
79. Moreover, as Randall (1994: 34) observed, '[p]aradoxically, since the electoral loss, revolutionary women have been able to break the binds of allegiance to male-oriented party politics. In an economy in shambles, with a conservative government in office, and amid a generalized depression that has seriously threatened everyone's sense of self, Nicaraguan women are getting together, questioning absolutely everything, developing new ways of looking at their reality and organizing to change what is wrong'.
80. Authors' interview with Blanca Sevilla, Director of the Unemployed Women's Centre, Estelí, June 1995.
81. Authors' interview with María Auxiliadora Chiong, Assistant Director of the Institute 'Women and Community', Estelí, June 1995.
82. Authors' interview with María Auxiliadora Romero Cruz, MC coordinator for the *centros infantiles*, Matagalpa, June 1995.
83. Authors' interview with María Auxiliadora Chiong, Assistant Director of the Institute 'Women and Community', Estelí, June 1995.
84. Vilas (1993: 42) refers to this as 'the moment of authoritarianism and forced depoliticization [in which] governmental agencies not only lost interest in encouraging popular participation, but they tried to crush it'.
85. Dore and Weeks (1992) argued that despite their Marxist ideology, the revolutions in Nicaragua and El Salvador completed a long transition from despotic feudalism to liberal capitalism.
86. Serra (1991: 56) points out that '… the party, government, or FSLN-oriented unions employed various tactics to prevent delegates from other unions from running for leadership positions. These included military conscription and firings to get rid of workers who were activists for competing unions'.
87. Authors' interview with MC national coordinator, Enrique Picado, Managua, January 1991.
88. The shift from a UNO legislative majority to so-called Sandinista–UNO '*cogobierno*' underlines the difficulties encountered by the right in consolidating the new regime.

Bibliography

Acevedo Vogel, Adolfo. 1994. *Algunas implicaciones de los acuerdos con el FMI y el Banco Mundial (ESAF y el ERC-II) para el país y la sociedad nicaragüense.* Documento de Trabajo 94/3. Managua: CRIES.

Aguilar, Renata and Asa Stenman. 1994. *Nicaragua 1994: Back into the Ranks.* Gothenburg, Sweden: Department of Economics, University of Gothenburg.

Albert, Michael and Robin Hahn. 1990. *The Political Economy of Participatory Economics.* Princeton, NJ: Princeton University Press.

Alvarez Montalván, Emilio. 1995. *Ensayo sobre los valores de la cultura política nicaragüense.* Managua: No Publisher.

Alvarez, Sonia E. 1990. *Endangering Democracy in Brazil.* Princeton, NJ: Princeton University Press.

Aptheker, Bettina. 1989. *Tapestries of Life: Women's Work, Women's Consciousness and the Meaning of Daily Experience.* Amherst, MA: University of Massachusetts Press.

Arana Mario, Richard Stahler-Sholk, Gerardo Timossi, and Carmen López. 1987. 'Deuda, estabilización y ajuste: La transformación en Nicaragua, 1979–1986'. *Cuadernos de Pensamiento Propio*, Serie Ensayos No. 15. Managua: CRIES.

Arnove, Robert. 1994. *Education as Contested Terrain – Nicaragua 1979–1993.* Boulder, CO: Westview Press.

Avendaño, Nestor. 1994. *La economía de Nicaragua: El año 2000 y las posibilidades de crecimiento.* Managua: Nitlapán/CRIES.

Banco Central de Nicaragua. 1994. Report. Managua.

Barberena, Edgar S. 1995. 'Abstencionismo a la vista!' *El Nuevo Diario.* 24 June.

Barricada. 1993. 'Las nicas en cifras', *Barricada.* 5 March.

——. 1995. 5 May.

——. 1995. 20 May.

——. 1996. 14 January.

Barricada Internacional. 1989. May.

——. 1992. 'Seeking Unity in Diversity'. 12 (347), March.

——. 1994. June.

——. 1995. February.

——. 1995. July.

——. 1995. 'The Community Movement's Autonomy: Our Most Precious Possession'. October.

——. 1995. December.

Baumeister, Eduardo. 1991. 'Agrarian Reform'. In Thomas W. Walker (ed.), *Revolution and Counterrevolution in Nicaragua.* Boulder, CO: Westview Press.

——. 1995. 'Farmers' Organizations and Agrarian Transformation in Nicaragua'. In Minor Sinclair (ed.), *The New Politics of Survival: Grassroots Movements in Central America.* New York: Monthly Review/EPICA.

207

Baumeister, Eduardo and Oscar Neira Cuadra. 1986. 'The Making of a Mixed Economy: Class Struggle and State Policy in the Nicaraguan Transition'. In Richard R. Fagen, Carmen Diana Deere and José Luis Coraggio (eds), *Transition and Development: Problems of Third World Socialism*. New York: Monthly Review Press and Center for the Study of the Americas.

BCN (Banco Central de Nicaragua). 1995. *Indicadores económicos*, 1 (4), April.

Bello, Walden. 1994. *Dark Victory: The United States, Structural Adjustment and Global Poverty*. Oakland, CA: Institute for Food and Development Policy.

Benería, Lourdes. 1982. 'Accounting for Women's Work'. In Lourdes Benería (ed.), *Women and Development: The Sexual Division of Labor in Rural Societies*. New York: Praeger.

Booth, John A. 1985. 'The National Governmental System'. In Thomas W. Walker (ed.), *Nicaragua: the First Five Years*. New York: Praeger.

———. 1985. *The End and the Beginning: The Nicaraguan Revolution*. Boulder, CO: Westview Press.

Boserup, Ester. 1970. *Women's Role in Economic Development*. New York: St. Martin's Press.

———. 1990. 'Population, the Status of Women, and Rural Development'. In Geoffrey McNicoll and Mead Cain (eds), *Rural Development and Population*. Oxford: Oxford University Press.

Brydon, Lynne and Sylvia Chant. 1989. *Women in Third World*. New Jersey: Rutgers University Press.

Cabezas Lacayo, Omar. 1988. 'Anuncios en asamblea realizada el 2 de Julio en la ocasión del décimo aniversario de los CDS'. Mimeograph.

———. 1988. 'Entrevista a Omar Cabezas' by Mariuca Lomba. In *Pensamiento Proprio*, 52, July–August.

Calderón, Fernando, Alejandro Piscitelli, and José Luis Reyna. 1992. 'Social Movements: Actors, Theories, Expectations'. In Arturo Escobar and Sonia E. Alvarez (eds), *The Making of Social Movements in Latin America: Identity, Strategy and Democracy*. Boulder, CO: Westview Press.

Castro, Vanessa. 1992. 'Electoral Results in the Rural Sector'. In Vanessa Castro and Gary Prevost (eds), *The 1990 Elections in Nicaragua and Their Aftermath*. Lanham, MD: Rowman and Littlefield.

Castro, Vanessa and Gary Prevost (eds). 1992. *The 1990 Elections in Nicaragua and Their Aftermath*. Lanham, MD: Rowman and Littlefield.

Cenzontle. 1990. *Mujeres: panorámica de su participación en Nicaragua*. Managua: CENZONTLE.

Chamorro, Amalia. 1989. 'La mujer: logros y límites en 10 años de revolución'. *Cuadernos de Sociología*, 9–10, January–August.

Chinchilla, Norma. 1990. 'Revolutionary Popular Feminism in Nicaragua: Articulating Class, Gender, and National Sovereignty'. *Gender and Society*, 4 (3), September.

Chuchryk, Patricia. 1991. 'Women in the Revolution'. In Thomas W. Walker (ed.), *Revolution and Counterrevolution in Nicaragua*. Boulder, CO: Westview Press.

CIA (Central Intelligence Agency). 1994. *World Fact Book 1994*. Washington, DC: Central Intelligence Agency.

CIERA (Centro de Investigaciones y Estudios de Reforma Agraria). 1984. *Las mujeres en cooperativas agropecuarias en Nicaragua*. Managua: CIERA.
——. 1988. *El debate sobre la reforma económica*. Managua: CIERA.
——. 1989. *Política económica y transformación social*. Managua: CIERA.
——. 'Tough Row to Hoe: Women in Nicaragua's Agricultural Cooperatives'. In Kathleen Staudt (ed.), *Women: International Development, Politics the Bureaucratic Mire*. Philadelphia. Temple University Press. 181–201.
CIPRES (Centro para la Investigación, la Promoción, y el Desarrollo Rural y Social). 1990. 'La instabilidad política y su impacto socioeconómico en el campo'. Managua: CIPRES, October.
——. 1992. *El acceso de la mujer a la tierra en Nicaragua*. San José, Costa Rica: Fundación Arias Para la Paz y el Progreso Humano, CIPRES.
Cofré, Jaime. 1992. 'La titulación asegura la tenencia de la tierra'. *Teosintle*, December.
Colburn, Forrest. 1992. 'The Fading of the Revolutionary Era in Central America'. *Current History*, 91, February.
Collinson, Helen. 1990. *Women and Revolution in Nicaragua*. London: Zed Books.
Conroy, Michael E. 1990. 'The Political Economy of the 1990 Nicaraguan Elections'. *International Journal of Political Economy*, Fall.
——. 1990. 'The Political Economy of the 1990 Elections'. Paper presented at the Coloquio sobre las Crises Económicas del Siglo XX. Madrid, Universidad Complutense de Madrid, April.
Cook, Mark. 1989. 'Unfit to Print about Nicaragua's Election'. *Extra*, 3 (1), October/November.
Coraggio, José Luis. 1985. *Nicaragua: Revolution and Democracy*. Boston: Allen and Unwin.
CORNAP (Corporaciones Nacionales del Sector Público). 1992. *Proceso de privatización de empresas: Evaluación de impacto económico y social*. Managua, May.
——. 1995. *Avance del proceso de privatización al 31 de diciembre de 1994*. Managua, March.
CRIES (Coordinadora Regional de Investigaciones Económicas y Sociales)/Equipo de Investigadores. 1992. 'La farsa del neoliberalismo'. *La Avispa*, 9, April–June.
Criquillon, Ana. 1989. 'La rebeldia de las mujeres nicaragüenses: semillero de una nueva democracia'. In *Construccion de la Democracia en Nicaragua*. Escuela de Sociologia de la Universidad Centroamericana. Managua.
Cronin, Thomas. 1989. *Direct Democracy, the Politics of Initiative, Referendum and Recall*. Cambridge, MA: Harvard University Press.
Cuadra, Scarlet and Leonardo Coca. 1994. 'Gains and Losses'. *Barricada Internacional*, October/November.
DeFranco, Mario. 1995. 'Nicaragua: Experiencia de privatización de empresas públicas'. Seminario Nacional sobre Privatizaciones organizado por CEPAL/ASDI y PNUD. Managua, 12 June.
Deighton, Jane *et al.* 1983. *Sweet Ramparts: Women in Revolutionary Nicaragua*. London: Spider Web Offset/War on Want, Nicaragua Solidarity Campaign.

Díaz Lacayo, Aldo. 1994. *El Frente Sandinista después de la derrota electoral*. Caracas: Ediciones Centauro.

Dore, Elizabeth and John Weeks. 1992. 'Up From Feudalism'. *NACLA Report on the Americas*, 26 (3), December.

Duarte, Vilma. 1993. 'University Crisis'. *Barricada Internacional*, August.

Dumazert, Patrick and Oscar Neira. 1994. *From Debt Burden to the Search for Development Alternatives: Could the Debt Be an Opportunity to Overcome the National Crisis in Nicaragua?* Managua: Nitlapán/CRIES, August.

Dye, David *et al.* 1995. *Contesting Everything, Winning Nothing*. Cambridge, MA. Hemispherie Initiatives.

ECLAC (UN Economic Commission for Latin America and the Caribbean). 1994. 'Nicaragua: An Economy in Transition'. LC/MEX/R.458. Mexico, 31 May.

———. 1995. 'Nicaragua: Evolución económica durante'. LC/MEX/R.519. Mexico, 8 May.

Edwards, Sebastian. 1992. 'Real Exchange Rates, Competitiveness and Macroeconomic Adjustment in Nicaragua: A Progress Report'. AID consultancy report. Managua, 20 February.

El Nuevo Diario. 1995. 15 February.

———. 1995. Interview with Luis Ramón. 25 March.

———. 1995. 22 May.

Enloe, Cynthia. 1989. *Bananas, Bases and Beaches*. Berkeley, CA: University of California Press.

Enríquez, Laura J. and Marlen I. Llanes. 1993. 'Back to the Land: The Political Dilemmas of Agrarian Reform in Nicaragua'. *Social Problems*, 40 (2), May.

Enríquez, Laura J. *et al.* 1991. 'Nicaragua: Reconciliation Awaiting Recovery. Politics, the Economy and U.S. Aid under the Chamorro Government'. Washington, DC: Washington Office on Latin America, April.

Escobar, Arturo and Sonia E. Alvarez. 1992. 'Introduction: Theory and Protest in Latin America Today'. In Arturo Escobar and Sonia E. Alvarez (eds), *The Making of Social Movements in Latin America: Identity, Strategy and Democracy*. Boulder, CO: Westview Press.

Escoto, René and Freddy Amador, 1990. *El contexto macroeconómico de la reforma agraria*. Managua: Departmento de Economía Agrícola de la Facultad de Ciencias Económicas, Universidad Nacional Autónoma de Nicaragua.

Evans, Trevor. 1993. 'Nicaragua: An Introduction to the Economic and Social Situation'. Managua: CRIES Working Paper, October.

———. 1995. 'Ajuste estructural y sector público en Nicaragua'. In Trevor Evans (ed.), *La transformación neoliberal del sector público: Ajuste estructural y sector público en Centroamérica y el Caribe*. Managua: CRIES/Latino Editores.

Fagen, Richard, Carmen Diana Deere, and José Luis Coraggio (eds). 1986. *Transition and Development*. New York: Monthly Review Press.

Fernández Poncela, Anna Fernandez. 1993. 'Los desajustes del ajuste: las mujeres en Nicaragua'. Unpublished paper.

FIDEG. 1994. 'El Observador Económica'. Managua.

Fisher, Jo. 1993. *Out of the Shadows: Women, Resistance and Politics in South America*. London: Latin America Bureau.

Flakoll Alegria, Daniel. 1994. 'Navigating Between the Currents'. *Barricada Internacional,* June.

FNT (Frente Nacional de los Trabajadores). 1991. 'Posición del FNT ante el FMI y BM'. Managua, 12 January.

Freire, Paolo. 1970. *Pedagogy of the Oppressed.* New York: Continuum Press.

FSLN (Frente Sandinista de Liberación Nacional). 1995. *Propuesta del FSLN para debatir la orientación de la economía nicaragüense.* Managua: May.

Gilbert, Dennis. 1988. *Sandinistas: The Party and the Revolution.* London: Blackwell.

Haggard, Stephan. 1986. 'The Politics of Adjustment: Lessons from the IMF's Extended Fund Facility'. In Miles Kahler (ed.), *The Politics of International Debt.* Ithaca, NY: Cornell University Press.

Haggard, Stephan, and Robert R. Kaufman. 1995. *The Political Economy of Democratic Transitions.* Princeton: University Press.

Harding, Sandra and Merrill Hintikka (eds). 1993. *Discovering Reality: Feminist Perspectives on Epistemology, Metaphysics, Methodology and Philosophy of Science.* Dordrecht: Reidel.

Harris, Richard and Carlos Vilas (eds). 1985. *Nicaragua: A Revolution Under Siege.* London: Zed Books.

Hartsock, Nancy C. M. 1983. *Money, Sex, and Power: Toward a Feminist Historical Materialism.* New York: Longman.

——. 'The Nature of Standpoint'. 1993. In Sandra Harding and Merrill Hintikka (eds). *Discovering Reality: Feminist Perspectives on Epistemology, Metaphysics, Methodology and Philosophy of Science.* Dordrecht: Reidel.

Haugaard, Lisa. 1991. 'In and Out of Power: Dilemmas for Grass-roots Organizing in Nicaragua'. *Socialism and Democracy,* 7 (3), Fall.

IDB (Inter-American Development Bank). 1991. *Nicaragua Trade and Finance Adjustment Loan (NI-0012).* Washington, DC, 20 September.

IDB/IBRD/FAO (Inter-American Development Bank/International Bank for Reconstruction and Development/Food and Agriculture Organization). 1992. *Nicaragua: Misión de identificación sectorial agropecuaria. Ayuda memoria.* Managua, 16 March.

IEN (Instituto de Estudios Nicaragüenses). 1994. 'La gobernabilidad y la democracia local en Nicaragua: Investigación sobre la opinión pública nacional'. Managua, 31 January.

——. 1995. 'La gobernabilidad y el acuerdo nacional en Nicaragua: Investigación sobre la opinión pública nacional'. Managua, 3 January.

IHCA (Central American Historical Institute). 1988. 'El pueblo de Nicaragua: Por la paz y por un modelo económico más popular'. *Envío,* 7 (85), July–August.

——. 1988. 'The New Economic Package'. *Envío,* September.

——. 1990. 'After the Poll Wars – Eplaining the Upset'. *Envío,* March/April.

——. 1990. 'UNO Plans a Market Economy'. *Envío,* May.

——. 1991. ¿Qué esperar del plan económico: Reactivación o recesión? *Envío,* 10 (117), July.

——. 1991. 'Privatización: Tres puntos de vista'. *Envío,* 10 (120), October.

——. 1991. 'Los pies de barro del plan económico'. *Envío,* 10 (121), November.

——. 1992. Managua, *Envío,* 11 (130), May.

——. 1995. 'The Foxes are Infighting; But the Hens Aren't Laughing'. *Envío*, 14 (157), April.

——. 1995. Managua, *Envío*, 14 (166), May.

——. 1995. 'En París, desfile de imágenes'. *Envío*, 14 (160), July.

——. 1995. 'Not Yet to the Root of the Crises'. *Envío*, 14 (161), August.

IMF (International Monetary Fund). 1989. *Nicaragua: Staff Report for the 1989 Article IV Consultation.* Washington, DC, 2 November.

——. 1991. *Nicaragua – Request for Stand-By Arrangement.* Washington, DC, 12 September.

——. 1994. *Enhanced Structural Adjustment Facility, Policy Framework Paper, 1994–97.* Washington, DC, 2 June.

——. 1994. *Nicaragua: Staff Report for the 1994 Article IV Consultation and Request for Arrangements under the Enhanced Structural Adjustment Facility.* Washington, DC, 2 June.

——. 1994. *Nicaragua: Recent Economic Developments.* Washington, DC, 13 June.

Jelin, Elizabeth. 1990. *Women and Social Change in Latin America.* London: Zed Books.

Joekes, Susan. 1987. *Women and the World Economy.* New York: Oxford University Press.

Kahler, Miles. 1990. 'Orthodoxy and Its Alternatives: Explaining Approaches to Stabilization and Adjustment'. In Joan M. Nelson (ed.), *Economic Crisis and Policy Choice: The Politics of Adjustment in the Third World.* Princeton, NJ: Princeton University Press.

LaRamée, Pierre. 1995. 'Differences of Opinion: Interviews with Sandinistas'. *NACLA Report on the Americas*, March/April.

LaRamée, Pierre and Erica Polakoff. 1990. 'Transformation of the CDS and Breakdown of Grassroots Democracy in Revolutionary Nicaragua'. *New Political Science*, 18/19, Fall/Winter.

LASA (Latin American Studies Association). 1990. *Electoral Democracy under International Pressure, The Report of the Latin American Studies Association Commission to Observe the 1990 Nicaraguan Election.* Pittsburg: University of Pittsburg Press.

Lowy, Michael. 1986. 'Mass Organizations, Party, and State: Democracy in the Transition to Socialism'. In Richard Fagen *et al.*, *Transition and Development.* New York: Monthly Review Press.

Marchetti, Peter E. 1986. 'Popular Participation and the Transition to Socialism: the Case of Nicaragua'. In Richard Fagen *et al.*, *Transition and Development.* New York: Monthly Review Press.

Martínez Cuenca, Alejandro. 1992. *Sandinista Economics in Practice: An Insider's Critical Reflections.* Boston: South End Press.

——. 1994. *El comportamiento inversionista en Nicaragua.* Materiales de Estudio y Trabajo No. 13. Managua: Fundación Friedrich Ebert, February.

McCoy, Jennifer. (1989). 'Nicaragua in Transition'. *Current History*, 90 (554), March.

MCE (Ministerio de Cooperación Externa). 1995. 'Nicaragua: Situación y perspectivas económicas 1994–1995 (Versión preliminar)'. Managua, January.

McMichael, David. 1990. 'U.S. Plays Contra Card'. *The Nation*, 5 February.

MEDE (Ministerio de Economía y Desarrollo). 1995. *La economía nicaragüense 1994.* Managua: MEDE.

Mies, Maria. 1986. *Patriarchy and Accumulation on a World Scale*. New Jersey: Zed Books.

Millett, Richard. 1994. 'Central America's Enduring Conflicts'. *Current History* 93 (580), February.

Ministry of Labour. 1994. 'La situación del empleo urbano en Nicaragua: resumen global de ocho ciudades'. Mimeograph. Managua: Ministry of Labour.

Mohanty, Chandra (ed.). 1991. *Third World Women and the Politics of Feminism*. Indiana: Indiana University Press.

Molyneux, Maxine. 1982. 'Mobilization without Emancipation? Women's Interests, State, and Revolution'. In Richard R. Fagen *et al.* (eds), *Transition and Development: Problems of Third World Socialism*. New York: Monthly Review Press and Center for the Study of the Americas.

——. 1985. 'Women'. In Thomas W. Walker (ed.), *Nicaragua: The First Five Years*. New York: Praeger.

Montealegre, Haroldo, *et al.* 1990. 'Programa de estabilización y ajuste estructural para Nicaragua 1990–1993'. Propuesta de la Comisión del Plan Económico. Managua, 17 September.

Moser, Carolyn. 1993. 'Adjustment from Below: Low-income Women, Time and the Triple Role in Guayaquil, Ecuador'. In Sarah Radcliffe and Sallie Westwood (eds), *ViVa: Women and Popular Protest in Latin America*. London: Routledge.

MRS (Movimiento Renovador Sandinista). 1995. *Estatutos, principios y programa*. Managua, 21 May.

Munck, Ronaldo. 1994. 'Workers, Structural Adjustment, and *Concertación Social* in Latin America. *Latin American Perspectives*, 21 (3), Summer.

NACLA Report on the Americas. 1995. 'Introduction to Hope: The Left in Local Politics'. 29 (1), July/August.

Neira Cuadra, Oscar and Adolfo Acevedo. 1992. *Nicaragua: hiperinflación y desestabilización. Análisis de la política económica 1988 a 1991*. Managua: Cuadernos CRIES, Serie Ensayos No. 21.

Nicaragua, República de. 1990. 'Documento presentado por el Gobierno de Nicaragua ante la conferencia de donantes en Roma'. Rome, June.

——. 1990. 'Acuerdos de la concertación económica y social y la política exterior del Gobierno de Nicaragua'. Managua, 26 October.

——. 1992. *Nicaragua: Medium-Term Development Strategy 1992–1996*. Document presented by the Government of Nicaragua at the Consultative Group Meeting. Washington, DC, 26 March.

——. 1995. *Plan nacional de desarrollo (Borrador preliminar para discusión en el comité técnico)*. Managua, 31 March.

Norsworthy, Kent and Tom Barry. 1990. *Nicaragua: A Country Guide*. Albuquerque: Central American Resource Center.

Núñez Soto, Orlando. 1986. 'Ideology and Revolutionary Politics in Transitional Societies'. In Richard Fagen *et al.*, *Transition and Development*. New York: Monthly Review Press.

——. 1992. 'La agenda de la revolución: Los nuevos sujetos económicos'. *La Avispa*, 9, April–June.

Ocampo, José Antonio. 1991. 'Collapse and (Incomplete) Stabilization of the Nicaraguan Economy'. In Dornbusch, Rudiger and Sebastian Edwards (eds), *The Macroeconomics of Populism in Latin America*. Chicago: University of Chicago Press.

O'Kane, Trish. 1995. 'New Automony, New Struggle: Labor Unions in Nicaragua'. In Minor Sinclair (ed.), *The New Politics of Survival: Grassroots Movements in Central America*. New York, Monthly Review/EPICA.

Padilla, Martha Luz and Nyurka Pérez. 1981. 'La mujer semi-proletaria'. Managua: CIERA.

Padilla, Martha Luz, Clara Marguialdy, and Ana Criquillon (eds). 'Impact of the Sandinista Agrarian Reform on Rural Women's Subordination'. In Carmen Diana Deere and Magdalena León (eds). *Rural Women and State Policy*. Boulder, CO. Westview Press. 124–41.

Parpart, Jane and Kathleen A. Staudt (eds). 1989. *Women and the State in Africa*. Boulder, CO: Lynne Rienner.

Pastor, Manuel. 1987. *The International Monetary Fund and Latin America: Economic Stabilization and Class Conflict*. Boulder, CO: Westview Press.

———. 1993. 'Managing the Latin American Debt Crisis: The International Monetary Fund and Beyond'. In Gerald Epstein, Julie Graham and Jessica Nembhard (eds), *Creating a New World Economy: Forces of Change and Plans for Action*. Philadelphia: Temple University Press.

Pérez-Alemán, Paola. 1990. *Organización, identidad y cambio: las campesinas en Nicaragua*. Managua: Centro de Investigación y Acción para la Promoción de los Derechos de la Mujer. Nicaragua: CIAM.

———. 1992. 'Economic Crisis and Women in Nicaragua'. In Lourdes Benería and Shelly Feldman (eds), *Unequal Burden: Economic Crises, Persistent Poverty, and Women's Work*. Boulder, CO: Westview Press.

Peterson, V. Spike and Anne Sisson Runyon. 1993. *Global Gender Issues*. Boulder, CO: Westview Press.

El Programa Historico del FSLN. 1981. Managua: FSLN.

La Prensa. 1995. 15 March.

———. 1995. 19 May.

Przeworski, Adam. 1992. 'The Neoliberal Fallacy'. *Journal of Democracy*, 3 (3), July.

———. 1995. *Sustainable Democracy*. Cambridge: Cambridge University Press.

Quandt, Midge. 1994. 'Sandinismo: A Tenuous Unity'. *Against the Current*, November/December.

———. 1995. 'Unbinding the Ties That Bind: The FSLN and the Popular Organizations'. In Minor Sinclair (ed.), *The New Politics of Survival: Grassroots Movements in Central America*. New York: Monthly Review/EPICA.

Radcliffe, Sarah and Sallie Westwood (eds). 1993. *ViVa: Women and Popular Protest in Latin America*. London: Routledge.

Ramírez, Noël, *et al*. 1995. *Nicaragua: La nueva estrategia económica 1997–2001*. Managua, n.p.

Randall, Margaret. 1994. *Sandino's Daughters Revisited*. New Brunswick: Rutgers University Press.

Randall, Margaret and Lynda Yanz. 1981. *Sandino's Daughters: Testimonies of Nicaraguan Women in Struggle*. Vancouver: New Star Books.

Renzi, María Rosa and Sonia Agurto. 1993. *¿Qué hace la mujer nicaragüense ante la crisis económica?* Managua: FIDEG.

Renzi, María Rosa with Mario J. Cangiani and Sonia Agurto. 1994. *Impacto de los proyectos FISE en las condiciones de vida de los nicaragüenses*. Managua: FIDEG.

'Resolution from El Crucero Assembly'. 1990. *Barricada Internacional*. 14 July.

Ricciardi, Joseph. 1991. 'Economic Policy'. In Walker, Thomas W. (ed.), *Revolution and Counterrevolution in Nicaragua*. Boulder, CO: Westview Press.

Robinson, William I. 1992. *A Faustian Bargain: U.S. Intervention in the Nicaraguan Elections and American Foreign Policy in the Post Cold-War Era*. Boulder, CO: Westview Press.

Roxborough, Ian. 1992. 'Neo-liberalism in Latin America: Limits and Alternatives'. *Third World Quarterly*, 13 (3).

Ruchwarger, Gary. 1985. 'The Sandinista Mass Organizations and the Revolutionary Process'. In Richard Harris and Carlos Vilas (eds), *Nicaragua: A Revolution under Siege*. London: Zed Books.

——. 1987. *People in Power*. Massachusetts: Bergin and Garvey.

Ruíz, Henry. 1995. 'Henry Ruíz rompe el silencio'. Interview by Jorge Katín with Cmdte. Henry Ruíz. *Semanario*, 29 June–5 July.

Ruíz, Henry and Dora María Téllez. 1992. '¿Apoya el FSLN el neoliberalismo en Nicaragua?' *La Avispa*, 9, April–June.

Ruíz, Henry *et al*. 1994. *Para una salida nacional a la crisis*. Managua: INPASA, November.

Saldomando, Angel. 1992. *El retorno de la AID: El caso de Nicaragua: condicionalidad y reestructuracíon conservadora*. Managua: CRIES.

Schrieberg, David. 1992. 'Nicaragua: After the Sandinistas'. *The Atlantic*, 270 (1), 1 July.

Serra, Luís Héctor. 1985. 'The Grass-roots Organizations'. In Thomas W. Walker (ed.), *Nicaragua: the First Five Years*. New York: Praeger Press.

——. 1991. 'The Grass-roots Organizations'. In Thomas W. Walker (ed.), *Revolution and Counterrevolution in Nicaragua*. Boulder, CO: Westview Press.

——. 1993. 'Democracy in Times of War and Socialist Crisis: Reflections Stemming from the Sandinista Revolution'. *Latin American Perspectives*, 20 (2), Spring.

Sklar, Holly. 1989. 'Washington Wants to Buy Nicaragua's Elections Again'. *Z Magazine*, December.

Spalding, Rose J. 1994. *Capitalists and Revolution in Nicaragua: Opposition and Accommodation, 1979–1993*. Chapel Hill, NC: University of North Carolina Press.

——. 1995. 'Economic Elites: The Chamorro Years'. *Latin Studies Association Meeting*, Washington, DC.

Spalding, Rose J. (ed.) 1987. *The Political Economy of Revolutionary Nicaragua*. Boston: Allen and Unwin.

Spoor, Max. 1995. *The State and Domestic Agriculture Markets in Nicaragua: From Intervention to Neo-Liberalism*. New York: St. Martin's Press.

Stahler-Sholk, Richard. 1990. 'Stabilization, Destabilization, and the Popular Classes in Nicaragua, 1979–1988'. *Latin American Research Review*, 25 (3), Fall.

——. 1994. 'El ajuste neoliberal y sus opciones: La respuesta del movimiento sindical nicaragüense'. *Revista Mexicana de sociología*, 56 (3), July–September.

———. 1995. 'The Dog that Didn't Bark: Labor Autonomy and Economic Adjustment in Nicaragua under the Sandinista and UNO Governments'. *Comparative Politics*, 28, October.

———. 1995. 'Sandinista Economic and Social Policy: The Mixed Blessings of Hindsight'. *Latin America Research Review*, 30 (2).

Stahler-Sholk, Richard and Max Spoor. 1989. 'Nicaragua: Las políticas macroeconómicas y sus efectos en la agricultura y la seguridad alimentaria'. Managua, July.

Standing, Guy. 1989. 'Global Feminization Through Flexible Labor'. *World Development*, 17 (7).

Taylor, Lance *et al.* 1989. *Report of an Economic Mission to the Government of Nicaragua.* Managua: Swedish International Development Authority, April.

Téfel, Reinaldo Antonio. 1995. 'La mancha más fea: la Piñata'. *La Prensa*, 19 July.

Timossi Dolinsky, Gerardo. 1993. 'Crisis y reestructuracíon: El balance centroamericano de los años ochenta'. In Carlos M. Vilas (ed.), *Democracia emergente en Centroamérica*. Mexico: UNAM.

Tinker, Irene. 1976. 'The Adverse Impact of Development on Women'. *Women and World Development*. Washington, DC, Overseas Council of Development.

Uhlig, Mark. 1991. 'Nicaragua's Permanent Crisis: Ruling from Above and Below'. *Survival*, 33 (5), September–October.

UNAG (Unión Nacional de Agricultores y Ganaderos). 1993. 'La estrategia de desarrollo agropecuario en Nicaragua: Una visión desde la UNAG'. Foro sobre una Estrategia de Desarrollo Agropecuario en Nicaragua. Managua, 23 February.

UNDP (United States Development Programme). 1992. *Human Development Report*. New York: Oxford University Press.

———. 1994. 'Statement for the Consultative Group Meeting on Nicaragua'. Paris, 16–17 June.

UNO (Unión Nacional Opositora). 1990. 'Agenda para el rescate de la economía nacional'. Managua, February.

———. 1990. 'Documento presentado por el gobierno de Nicaragua en la Conferenciá de Donantes en Roma'. June.

———. 1990. 'Programa de estabilización y ajuste estructural para Nicaragua, 1990–93'. September.

Urcuyo, Braulio. 1994. *Casas comunales del niño*. Managua: Valdez y Valdez.

USAID (United States Agency for International Development)/Nicaragua. 1991. *Country Development Strategy Statement, USAID/Nicaragua 1991–1996*. Managua, June.

———. 1992. 'USAID Programs in Nicaragua: A Brief Description and Current Status'. Managua: USAID, June.

———. 1995. *Nicaragua 2000: Challenges for Developing a Stable, Democratic Prospering Society*. Managua: USAID, March.

Utting, Peter. 1991. *Economic Adjustment under the Sandinistas: Policy Reform, Food Security and Livelihood in Nicaragua*. Geneva: UNRISD.

Vanden, Harry E. 1990. 'Law, State Policy, and Terrorism'. *New Political Science*. Fall/Winter.

——. 1991. 'Foreign Relations'. In Thomas Walker (ed.), *Revolution and Counterrevolution in Nicaragua*. Boulder, CO: Westview Press.

Vanden, Harry E. and Thomas Walker. 1991. 'The Reimposition of U.S. Hegemony over Nicaragua'. In Kenneth M. Coleman and George C. Herring (eds), *Understanding the Central American Crisis*. Wilmington: Scholarly Resources.

Vanden, Harry E. and Gary Prevost. 1993. *Democracy and Socialism in Sandinista Nicaragua*. Boulder, CO: Lynne Reiner.

Vanderlaan, Mary. 1993. 'Nicaragua in the New World (Disorder): Free Trade Liberalism, Security, and the Crisis of Development'. *New Political Science*. 26, Fall.

Vargas, Virginia. 1989. *El aporte de la rebeldía de las mujeres*. Santo Domingo: CIPAF.

Vickers, George R. 1990. 'A Spider's Web'. *NACLA – Report on the Americas*. 30 (1), June.

Vickers, George R., and Jack Spence. 1992. 'Nicaragua: Two Years After the Fall'. *World Policy Journal*, 9 (3).

Vilas, Carlos. 1986. *The Sandinista Revolution, National Liberation and Social Transformation in Central America*. New York: Monthly Review Press.

——. 1986. 'The Mass Organizations in Nicaragua: The Current Problematic and Perspectives for the Future'. *Monthly Review*, November.

——. 1990. 'What Went Wrong'. *NACLA Report on the Americas*, 30 (1), June.

——. 1991. 'The Revolution that Fell from the Grace of the People'. *Socialist Register 1991*. London.

——. 1992. 'Family Affairs: Class, Lineage and Politics in Contemporary Nicaragua'. *Journal of Latin American Studies*, 24 (2), May.

——. 1993. 'The Hour of Civil Society'. *NACLA Report on the Americas*, 27 (2), September.

——. 1995. 'Entre la democracía y el neoliberalismo: los caudillos electorales de la posmodernidad'. *Socialismo y Participación*. Lima, Peru: 69, March.

Walker, Thomas W. (ed.) 1982. *Nicaragua in Revolution*. New York: Praeger.

——. 1985. *Nicaragua: the First Five Years*. New York: Praeger.

——. 1991. *Revolution and Counterrevolution in Nicaragua*. Boulder, CO: Westview Press.

Walton, John. 1989. 'Debt, Protest, and the State in Latin America'. In Susan Eckstein (ed.), *Power and Popular Protest: Latin American Social Movements*. Berkeley: University of California.

Webbels, Erik. 1993. 'Misguided Aid Policy toward Nicaragua'. *Nicaragua Monitor*, November.

Weeks, John. 1987. 'The Mixed Economy in Nicaragua: the Economic Battlefield'. In Rose J. Spalding (ed.), *The Political Economy of Revolutionary Nicaragua*. Boston: Allen and Unwin.

Westwood, Sallie and Sarah Radcliffe. 1993. 'Gender, Racism, and the Politics of Identity'. In Sarah Radcliffe and Sallie Westwood (eds), *ViVa: Women and Popular Protest in Latin America*. London: Routledge.

Wheelock, Jaime. 1984. *El Gran Desafío*. Managua: Editorial Vanguardia.

——. 1984. *Entre la crisis y la agresión: la reforma agraria Sandinista*. Managua: MIDINRA (Ministry of Agriculture and Agrarian Reform).

Williams, Harvey. 1991. 'Social Reforms'. In Thomas W. Walker (ed.), *Revolution and Counterrevolution in Nicaragua.* Boulder, CO: Westview Press.

Williams, Philip. 1994. 'Dual Transitions from Authoritarian Rule: Popular and Electoral Democracy in Nicaragua'. *Comparative Politics,* January.

Williamson, John. 1990. 'What Washington Means by Policy Reform'. In John Williamson (ed.), *Latin American Adjustment: How Much Has Happened?* Washington, DC: Institute for International Economics.

Witness for Peace. 1995. 'Structural Adjustment in Nicaragua'. Managua: Witness for Peace.

World Bank. 1992. *Nicaragua: Managing the Transition from Stabilization to Sustained Economic Growth.* Washington, DC, 26 March.

——. 1993. *Nicaragua – Stabilization and Adjustment: Enabling Private Sector-Led Growth.* Consultative Group Meeting for Nicaragua. Paris, 2 April.

——. 1993. *Nicaragua: Opciones de política económica en el marco de perspectivas de ayuda extranjera decreciente.* Managua, October.

——. 1993. *The Who, What and Where of Poverty in Nicaragua.* Washington, DC, 24 November.

Yanz, Lynda. 1981. 'Preface'. In Margaret Randall and Lynda Yanz. *Sandino's Daughter's: Testimonies of Nicaragun Women in Struggle.* Vancouver: New Star Books.

Zeledón, Dora. 1993. 'Mujer y poder'. *Barricada,* 2 October.

Index